TEACHING
LGBTQ
PSYCHOLOGY

Perspectives on Sexual Orientation and Diversity
Maria Lucia Miville, Series Editor

TEACHING
LGBTQ
PSYCHOLOGY

QUEERING INNOVATIVE PEDAGOGY AND PRACTICE

EDITED BY
THEODORE R. BURNES AND **JEANNE L. STANLEY**

AMERICAN PSYCHOLOGICAL ASSOCIATION • *Washington, DC*

Published by
American Psychological Association
750 First Street, NE
Washington, DC 20002
www.apa.org

To order
APA Order Department
P.O. Box 92984
Washington, DC 20090-2984
Tel: (800) 374-2721; Direct: (202) 336-5510
Fax: (202) 336-5502; TDD/TTY: (202) 336-6123
Online: www.apa.org/pubs/books
E-mail: order@apa.org

In the U.K., Europe, Africa, and the Middle East, copies may be ordered from
American Psychological Association
3 Henrietta Street
Covent Garden, London
WC2E 8LU England

Typeset in Meridien by Circle Graphics, Inc., Columbia, MD

Printer: Sheridan Books, Chelsea, MI
Cover Designer: Naylor Design, Washington, DC

The opinions and statements published are the responsibility of the authors, and such opinions and statements do not necessarily represent the policies of the American Psychological Association.

Library of Congress Cataloging-in-Publication Data

Names: Burnes, Theodore R., editor. | Stanley, Jeanne L., editor.
Title: Teaching LGBTQ psychology : queering innovative pedagogy and practice
    / edited by Theodore R. Burnes and Jeanne L. Stanley.
Description: Washington, DC : American Psychological Association, [2017] |
    Series: Perspectives on sexual orientation and diversity | Includes
    bibliographical references and index.
Identifiers: LCCN 2016038777 | ISBN 9781433826511 | ISBN 1433826518
Subjects: LCSH: Sexual minorities—Mental health. | Sexual
    minorities—Psychology. | Sexual minorities—Counseling of.
Classification: LCC RC451.4.G39 T469 2017 | DDC 616.890086/6—dc23 LC record available at
https://lccn.loc.gov/2016038777

British Library Cataloguing-in-Publication Data
A CIP record is available from the British Library.

Printed in the United States of America
First Edition

http://dx.doi.org/10.1037/0000015-000

Contents

Contributors

Jay N. Bettergarcia, PhD, is a recent graduate of the Counseling, Clinical, and School Psychology PhD program at the University of California, Santa Barbara. Dr. Bettergarcia's research focuses on transgender-affirming therapy, nonbinary gender identities, nondominant narratives in trans communities, and receptiveness and resistance to teaching and training about diversity-related topics. Dr. Bettergarcia teaches courses such as multicultural psychology and the helping relationship.

Caroline Carter, PsyD, is a registered postdoctoral psychological assistant with the Los Angeles Gender Center in Los Angeles, California, where she works with LGBQIA, transgender, and gender diverse children, adolescents, and adults. She completed her doctorate in clinical psychology at Azusa Pacific University. Her clinical interests are in gender, sexuality, religion, spirituality, and the interplay of gender and sexual identity with god image.

Cadyn Cathers, MA, is a female-to-male transgender clinician. He is a psychological assistant at the Los Angeles Gender Center in Los Angeles, California. He is an affiliate faculty member at Antioch University Los Angeles in the LGBT Specialization MA Psychology Program, where he teaches courses on LGBT affirmative theory and practice, and he is an adjunct faculty at Alliant International University and Mount Saint Mary's University. His doctoral research at the Chicago School of Professional Psychology focused on internalized transphobia and the therapeutic alliance of transgender clients with a cisgender therapist. His areas of interest include affirmative relational psychoanalytic theory, LGBTQIA identities, disordered eating, and transgenerational trauma.

Courtney M. Dunne, EdD, is the director of a deaf and hard-of-hearing program for EDCO Collaborative in Newton, Massachusetts, serving secondary students in the greater Boston area. She earned her master's degree in deaf education from Teachers College, Columbia University, and her doctorate in educational leadership from the University of Pennsylvania. Dr. Dunne's doctoral work looked at the lived intersectional experiences of deaf lesbian students of color at an urban school for the deaf on the East Coast. Dr. Dunne has been instrumental in helping to establish and support antioppressive environments for a diverse group of faculty, students, and families.

Paul N. T. Hovanesian, PhD, is a graduate of the Clinical Psychology Doctoral Program at the California School of Professional Psychology at Alliant International University. He has experience in the domains of severe and persistent mental illness, substance dependence/addiction, sexual violence risk assessment, group psychotherapy, and forensics. His past research includes analyzing the relationship between gender, perceived parent–child bonding during adulthood, and substance use among the Armenian American population. Additional research interests include group process, equality, supervision, trauma, violence and risk factors for recidivism, and factors of acculturation.

Kim Lee Hughes, PhD, is an assistant professor in the Department of Counseling at the University of Texas at San Antonio. She received her doctorate in counseling and student personnel services from the University of Georgia in 2015. Her clinical, research, and advocacy interests include qualitative research, the empowerment of queer women of color, and counseling ethics and professional development. Dr. Hughes is the chair of the Association of Multicultural Counseling and Development Day of Service and a Task Force Chair with the Association of Lesbian, Gay, Bisexual, and Transgender Issues in Counseling.

Tania Israel, PhD, is a professor of counseling, clinical, and school psychology at the University of California, Santa Barbara. She conducts research relevant to scholarship, policy, and practice on interventions to support the mental health and well-being of LGBTQ individuals and communities. Dr. Israel has received honors for her research and advocacy from the American Psychological Association, the California Asian and Pacific Islander Legislative Caucus, and her local LGBT community. She teaches courses on counseling LGBT clients and pedagogy in applied psychology, among others.

Nicholas Ladany, PhD, is dean of the School of Leadership and Education Sciences at the University of San Diego in California. Dr. Ladany holds a PhD in counseling psychology from the University at Albany, State University of New York, and a BS in psychology from the University of Maryland. He is the author of five books and more than 80 publications and has given over 200 national and international presentations in more than 20 countries on the effectiveness of counselor education and supervision, school-based mental health awareness, multicultural competence, and social justice.

Susan P. Landon, MA, LMFT, is director of the Child and Adolescent Program at the Los Angeles Gender Center in Los Angeles, California. She is on the advisory board of Transforming Family and facilitates their monthly parent meeting. She has presented at conferences and led training nationally on comprehensive health care for gender diverse children and teens. In addition to her work with the Los Angeles Gender Center, she has been in private practice for 30 years counseling individuals, couples, children, and families in Santa Monica, California. She is a member of the California Association of Marriage and Family Therapists and the World Professional Association for Transgender Health. Ms. Landon trains administrative staff and teachers at schools in the Los Angeles area about how to welcome gender nonconforming children and transgender adolescents into their school communities.

Tiffany O'Shaughnessy, PhD, is an assistant professor of counseling at San Francisco State University in California. She received a PhD in counseling psychology from Lehigh University. She also maintains a therapy practice in Berkeley, California, and serves as a volunteer supervisor and trainer for The Pacific Center for Human Growth, a queer community mental health center that provides sliding-scale therapy to foster the well-being of the LGBTQ community.

Carlton W. Parks, PhD, is a professor in the California School of Education at Alliant International University, Los Angeles. Dr. Parks is a Fellow of the American Psychological Association (APA) and a Fellow of APA Divisions 9 (Society for the Psychological Study of Social Issues), 27 (Society for Community Research and Action: Division of Community Psychology), 35 (Society for the Psychology of Women), 44 (Society for the Psychological Study of Lesbian, Gay, Bisexual and Transgender Issues), and 45 (Society for the Psychological Study of Culture, Ethnicity and Race).

Anneliese A. Singh, PhD, is an associate professor and associate dean for Diversity, Equity, and Inclusiveness in the College of Education at the University of Georgia in Athens as well as cofounder of the Georgia Safe Schools Coalition and Trans Resilience Project. Her research, practice, and community organizing have centered on the resilience of trans youth and people of color, queering educational systems, South Asian survivors of child sexual abuse, qualitative and mixed methods, and social justice and empowerment training and pedagogy. She has worked on several national competencies and guidelines projects for the American Counseling Association (ACA) and American Psychological Association (APA; e.g., APA's "Guidelines for

Psychological Practice With Transgender and Gender Nonconforming People," ACA's "Competencies for Counseling With Transgender Clients," and ACA's "Multicultural and Social Justice Counseling Competencies").

Jacqueline (Jackie) S. Weinstock, PhD, received her doctoral degree in developmental psychology and is an associate professor in the Human Development and Family Studies Program at the University of Vermont in Burlington. She coedited (with Esther Rothblum) *Lesbian Ex-Lovers: The Really Long-Term Relationships* (2004) and *Lesbian Friendships: For Ourselves and Each Other* (1996). Her current scholarship focuses on assessing and promoting undergraduate students' critical thinking skills and social justice understanding and identifying pedagogical activities and approaches most effective for promoting these aspects of personal, interpersonal, and professional development and practice.

List of Activities

Preface

This book has had a long history in the making. Both of us have spent most of our professional careers teaching students; educators; and community members about affirming lesbian, gay, bisexual, transgender, queer, and/or questioning (LGBTQ) individuals. Throughout our careers, teaching LGBTQ psychology has also been a focal point of our professional work. Theo has taught in and been appointed the director of a track within a clinical psychology master's program that focuses on LGBTQ mental health. Jeanne has served as a graduate professor and the director of an institute focused on training mental health and educational providers about creating affirmative environments for LGBTQ youth.

These histories were the context for our work together to gain approval for, create, and then implement the first graduate-level LGBTQ psychology course taught at the University of Pennsylvania's Graduate School of Education. At that time, we were each serving as directors of two related graduate psychology programs and teaching counseling courses in one another's program. As we had many times before, we provided a strong rationale for this course; however, we noticed the absence of literature that would help us to design and implement such a course. After gaining approval for the course, we went into an empty classroom and, within 10 minutes, had mapped out the entire course across the blackboard. At that moment, we solidified our collective passion for educating about LGBTQ psychology, life-long commitment to social justice, and slightly skewed senses of humor. These three key ingredients meant that we would work together for many years with the shared goal of educating others about the best practices for supporting and affirming LGBTQ people. However, in the midst of cementing our professional relationship, at that time, we both posed the following questions: Where is the literature to help us understand the best practices for teaching this material? Where are the articles that reflect the difficulty in teaching sensitive material regarding sexuality and gender?

Our friendship and professional work have meant that we both continue to teach, train, and write about LGBTQ issues—Theo on the West Coast and Jeanne on the East Coast. During one of our many phone calls, we decided that we could not wait any longer and we had to write the material that we had so often needed. This book was the perfect extension of getting information and resources out to others, but it was important for us to involve other authors who also had a passion for the topic and who are outstanding educators and service providers in the field. It is our goal that this book will help our readers in their work to expand support and affirmation for LGBTQ people via education in all its various forms.

This book would not be possible without the many mental health professionals in the world who have taught about LGBTQ psychology for decades in colleges, universities, mental health agencies, K–12 schools, religious organizations, hospitals, clinics, and many other environments using teaching practices that range in formality and structure. Whether a part of an organization or brought in as an expert, LGBTQ psychology is full of bright, innovative educators who have paved the way with their hard work to understanding LGBTQ people, cultures, and communities. Such people are a pivotal part of this book's creation, and they inspire us.

This book would also not have been possible without Dr. Marie Miville. In her capacity as the American Psychological Association (APA) Division 44 (Society for the Psychological Study of Lesbian, Gay, Bisexual and Transgender Issues) book series editor, we have been fortunate enough to benefit from her mentoring, continuous supportive feedback, and check-ins that made this project move from a dream to reality. Thanks to Christopher Kelaher and Neelima Charya at APA Books for answering our many questions and providing helpful feedback throughout our writing process. Special thanks to Susan Herman at APA for her amazing editing skills and her care for creating change in a supportive way for many via the information in this book. Thanks also to Dr. Angela Gillem and to Dr. Diane Hall, who were kind enough to be reviewers for two chapters in the book.

We would like to thank the authors who contributed to this book and who care tremendously about supporting and affirming LGBTQ people. Their consistent openness to feedback and their unwavering desire to document their stellar teaching practices have made putting this book together a complete delight and make us excited (and thankful!) for the students in their respective educational environments. The book would not have been possible without their knowledge, commitment, and care for the well-being of others.

Theo would like to thank a variety of people who have made this project possible, including the wonderful editorial staff at APA Books who have made this project a reality. He would like to thank the many students across their (and his) professional lifespan (K–12, undergraduate, and graduate) who have challenged, inspired, and grown with him in a variety of learning environments. Whether it has been working in a kindergarten class, a doctoral level course on therapy, or working with school counseling students on antibullying curricula for LGBTQ students, his career has been a beloved part of his life because of all of these students. He thanks Dr. Jeanne Stanley, who has been a mentor, a constant personal and professional support, a soul sister, and one of the most intelligent people he knows, for always believing in him, being patient with him as he grows, and challenging him to live authentically, have fun, and to always know the location of the nearest Starbucks, wherever they are at any given moment. Sam Cooper, is truly the embodiment of friendship, and Theo is so thankful that Sam is continuously in his life. And, he thanks Craig Bauer, the man who helped him to believe that his best friend and his boyfriend could be the same person. Craig's support has allowed him to do the work that he does. He loves him more every day.

There have been many individuals throughout various points of Theo's life who, as mentors, colleagues, clinical supervisors, friends, and change agents, have challenged him to think critically about being an L, G, B, T, and/or Q individual with humility, respect, and love. He would like to thank these people, who include (but are certainly not limited to): Julie Collins, Matthew Shepard, Fran McDaniel, Robert Midkiff, Cindy Peltier, Marco Sausa, Jeanne Stanley, Tania Israel, Simone Chess, Max Matthies, Tiffany Willoughby-Herard, Ingrid Banks, Xochitl Tafoya, Anneliese Singh, lore dickey, Konjit Page, Dan Walinsky, Peter Russell, Cathy Thompson, Jeanne Manese, Kathy Bieschke, Kate Richmond, Dahomey Abanishe, Erin Cross, Cindy Boyd, Karlene Burrell-McCrae, Judy Holloway, Ron Duran, Carlton Parks, Morgan Sammons, Sylvie Taylor, Charley Lang, Heather Huff, Marie Keller, Elise Turen, and Aydin Kennedy. Each of them has had a critical part in shaping his attitudes, knowledge, and skills about serving LGBTQ people through the way they teach, the way they live, the questions that they ask about the world and the people in it, and the questions that they ask him.

Jeanne would like to thank the many graduate students, community members, K–12 students, teachers, and educators who helped her learn and continually finesse the best ways to expand the support and affirmation for LGBTQ people. It is an honor to be an educator and trainer at a time in history when LGBTQ rights are expanding because of the many people in the LGBTQ community and supporters who worked so hard to make our work today possible. Jeanne thanks the many educators, supervisors, and mentors over the years who have taught her how to bring about positive change, no matter how small or large, whenever and wherever possible. She thanks the amazing editorial staff at APA Books for their care and commitment to this book. And huge thanks are due to Dr. Theodore Burnes; there was a reason he was her wing/ring man at her wedding. He is in the true sense a friend and an amazing advocate. He is a role model on how to maintain one's values while promoting social justice and bringing about change. Jeanne thanks him also for his wicked sense of humor and many voice messages that liven up her days. She is glad they have been and continue to be on this professional journey together. She would also like to thank her family and friends who continuously supported her in this endeavor. Finally, to her wife, Julia Sawabini, who for over 23 years has provided the continual support and love that made being an educator about LGBTQ issues possible: Jeanne could not have been half as effective in teaching, training, writing, and providing psychological services without Julia's unwavering support. She loves and thinks the world of her each and every day.

Finally, Theo and Jeanne would both like to thank the many members of APA Division 44 and the American Counseling Association's Association of LGBT Issues in Counseling, who, through years of their caring and tenacity, made this book even possible.

TEACHING
LGBTQ
PSYCHOLOGY

Theodore R. Burnes and Jeanne L. Stanley

Introduction

1

Dr. Coltin receives the call early on a Monday morning: an offer to do a training series at a community mental health agency on "LGBTQ mental wellness" as part of the agency's commitment to educating its clients and communities about their various diverse identities. Dr. Coltin, an early career African American psychologist who has been an adjunct professor and a practicing psychologist for almost five years, has some knowledge about diversity from his doctoral studies and continuing education seminars. Given some of his experiences in his graduate coursework (e.g., comments made by classmates in his learning experiences about LGBTQ people), he knows that teaching an entire 2-hour seminar about LGBTQ psychology may be more challenging than other types of teaching in which he has engaged previously. Specifically, how will he begin to structure content in his training seminar? What ethical issues should he cover in his training for consumers of mental health services, and why? Further, given that there may be a wide range of knowledge and attitudes about lesbian, gay, bisexual, transgender, queer, and questioning

http://dx.doi.org/10.1037/0000015-001
Teaching LGBTQ Psychology: Queering Innovative Pedagogy and Practice, T. R. Burnes and J. L. Stanley (Editors)

people in the room, what are the ways that he might
need to navigate difficult reactions, emotions, or learning
processes in the room? Dr. Coltin begins to experience
feelings of doubt.

The Movement Advancement Project of GLAAD (2016) notes that
there is an increasing visibility of lesbian, gay, bisexual, transgender,
and queer or questioning (LGBTQ) people in society, and that this discernibility has been greater than in previously documented periods of
history. Such increased visibility brings with it the need for more education about LGBTQ psychology, including training for mental health providers (MHPs; including psychologists, professional counselors, social
workers, marriage and family therapists, and other MHPs). As depicted
in the vignette with Dr. Coltin, there is a corresponding need for more
information about teaching LGBTQ psychology. Although scholars and
practitioners in mental health services have long called for education
in the area of LGBTQ psychology, there is still a dearth of information
available (ALGBTIC LGBQQIA Competencies Taskforce, 2013; American Psychological Association, 2012; Vaughan et al., 2014) and a lack
of systemic institutionalization of LGBTQ training and education in
psychological practice (including graduate training programs, accreditation, predoctoral internship programs, licensure exams, etc.).

Historically, training for MHPs in LGBTQ issues has centered on theoretical models of LGBTQ identity development as part of overall cultural
competence training (Sue & Sue, 2015). However, we contend that current sexuality and gender-focused education and training in psychology
must expand to thoroughly address the clinical skills that are needed
to practice competently with LGBTQ people. The term *queer* (Fassinger
& Arseneau, 2007) often reflects a move away from traditional norms
that may not allow for multiple realities and differing perspectives on
gender and sexuality. The term also partially originated from activist contexts, having to do with practices and identities that subverted norms of
patriarchy, gender dichotomy, sexual expression within heteronormative relationships, and traditional gender expression (Laing, Pilcher, &
Smith, 2015). As the title of this book involves queering pedagogy and
practice, we contend that the queering must occur not only with educational content but also with educational process. Specifically, the teaching
of gender and sexuality in a contemporary context must include the ability to radically include multiple perspectives simultaneously in a classroom or other learning space, even when these views oppose each other.
Further, queering classroom process also means transcending traditional
methods (and questioning basic assumptions of education hierarchies)
and modes of instruction to include the learner in the development of
the learning space, learning goals, and methods of learning assessment.

Such a shift in pedagogy, education, and training is necessary to meet the evolving demands of mental health practice in diverse settings and communities. Further, theoretical and empirical writings about such a shift are in critical need given the necessity for competent teaching practice.

The literature (e.g., Prilleltensky & Nelson, 2002) has suggested that traditional models of sexuality and gender-focused education may not work in increasingly diverse settings and across a wide range of educational and professional environments. As there are increasing online educational environments across a range of settings (Braunsberger, McCuiston, Patterson, & Watkins, 2016), the need to include topics related to LGBTQ psychology has become increasingly critical. Online learning also occurs in a diversity of formats, from on-ground courses that use online supplemental platforms for discussion and reading (e.g., Blackboard, Moodle) to courses that are entirely online using applications such as GoToMeeting (Dabbagh et al., 2016). This diversity of online education formats and the plethora of settings in which online learning about LGBTQ mental health occurs necessitate the queering of both educational content and process. Further, how educators not only assess learning in online environments but also maintain student safety from oppression and marginalizing content in an online forum necessitate that MHPs teaching LGBTQ psychology learn how they adapt their teaching pedagogy and practice for use in online platforms.

Recognition of LGBTQ cultures and communities around the world necessitates the application of global perspectives to LGBTQ-focused instruction and pedagogy (Platt & Laszloffy, 2013). Although some have used the term *culture* to talk solely about race and ethnicity, scholars have broadened *culture* to address many sociocultural identities, including sexual orientation and gender identity (Sue & Sue, 2015). Moreover, the specific needs for professional care among LGBTQ individuals outside the United States are vastly different from those in the United States. Understanding the range of care needs people bring with them is imperative for training the next generation of providers in various disciplines (Daulaire, 2014). Similarly, training may also be different for MHPs in regard to various settings and global locations (e.g., how a social worker is trained in Bangkok is different from how a clinical psychologist is trained in London).

In addition to incorporating global perspectives, educators also have to make the understanding of how sexuality and gender may differ in various disciplines of mental health (e.g., psychology, social work, clinical counseling; Burnes, Rowan, & Paul, 2017) a priority. Such differences are a topic in need of further understanding, assessment, and evaluation. Such differences point to the necessity of understanding not only how constructs of sexual orientation and gender affect mental health work but also how different disciplines have varying abilities and ideas about how to incorporate these various constructs—both pedagogically as well as politically (Tower, 2016).

Scholars (e.g., Adams, Bell, & Griffin, 2007; Nelson & Prilleltensky, 2010) have noted the importance of teaching about diversity and multiculturalism in settings outside the classroom. Examples of community settings in which mental health services are provided include clinical settings within universities (e.g., university counseling centers) and community spaces that are not traditionally viewed as education spaces but in which clinical education may often occur (e.g., a religious organization that hosts a psychoeducational workshop about mental health issues for diverse communities).

This expansion in the numbers of settings and in the inclusion of intersecting multicultural identities results in the need to incorporate social justice into the teaching of LGBTQ psychology. *Social justice*, or the application of multicultural knowledge, attitudes, and awareness to create systemic change with the goal of dismantling various types of cultural marginalization and cultural privilege, is both a process and a goal within educational settings (Burnes & Manese, 2008). Although social justice has been documented as a helpful tool in training trainees in psychology to learn about multicultural issues (Burnes & Singh, 2010) such as LGBTQ psychology, educational and psychology literatures still lack application-focused writings that help LGBTQ psychology educators to apply social justice–focused content to their work.

Although the American Psychological Association (APA) has constructed several sets of guidelines for culture-specific training in professional practice competencies (e.g., the *APA Guidelines on Multicultural Education, Training, Research, Practice and Organizational Change for Psychologists*, 2002; *Guidelines for Psychological Practice With Lesbian, Gay, and Bisexual Clients*, 2012; *Guidelines for Prevention in Psychology*, 2014; *Guidelines for Psychological Practice With Transgender and Gender Nonconforming People*, 2015), there is still a lack of resources regarding how educators in these settings may best teach about mental health and wellness for LGBTQ populations. Trainees within the various mental health disciplines are at differing professional developmental levels: practicum, pre- and post-doctoral internships, and professional continuing education. Within this range of knowledge, attitudes, and skills, information and training approaches that are scaffolded and graded in complexity are essential for educators to adequately teach and train about LGBTQ psychology.

Compounding the lack of resources is the lack of agreed-on competencies needed for educators and trainers who are teaching LGBTQ psychology. Our professional networks are filled with stories of MHPs who personally identify somewhere on the LGBTQ spectrum of identities and on the basis solely of their identity are asked to teach LGBTQ psychology-focused courses, lectures, in-service training, and work-shops. Identification within LGBTQ cultures and communities is not the same as competence for teaching and training in LGBTQ psychology. Further, an individual's competence in teaching LGBTQ psychology is not a direct reflection or result of the educator's identity. With strong training in teaching LGBTQ psychology, all MHPs can become competent in working with LGBTQ clients, and an increasing number of educators from across different sexual orientations and gender identities can foster such competence. The historical myths and stereotypes that link the content of one's teaching to one's identity necessitate a greater understanding of the unique theoretical frameworks, skills, awareness, and resource knowledge needed for the effective teaching of LGBTQ psychology and for professionals to learn such competence and in turn work with LGBTQ clients.

Not only is there a lack of awareness related to instructor competence, but literature (e.g., Obedin-Maliver et al., 2011) also consistently documents a lack of competence related to the integration of LGBTQ-related content in the classroom. Specifically, educators note that there is a consistent tension between the integration of LGBTQ psychology content into teaching and training and the lack of stand-alone courses, training modules, and fieldwork related to LGBTQ mental health in various mental health disciplines. As we have prepared this volume and shared our ideas about its content with multiple people, we have been consistently reminded of the need for mental health agency administrators, academic program chairs, and leaders in various community settings to create specific training modules that focus on LGBTQ psychology while also being mindful of including such content in a variety of different courses that may not be specific to LGBTQ individuals and communities.

Our purpose in creating this volume is that the content, processes, tips, and strategies presented here can be used in the creation of stand-alone courses and training modules while being intentionally and purposely integrated into courses and training modules in which LGBTQ psychology is not the sole focus. For example, the Gender Unicorn (see Chapter 7, Activity 7.1) is a one-page education tool that can be used in multiple educational settings, from classrooms to community training, as a quick reference to assist people in learning some of the foundational terminology in regard to sexual and gender identities. Another example is the spectrum model of sex, gender, and sexuality (see Chapter 8, Figure 8.1 and Activity 8.2). This activity can be synthesized with a wide variety of topics but can also be used to help individuals with various degrees of content knowledge about LGBTQ mental health to reflect on the identities of the people they serve from a place of curiosity and insight.

In this edited volume, we provide a theoretical and practical guide for instructors who are teaching about LGBTQ issues in a variety of contexts and settings. The book is a resource for those who teach and train MHPs. However, we believe that the content is also relevant and helpful for professionals in various disciplines who are teaching in academic settings, for MHPs who deliver community outreach and/or psychoeducational programs in various settings (including, but not limited to, religious organizations, youth-centered social services, and political organizations), and for MHPs who conduct research related to LGBTQ issues. This book is intended also as a resource for those who are designing, implementing, and evaluating continuing education programs for MHPs. The chapters include recommendations, teaching activities, and best practices to empower educators.

Our Goals in Writing This Book

The goal of this book is to expand instructors' pedagogy and teaching practice when educating about psychological intervention(s), sexual orientation, and gender identity. Presenting innovative strategies for teaching LGBTQ psychology is a critical part of this volume, but we also understand that such an emphasis is not enough to ensure a text that will assist in developing quality teaching practice. Specifically, we must be able to ensure also that students are learning in meaningful ways. Scholars have increasingly cited the need to have innovative instructional strategies that also consider how teaching practice contributes to student learning (Bain, 2004).

The literature on teaching has documented the importance of educators' engagement, personality, and teaching as part of the educational process. In one classic study, students were divided into two separate classrooms. In one classroom, an actor given the name of Dr. Fox gave a lecture in a monotone voice about game theory and physical education; in the other classroom, a scientist with expertise also gave the same lecture in a monotone voice. When students were tested on the information, they learned more from the scientist than from Dr. Fox. However, in the second half of the study, Dr. Fox gave the lecture in an engaged manner and the scientist again gave the lecture in a monotone voice. This time, students rated Dr. Fox higher than the scientist. Such lack of correlation between content coverage and ratings under conditions of connection to the instructor has become known as the *Dr. Fox effect* (Naftulin, Ware, & Donnelly, 1973). The literature rarely documents, however, to what extent such factors and corresponding teaching processes affect actual student learning (Huang & Lin, 2014). We hope that this book will empower educators to engage learners and create socially just classrooms while implementing rigorous learning goals, corresponding classroom activities, and equally rigorous evaluation strategies. We also hope that this text will help to begin to create a body of knowledge about how students learn deeply and critically about sexual orientation and gender identity.

We have a related and equally important goal of reducing minority stress and cultural marginalization for LGBTQ people by heightening the awareness of individuals who train and teach MHPs and researchers to provide effective mental health services with them. To do this, we asked contributors to focus on informing readers about culturally competent training related to LGBTQ psychology and education. The chapters cover a variety of topics related to educating about LGBTQ issues, including training of clinical skills, designing psychoeducation programs related to LGBTQ issues, teaching about sexual orientation and gender identity in community settings, managing various classroom dynamics, and facilitating difficult dialogues related to LGBTQ issues.

We also asked our contributors to provide a foundation for further developing the theory, research, and evidence-based practice for teaching LGBTQ psychology by highlighting existing strategies, teaching activities, and theoretical writings about previously undocumented phenomena related to teaching. Therefore, experts in the areas of pedagogy and LGBTQ psychology have reviewed the extant literature and provided practical strategies for teaching about work with LGBTQ populations, emphasizing the importance of collaborative education to address medical, psychosocial, educational, ethical, and legislative matters. Critical to this text is the inclusion of empirical research that supports innovative pedagogy and practice. Thus, we address empirical research in each of the chapters and synthesize the empirical literature and related content in a separate final chapter.

MHPs using this edited volume will find current information on teaching about LGBTQ cultures and communities. In particular, they will be able to use this text to address issues related to, but not limited to, teaching foundational information regarding identity development; affirmative language and terminology; coming out issues for LGBTQ individuals; interventions and prevention efforts that are relevant to LGBTQ communities; LGBTQ history, culture, and community and how history, identity, culture, and community may affect various aspects of functioning for LGBTQ individuals; and intersections of identity development for individuals with various privileged and marginalized identities.

Thematic Framework

With these goals, we as editors of this text created a theoretical framework comprising six themes. We use these themes to organize the text and to create consistency in educators' learning.

THEME 1. INTERSECTING, MULTIPLE IDENTITIES

All chapters in this volume have highlighted the multiple cultural identities (e.g., race, ethnicity, class, gender, sexual orientation, religion, country of origin) of teachers and learners as well as the multiple professional identities (e.g., instructor/student, supervisor/supervisee, workshop facilitator/attendee) that are relevant when teaching LGBTQ issues in a variety of contexts. The book also addresses the importance of teaching about the intersection of sociocultural identities for LGBTQ people (Stanley, 2004). For example, religious and spiritual identities can be a source of positive perspectives for some LGBTQ people and, therefore, educators may want to address such multiple intersections as that of religions and LGBTQ identities.

THEME 2. STRENGTH-BASED, EMPOWERMENT-FOCUSED LEARNING

Because scholars are increasingly focusing on a shift away from a pathology-focused model of sexual orientation and gender identity (Vaughan & Rodriguez, 2014), the authors in this text explore ways that mental health educators and practitioners can consider and address professional development level, diverse learning styles, and existing strengths of those who are learning. Although it is important to discuss how educators include and facilitate learning about prejudice and discrimination (see the next section), the authors in this book also focus on teaching about LGBTQ people from a resilience, wellness-focused framework.

THEME 3. IDENTIFYING AND OUTLINING DIFFERENCES BETWEEN SEXUAL ORIENTATION AND GENDER IDENTITY

Several scholars (e.g., Alderson, 2013) have noted the absence of differentiation between sexual orientation and gender identity diversity in many LGBTQ training resources. However, we recognize the diversity and critical within-group differences when teaching about sexual orientation, gender diversity, and LGBTQ psychology. In this book, we take into account the conceptual and practical differences between sexual orientation and gender identity in our explorations of empirical research, conceptual and pedagogical frameworks, and applied teaching strategies. The authors explore ways that educators who teach about working with LGBTQ clients may conceptualize or use teaching interventions that are different when addressing sexual orientation than when they teach about gender identity.

THEME 4. TEACHING PRACTICE

Although there is existing literature that has found that students in social science programs have an increased understanding of sexuality (Stombler, Baunach, Simonds, Windsor, & Burgess, 2013) and gender (Zosuls, Miller, Ruble, Martin, & Fabes, 2011), there is no literature that discusses the practice of teaching about LGBTQ issues and specifically not about LGBTQ issues in psychology. The authors in this text include a focus on the practice of teaching, including examples of classroom discourse, innovative teaching tools, and exercises. Each chapter includes Activities that educators can use in their classrooms. These activities are also available for download online (http://pubs.apa.org/books/supp/burnes).

THEME 5. MINORITY STRESS AND MARGINALIZATION

Meyer (2003) noted the importance of psychologists' understanding of minority stress: chronically high levels of stress faced by members of stigmatized minority groups. Meyer stated that such stress may be caused by a number of factors, but the most well-understood causes of minority stress are interpersonal prejudice and discrimination. It is critical that educators help trainees understand the impact of minority stress on the lived experiences of LGBTQ people. Therefore, within the context of their respective chapters, the authors identify innovative strategies that instructors can use to explain the concepts of marginalization and minority stress to trainees while accommodating various learning styles.

THEME 6. RESEARCH AND EMPIRICALLY INFORMED PEDAGOGY

Paramount to the creation of this book is the inclusion of empirical research that supports innovative teaching pedagogy and practice. Thus, the authors address empirical research in each of their chapters and a synthesis of the empirical literature in the final chapter.

In addition to these six themes, we want to explicitly note the use of terminology throughout the book. Authors will use the acronym *LGBTQ* for lesbian, gay, bisexual, transgender, questioning, and queer. Such language is meant to be inclusive given the current lexicon. Although various other letters may be added to the initials depending on community and context, no specific letter per se represents each individual person's multidimensional identities. We acknowledge that LGBTQ may feel representative of some people and not others. Further, we do not use the term *homosexual* in this volume because it is a medically constructed identity label with pathology-focused connotations embedded in its use. Because there is historical significance to this word, the word *homosexual* will only be used in the book when addressing its historical underpinnings or when referencing a respective author's terminology.

Similarly, an acronym that addresses all gender identities and expressions would fill this page and still not speak to every person. We have chosen to use the acronym GET, with the GE for gender expansive and the T for transgender. As language continues to evolve and change with regard to gender and sexual identity over time, environment, and culture (Fassinger & Arseneau, 2007), we recognize that these acronyms may not be inclusive of individuals of certain identities, generations, and geographic origins; we use it with the best of intentions for inclusivity.

The Chapters in This Book

Using these goals and themes, the chapters herein provide a wide range of information about the teaching of sexual orientation and gender identity from an LGBTQ-focused framework. The first section of the text, Chapters 2 to 5, provides theoretical and historical contexts to help the reader understand the current context in teaching LGBTQ psychology. In Chapter 2, Jeanne L. Stanley, Theodore R. Burnes, and Jacqueline S. Weinstock provide historical and contextual information about how teaching LGBTQ psychology has changed over time. Building on these historical foundations in Chapter 3, Courtney M. Dunne presents current theoretical perspectives related to pedagogy for those who are teaching about LGBTQ individuals, cultures, and communities. In Chapter 4, Jeanne L. Stanley addresses ethical and legislative issues to be aware of when teaching LGBTQ psychology in various contexts. Building on these first four chapters, Anneliese A. Singh and Kim Lee Hughes concretely present a social justice framework for teaching LGBTQ psychology in Chapter 5 and begin to identify ways that systemic change can be introduced. The authors outline a teaching pedagogy that includes active dismantling of intersecting privileges and oppressions. They show how such dismantling can provide a strong foundation for effective teaching in LGBTQ psychology.

In the second section of the book, the authors of Chapters 6 to 10 discuss specific tools for teaching LGBTQ psychology using the increasing knowledge, skills, and awareness gained from previous chapters. In Chapter 6, Carlton W. Parks and Theodore R. Burnes describe effective strategies for classroom management and the facilitation of difficult dialogues when teaching about the psychological functioning of LGBTQ individuals, cultures, and communities. In Chapter 7, Theodore R. Burnes and Paul N. T. Hovanesian introduce the reader to psychoeducation groups as a way of teaching about LGBTQ psychology. In Chapter 8, three community practitioners, Cadyn Cathers, Caroline Carter, and Susan P. Landon, address how educators can teach about LGBTQ psychology in community-based settings using exercises that are geared toward broader audiences. Chapter 9, by Tiffany O'Shaughnessy and Nicholas Ladany, focuses on the importance of MHPs' educational roles when providing clinical supervision through the use of models, cultural self-awareness, and clinical strategies. Finally Chapter 10, by Tania Israel and Jay N. Bettergarcia, addresses evidence-based teaching of LGBTQ issues in psychology. The authors review current research that enables the reader to contextualize the teaching of LGBTQ psychology using a merging of science and teaching practice.

References

Adams, M., Bell, L. A., & Griffin, P. (Eds.). (2007). *Teaching for diversity and social justice*. New York, NY: Routledge.

Alderson, K. (2013). *Counseling LGBTI clients*. Thousand Oaks, CA: Sage.

ALGBTIC LGBQQIA Competencies Taskforce. (2013). Association for Lesbian, Gay, Bisexual, and Transgender Issues in Counseling Competencies for Counseling With Lesbian, Gay, Bisexual, Queer, Questioning, Intersex, and Ally Individuals. *Journal of LGBT Issues in Counseling*, 7, 2–43. http://dx.doi.org/10.1080/15538605.2013.755444

American Psychological Association. (2002). *APA guidelines on multicultural education, training, research, practice and organizational change for psychologists*. Retrieved from http://www.apa.org/pi/oema/resources/policy/multicultural-guidelines.aspx

American Psychological Association. (2012). Guidelines for psychological practice with lesbian, gay, and bisexual clients. *American Psychologist*, 67, 10–42. http://dx.doi.org/10.1037/a0024659

American Psychological Association. (2014). Guidelines for prevention in psychology. *American Psychologist*, 69, 285–296. http://dx.doi.org/10.1037/a0034569

American Psychological Association. (2015). Guidelines for psychological practice with transgender and gender nonconforming people. *American Psychologist, 70,* 832–864. http://dx.doi.org/10.1037/a0039906

Bain, K. (2004). *What the best college teachers do.* Cambridge, MA: Harvard University Press.

Braunsberger, K., McCuiston, V., Patterson, G., & Watkins, A. (2016). Perceived risks and psychological well-being in online education: Implications for grade expectations and future enrollment. In M. D. Groza & C. B. Ragland (Eds.), *Marketing challenges in a turbulent business environment* (pp. 487–488). http://dx.doi.org/10.1007/978-3-319-19428-8_123

Burnes, T. R., & Manese, J. E. (2008). Social justice in an accredited internship in professional psychology: Answering the call. *Training and Education in Professional Psychology, 2,* 176–181. http://dx.doi.org/10.1037/1931-3918.2.3.176

Burnes, T. R., Rowan, S. F., & Paul, P. L. (2017). Clinical supervision with TGNC clients in health service psychology. In A. A. Singh & l. m. dickey (Eds.), *Affirmative counseling and psychological practice with transgender and gender nonconforming clients* (pp. 175–190). Washington, DC: American Psychological Association.

Burnes, T. R., & Singh, A. A. (2010). Integrating social justice training into the practicum experience for psychology trainees: Starting earlier. *Training and Education in Professional Psychology, 4,* 153–162. http://dx.doi.org/10.1037/a0019385

Dabbagh, N., Benson, A. D., Denham, A., Joseph, R., Al-Freih, M., Zgheib, G., . . . Guo, Z. (2016). Evolution of learning technologies: Past, present, and future. In N. Dabbagh, A. D. Benson, A. Denham, R. Joseph, M. Al-Freih, G. Zgheib, . . . Z. Guo (Eds.), *Learning technologies and globalization* (pp. 1–7). New York, NY: Springer.

Daulaire, N. (2014). The importance of LGBT health on a global scale. *LGBT Health, 1,* 8–9. http://dx.doi.org/10.1089/lgbt.2013.0008

Fassinger, R. E., & Arseneau, J. R. (2007). "I'd rather get wet than be under that umbrella": Differentiating the experiences and identities of lesbian, gay, bisexual, and transgender people. In K. J. Bieschke, R. M. Perez, & K. A. DeBord (Eds.), *Handbook of counseling and psychotherapy with lesbian, gay, bisexual, and transgender clients* (2nd ed., pp. 19–49). http://dx.doi.org/10.1037/11482-001

GLAAD. (2016). *Studio responsibility index 2016.* Retrieved from http://www.glaad.org/files/2016_SRI.pdf

Huang, Y.-C., & Lin, S.-H. (2014). Assessment of charisma as a factor in effective teaching. *Journal of Educational Technology & Society, 17,* 284–295.

Laing, M., Pilcher, K., & Smith, N. (Eds.). (2015). *Queer sex work.* Milton Park, England: Routledge.

Meyer, I. H. (2003). Prejudice, social stress, and mental health in lesbian, gay, and bisexual populations: Conceptual issues and research evidence. *Psychological Bulletin, 129*, 674–697. http://dx.doi.org/10.1037/ 0033-2909.129.5.674

Naftulin, D. H., Ware, J. E., & Donnelly, F. A. (1973). The Doctor Fox lecture: A paradigm of educational seduction. *Journal of Medical Education, 48*, 630–635. http://dx.doi.org/10.1097/00001888-197307000-00003

Nelson, G., & Prilleltensky, I. (Eds.). (2010). *Community psychology: In pursuit of liberation and well-being* (2nd ed.). Basingstoke, England: Palgrave Macmillan.

Obedin-Maliver, J., Goldsmith, E. S., Stewart, L., White, W., Tran, E., Brenman, S., . . . Lunn, M. R. (2011, September 7). Lesbian, gay, bisexual, and transgender-related content in undergraduate medical education. *JAMA, 306*, 971–977. http://dx.doi.org/10.1001/ jama.2011.1255

Platt, J. J., & Laszloffy, T. A. (2013). Critical patriotism: Incorporating nationality into MFT education and training. *Journal of Marital and Family Therapy, 39*, 441–456. http://dx.doi.org/10.1111/j.1752-0606.2012.00325.x

Prilleltensky, I., & Nelson, G. (2002). *Doing psychology critically: Making a difference in diverse settings*. New York, NY: Palgrave Macmillan.

Stanley, J. L. (2004). Biracial lesbian and bisexual women: Understanding the unique aspects and interactional processes of multiple minority identities. In A. R. Gillem & C. A. Thompson (Eds.), *Biracial women in therapy: Between the rock of gender and the hard place of race* (pp. 159–171). New York, NY: Haworth Press.

Stombler, M., Baunach, D. M., Simonds, D., Windsor, E., & Burgess, E. O. (Eds.). (2013). *Sex matters: The sexuality and society reader* (4th ed.). New York, NY: Norton.

Sue, D. W., & Sue, D. (2015). *Counseling the culturally diverse: Theory and practice* (7th ed.). New York, NY: Wiley.

Tower, K. (2016). Third gender and the third world: Tracing social and legal acceptance of the transgender community in developing countries. *CONCEPT, 39*. Retrieved from http://concept.journals.villanova. edu/article/view/2082/1857

Vaughan, M. D., Miles, J., Parent, M. C., Lee, H. S., Tilghman, J. D., & Prokhorets, S. (2014). A content analysis of LGBT-themed positive psychology articles. *Psychology of Sexual Orientation and Gender Diversity, 1*, 313–324. http://dx.doi.org/10.1037/sgd0000060

Vaughan, M. D., & Rodriguez, E. M. (2014). LGBT strengths: Incorporating positive psychology into theory, research, training, and practice. *Psychology of Sexual Orientation and Gender Diversity, 1*, 325–334. http:// dx.doi.org/10.1037/sgd0000053

Zosuls, K. M., Miller, C. F., Ruble, D. N., Martin, C. L., & Fabes, R. A. (2011). Gender development research in sex roles: Historical trends and future directions. *Sex Roles, 64*, 826–842. http://dx.doi.org/10.1007/ s11199-010-9902-3

Jeanne L. Stanley, Theodore R. Burnes, and Jacqueline S. Weinstock

Teaching the History of LGBTQ Psychology

2

The discipline of lesbian, gay, bisexual, transgender, queer, and questioning (LGBTQ) psychology is defined as "a branch of psychology that is affirmative of LGBTQ people" and that "seeks to challenge prejudice and discrimination against LGBTQ people" while offering "a range of psychological perspectives on the lives and experiences of LGBTQ people and on LGBTQ sexualities and genders" (Clarke, Ellis, Peel, & Riggs, 2010, p. 6). What is the history of this relatively new discipline, and how might psychology educators effectively teach this history to mental health practitioner (MHP) trainees? Such teaching and corresponding student learning are especially challenging when it may be easier and more common for the current generation of students to write off their elders' views and even earlier perspectives about LGBTQ issues as naïve, ill-informed, or downright bigoted (Orel & Fruhauf, 2014).

Scholars have documented that educators consistently face struggles related to teaching historical content about topics because it may force learners to adapt their existing knowledge

http://dx.doi.org/10.1037/0000015-002
Teaching LGBTQ Psychology: Queering Innovative Pedagogy and Practice, T. R. Burnes and J. L. Stanley (Editors)

to incorporate different historical perspectives (Bain, 2004). Further, there is literature noting that teaching historical context related to social and cultural identities requires learners to become more fully aware of discrimination and oppression that individuals with marginalized identities have experienced (Spring, 2012). Specifically, it can take more effort for individuals learning about LGBTQ psychology to understand the nature of early beliefs about sexuality and gender and the factors that contributed to their development and endorsement than to only engage with current knowledge and attitudes about LGBTQ people. Still harder is recognizing that the roots of these early beliefs are still present in misconceptions and surreptitious prejudice and discrimination surrounding LGBTQ people and even in current, seemingly more progressive perspectives within psychology. For all these reasons, there is much to be gained by teaching the history of LGBTQ issues in psychology to students.

It is important that individuals engaging with this chapter understand that it is in no way a complete history (or even a thorough overview) of LGBTQ history. Books such as Jonathan Katz's (1978) classic, *Gay American History*; Lillian Faderman's *The Gay Revolution: The Story of the Struggle* (2015) and *Odd Girls and Twilight Lovers: A History of Lesbian Life in 20th-Century America* (2012); and Marc Stein's (2004) *Encyclopedia of Lesbian, Gay, Bisexual, and Transgender History in America* are excellent resources for gaining a more detailed history of LGBTQ people in relation to psychology. The material covered in this chapter is meant to assist the educator with understanding trends that still affect how psychology views and works with LGBTQ people, and we offer recommendations for how to teach the history of LGBTQ psychology.

Historical Trends in LGBTQ Psychology

Tracing the relationship between the historical shifts in how society has viewed LGBTQ people and how psychology has presented and taught about LGBTQ individuals provides students with the opportunity to understand better the integral role psychology has had in the past century in the portrayal of LGBTQ individuals. Critical race theory scholars (e.g., Lynn & Dixson, 2013; Marable, 2015) have noted the importance of challenging historicism in classrooms as part of social justice education, noting that providing a space for people to learn history helps individuals to grapple with privilege and oppression instead of pretending that historical oppression does not exist. Marable (2015) noted that when such lack of historical knowledge exists, individuals have the privilege of not having to understand how historical inequality has greatly contributed to present-day systemic and cultural dynamics. Such a framework can also be used for LGBTQ psychology. Consider how psychology has traversed past ruts created by religion, law, and medicine's treatment of homosexuality, bisexuality, and transgender identity as a sin, a crime, and an illness to arrive at today's affirmative approaches toward LGBTQ individuals. Consider as well how conceptualizations of sexual identities and gender identities (and related terms for these identities) have changed. As described in Activity 2.1, introducing students to some of these changing conceptualizations and related measurement issues as they emerged in historical contexts may be a useful in-class exercise.

It is important to note that many individuals learning about LGBTQ psychology's history focus only on European historical trends without reviewing the many ways that diverse sexuality and gender have been presented in non-Western cultures (Wiesner-Hanks, 2010). For example, learners in community settings may refer to transgender identities as a "new phenomenon" given that transgender people have gained increased attention in Western media in the past 5 years. Educators in these settings may find it helpful to include information and discussions on the hijras of India and their historical impact on the understanding of gender in South Asian communities at various points in history (Reddy, 2010). Teaching these historical paradigms (and the subsequent paradigm shifts) is an important part of the LGBTQ psychology learning experience.

RELIGION: SIN

It is important for students to understand that, with respect to early religious views in the United States toward homosexuality, bisexuality, and transgender identity, the dominant perspective was that homosexual acts were sinful, and those engaging in such acts were therefore by definition sinners. Some religious doctrines continue to uphold these beliefs, although thought continues to be changed and shaped within various organized religious institutions that are more affirmative and/or celebratory of LGBTQ identities. Those transgressing binary sex and gender categories, as well as heterosexual expectations, were viewed as going against the will of God and threatening the moral and social fabric of society (Beere, 1990). From these beliefs flourished the message that homosexual acts were not only a choice but also an immoral choice. Negative religious views and this "choice" stance have affected and continue to affect the provision of mental health services with the aim of repairing, converting, and altering the person on the basis of their "free choice" regarding their sexual/gender orientation (Haldeman, 1994). Educators may find that students who have had personal histories that are embedded in these religious contexts have difficulty confronting certain organized religions' oppressive attitudes. Guilt and shame related to cultural privilege may also emerge and take many forms. Thus, educators' creation of safe spaces and structured activities is necessary for learners to process and learn historical context, historical trauma, and patterns of historical marginalization within various religions institutions.

LAW: ILLEGAL

Early secular laws against same-sex acts were rooted in these religious views; for example, in England in 1533 the first secular law was put in place that criminalized same-sex sex acts, and it was soon adopted by many of the colonies in America (Group for the Advancement of Psychiatry [GAP], 2012). Some of the colonies "simply cited Leviticus as the basis for establishing sodomy as a capital offense," reflecting how tied to each other religious and criminal conceptions of homosexuality were in burgeoning America (GAP, 2012, "Sodomy and Other 'Crimes Against Nature,'" para. 3).

By the turn of the century, homosexuals were no longer just deviants, but threats to America's youth. Psychology and psychiatry were resources used by the legal system to identify homosexual men and women who were considered predators. Incarceration and other forms of punishment were enacted to control what was considered immoral or antisocial behavior. These punishments were also enacted to separate homosexuals from the mainstream to prevent the spread of such behavior to the young and the vulnerable because homosexuality was considered by some to be contagious (Knauer, 2000; Rousseau, 2013). Similar approaches were in evidence a half a century later during the HIV/AIDS crisis when religious leaders and politicians again rallied, recommending incarceration and seclusion of homosexuals to control the spread of the virus that was seen as "God's punishment" against immoral and illegal life choices.

Teaching these legal–historical underpinnings can be a useful tool to highlight the ways that privilege and oppression currently exist in contemporary LGBTQ psychology. Although students may think that the treatment of LGBTQ people as criminals is long in the past, it is useful to point out that it was only in 2003 that the U.S. Supreme Court ruling in *Lawrence v. Texas* (2003) struck down the sodomy law in Texas. It was not until this time that same-sex activity between consenting adults was legal nationwide. The step-by-step history of legal changes toward this end and the role that various mental health disciplines played in making the case for homosexual, bisexual, and transgender identities as natural and celebratory expressions offer a good example of the early interplay between social sciences and politics.

Some learners may also be under the misimpression that the 2015 landmark decision by the U.S. Supreme Court for marriage equality marked the end of unequal rights for LGBTQ individuals in the United States. It is useful for individuals learning about LGBTQ psychology in various settings to understand how history still strongly affects current attitudes and behavior toward LGBTQ individuals. Educators can give assignments such as having students compare and contrast past laws with current anti-LGBTQ legislation that restricts the rights of LGBTQ people. For example, students can compare the racial segregation laws regarding public bathrooms in the mid-20th century in the United States with the wave of anti-gender expansive and transgender (GET) laws that burgeoned in 2016 regarding bathroom access for people who are transgender. Students can also examine the proliferation of anti-LGBTQ legislation that arises in reaction to the expansion of LGBTQ rights. For example, in 2015, there were approximately 100 anti-LGBTQ proposed legislation acts across United States. Yet when same-sex marriage was legalized at the federal level in the middle of 2015, the first 10 weeks of 2016 saw nearly 200 anti-LGBT bills proposed in 34 states (Griffin, 2016). Another assignment could involve students comparing past anti-LGBTQ practices and laws with that of current legislation, such as the bill that was signed into law in 2016 in Tennessee that allows counselors to refuse to work with clients who have "goals, outcomes or behaviors that conflict with the sincerely held principles of the counselor or therapist" (Meyers, 2016, para. 1; see also Chapter 4 of this volume for a more detailed discussion).

For educators, presenting learners with psychological research that was and continues to be instrumental in demonstrating the equal status of gay and heterosexual couples and used as evidence in *Obergefell v. Hodges* (2015) to support LGBTQ rights can be a useful tool in teaching the history of LGBTQ psychology. Asking students to read specific articles and rulings can assist them in understanding the definite impact (both positive and negative) that psychology has had on LGBTQ civil rights. For example, articles documenting the work of Evelyn Hooker (1957, 1993) or the American Psychological Association's (APA; 2013) amicus brief in support of the *United States v. Windsor* (2013) Supreme Court case are important sources for students to learn how psychology has affected such legal processes.

PSYCHIATRY AND PSYCHOLOGY: MENTAL ILLNESS

In the later part of the 19th century, the field of psychology emerged from the study of philosophy as a separate discipline as part of the trend of Western physicians, scientists, and philosophers to "replace traditional religious explanations of human behavior with scientific and medical understanding" (Drescher, 2014b, p. 1472). Herek (1997–2012) noted that "by the end of the 19th century, medicine and psychiatry were effectively competing with religion and the law for jurisdiction over sexuality" (para. 3), thereby expanding the view of homosexuality beyond sin and crime to that of a pathology that should be treated. Various treatment approaches were developed and used, from behavioral treatments (e.g., vigorous exercise, "the rest cure," and for men, visiting prostitutes and marrying a woman), psychoanalytic approaches (e.g., reorientation therapy), and various medical approaches ranging from drug and hormone therapy to the extreme of lobotomies (Murphy, 2003).

In 1864, almost a decade before Wilhelm Wundt published his landmark book *Principles of Physiological Psychology* (1864/1910; considered by many as the marker of psychology as a separate discipline), Karl Heinrich Ulrich (1864/1994) published his works, a radical departure from the criminalization, sin/sodomy, and illness messages of homosexuality. Ulrich's stance was that same-sex desires, rather than being an acquired vice, had a biological basis and "inborn nature" and were, therefore, as natural as heterosexuality (Kennedy, 1997, p. 30). Ulrich's third sex theory also incorporated notions of gender identity and expression: He described how some men were born with a woman's spirit trapped in their bodies (Dresher, 2015). By 1869, Karl Maria Kertbeny, an early sex-law reformer, coined and publicly wrote about the terms *homosexual* and *heterosexual* (Dresher, 2015, p. 568). From this point forward, homosexuality was no longer considered a simple act or behavior; it was viewed as a distinct identity (Katz, 1983).

As psychology gained a foothold and sought to establish itself as a science, the field often fell in line with the medical establishment's illness model with the goal of curing mental illnesses. Under the cure model, psychology's goal was to alter a person's "homosexual orientation" to that of the perceived healthy heterosexual. In the 1940s, psychiatrists and psychologists alike were involved in rooting out homosexuals serving in the military, relying largely on prevailing gender stereotypes and the Rorschach test (Hegarty, 2003). Psychology gained in reputability during and after World War II as psychologists took on the role of "gatekeepers," protecting the contamination of the military by evaluating and foraging out homosexuals, theoretically ridding the military services of those who were thought to be easily blackmailed and vulnerable to becoming spies. Students may want to learn in more detail about the specific changes and patterns of intersection between psychology and LGBTQ identities. Educators in community settings may also want to embed historical knowledge about LGBTQ people from across various cultural groups.

Evolving Diagnoses Related to Sexual Orientation and Gender Identity

Teaching the history of LGBTQ psychology must include a critical examination of the diagnoses related to homosexuality and transgender identities and experiences as evidenced in the first edition of the *Diagnostic and Statistical Manual of Mental Disorders* (*DSM*; American Psychiatric Association, 1952) through to the most recent version. The *DSM* has been the prominent taxonomy reference for mental health disorders in the United States. The World Health Organization's (2016) *International Classification of Diseases* (10th rev.) is the other established classifier of mental disorders; however, until more recently, it has been used less by MHPs in the U.S., who have predominantly used the *DSM*.

There are five versions of the *DSM*, starting with the first *DSM* (American Psychiatric Association, 1952) and ending with the most recent version, the *DSM–5* (American Psychiatric Association, 2013). Most of the published research in psychology prior to and during the years when the first three editions of the *DSM* were in use focused on exploring three main questions: whether homosexuals were mentally ill, what caused homosexuality, and how homosexuals could be identified (Morin, 1977). These questions reflected and reinforced medical diagnostic assumptions that also supported the belief that one's sexual proclivities and activities were under the control of the person and, thus, could be changed or prevented through appropriate moral teachings, social expectations, punishment, or psychological and medical treatments. Barbara Gittings (2007), an LGBTQ activist, stated,

> It's difficult to explain to anyone who didn't live through that time how much homosexuality was under the thumb of psychiatry. The sickness label was an albatross around the neck of our early gay groups. . . . Anything we said on our behalf could be dismissed as "That's just your sickness talking." (p. xv)

The work of researchers such as Dr. Alfred Kinsey and Dr. Evelyn Hooker and activists such as Barbara Gittings and Frank Kameny as well as MHPs—in particular, Dr. John Fryer (initially known as "Dr. Anonymous"), who presented his experiences of homophobia and oppression from within the field of psychiatry and psychology—was instrumental in the Board of Trustees of the American Psychiatric Association's voting to remove homosexuality as a category of disorder in 1973. Until this point, LGBTQ people experienced persecution and untenable treatments with the goal of correcting their perceived disorder.

It is essential for students to learn how the efforts of social justice advocates changed for so many the understanding of LGBTQ people as disordered to normal.

Revision and removal of the diagnosis of gender identity as a disorder, however, has lagged behind that of homosexuality and bisexuality. After a great deal of debate and advocacy, the *DSM–5* changed the wording from *gender identity disorder* to *gender dysphoria*, dropping the stigmatizing *disorder* terminology. The diagnosis was also moved from the former category of sexual disorders and placed into its own category at the level of a primary diagnosis. With the addition of an adolescent and adult category and additional specifiers, more clarity exists, yet the continued presence of a mental diagnosis does not "completely reconcile a narrative of normality (no stigma attached to phenomenon) with one of pathology" (Drescher, 2014a, p. 12). However, access to care may be easier with this compromise.

Educators should highlight the continued debate in psychology between psychologists and GET activists regarding the current version of the *DSM* and related best practices. Especially useful is connecting current struggles related to gender identity with a pathological past and present with the history of homosexuality in the *DSM* and LGB activism (e.g., Lev, 2005, 2013). Asking learners to engage with their understanding of these shifts in diagnostic history may yield much discomfort—especially for individuals beginning their training as therapists and taking a course in diagnosis as one of their first classes. Educators should be prepared to address explicitly such difficulty and the subsequent feelings that might emerge.

Before the removal of the diagnosis of homosexuality from the *DSM*, diagnosing the disease led to the treatment of the illness of homosexuality, bisexuality, and gender "confusion." Murphy (2003) examined the underlying reasons offered in support of these "treatments" and how the rationales have changed as psychological and cultural attitudes toward homosexuality have transformed throughout U.S. history. Murphy noted that some of the earliest identified causes were considered biological or genetic; however, as the range of theoretical orientation options grew, so did the causation and related treatment options for LGBTQ clients. For example, as behaviorism gained as a leading treatment post–World War II, the focus was on sensitization therapies aimed at pairing repulsivity with same-sex sexual desire. Learners of the history of LGBTQ psychology should also understand that MHPs collaborated with physicians supporting the use of a range of methods, including chemical castration, electroshock, and ice pick lobotomies, as treatments to "cure" LGBTQ individuals (Milar, 2011). Whether termed *conversion therapy*, *reparative therapy*, or in the latest terminology, *sexual identity therapy*, there are still some MHPs who continue to treat with the goal of changing the state of a client's sexual orientation and/or gender identity. However, as of early

2016, most mental health organizations, U.S. President Barack Obama, five state legislatures, and several court cases have come out against these types of therapies (Burbank, 2016; Jarrett, 2015; Moss, 2014). There has also been substantial research evidence that such approaches are not only ineffective but also unethical and harmful (American Psychological Association, 2009).

How LGBTQ Identities Have Been Celebrated Over Time

The field of mental health in the past century has shifted toward becoming more accepting and affirming of LGBTQ people. That fact itself makes it worth the effort to teach students how social justice, advocacy, political engagement, and support from allies work to bring about change. Educators teaching the history of LGBTQ psychology should also include information related to these paradigm shifts.

Alfred Kinsey's (Kinsey, Pomeroy, & Martin, 1948, 1953) research was influential in shifting the perspective regarding LGB individuals. Kinsey's research examined sexuality among the general population and was, therefore, a critical influence in informing the debates in psychiatry, psychology, and the larger society about the normalcy of homosexuality. Kinsey's work also allowed for and made visible the experience of bisexuality in a paradigm that had polarized sexuality for multi-sex and same-sex experiences. He argued that all individuals have a bisexual potential, and he challenged the prevailing view that bisexuality did not exist and was only a way for those who were homosexual to try to fit in with societal norms (Bullough, 1995). Klein's (1993) Sexual Orientation Grid later expanded Kinsey's continuum to account for more than just sexual behavior (e.g., sexual attraction, self-identification) and took into account the fluidity of sexuality for some individuals over time. These and more recently constructed sexual identity labels, including no label, may be compiled and reviewed with students to demonstrate the progression of thinking in psychology and the culture (see Activity 2.1). A similar sequence of understandings may be developed and reviewed regarding gender identities and expressions.

Evelyn Hooker was also instrumental in moving the fields of psychology and medicine away from a pathology stance toward LGB people. Instead of accepting the prevailing belief in the early 1950s that homosexuals were maladjusted, she chose to test this conjecture using the scientific research method (Herek, 2014). Her research, in particular, has been recognized as instrumental in the removal of homosexuality from the *DSM* (Milar, 2011). By the 1960s and early 1970s, the shift had affected mental health therapies and treatment, which adopted a more acceptance-based approach toward working with LGB people.

It is also important for MHP trainees to recognize the role social movements have had in changing the understanding of sexual orientation and gender identity throughout history. Throughout global history, connected social groups (such as those involved in the South Asian understanding of gender fluidity and Magnus Hirschfeld's mobilization of social understanding of gay male identity through the Scientific Humanitarian Committee) and social justice movements have shaped how LGBTQ identities have been understood by psychology (Bullough, 2014).

The historical growth away from pathology to affirmation still varies within the subdisciplines of the mental health profession and is an important consideration for individuals learning about LGBTQ psychology within a historical context. For example, those using more traditional biomedical models within psychiatry may at times struggle in taking a wellness-model-based approach to conceptualizing a GET person's care. It may take advocating on the part of professors, instructors, and supervisors to integrate LGBTQ content into more traditionally based training programs. Educators should focus on resources from professional associations such as the APA and American Counseling Association and from evidence-based research and practice (see Chapter 10 of this book for a more detailed discussion) to garner information to use in making their case to committees on instruction and content course committees as well as to program directors, chairs, and deans about the benefits of addressing the historical transition to today's wellness approach toward LGBTQ individuals.

Teaching Strategies Focusing on the History of LGBTQ Issues in Relation to Psychology

Thus far, we have documented major historical trends in LGBTQ psychology and the importance of including these in LGBTQ psychology education. This section offers teaching ideas and opportunities to expand students' understanding and perspective of historical foundations and trends that have affected the link between LGBTQ people and psychology.

Religion, law, and medicine were used to restrict sexual and gender diversity and uphold power differentials in society. This point is quintessential for students to gain an understanding that any transgressions against the norm of power (often White, heterosexual, Christian, males) were for all purposes a threat against the loss of this power and, therefore, had to be negated. Such opportunities to teach about stereotyping, oppression, power, privilege, prejudice, and discrimination are made available by gaining a deeper understanding of the history of LGBTQ psychology. For example, a time period article (e.g., Weitz, 1984) that challenges students to examine those with power and privilege and their attempts to control perceived threats to their existing power could serve as the basis for a class discussion in the form of a debate, where students take on the role of historical trends in psychology from this period in relation to today. Such an activity can assist students to realize processes from the past still exist in psychology today in regard to LGBTQ people.

Teaching about LGBTQ history, psychology, and identification also provides an opening for conversations about identity far beyond that of just one's behavior. It also allows students to move beyond binary categories and learn about a continuum and fluid understanding of identities for LGBTQ people. Kinsey (Kinsey et al., 1948, 1953) and Klein's (1993) scales, along with more recent self-identification means, are useful handouts (see Activity 2.1). As students compare the items, they move from earlier, simpler, and narrow assessments (e.g., a two-option choice: I am heterosexual; I am homosexual) to more complex and varied ways of describing one's sex, sexual and gender identities, behaviors, social roles, and so forth. Whether used in a research course or an assessment course, discussion can be raised about the benefits and drawbacks of each method and the historical contexts out of which each assessment emerged. It also may lead to a discussion about how available categories and scales themselves shape our choices and affect our self-understanding.

It is critical as part of LGBTQ psychology to examine the history of anti-LGBTQ attitudes from various religious doctrines and teachings to comprehend the past and the current assertions that increasing the rights of LGBTQ people infringes on religious freedom. Questioning the prevailing stereotype among LGBTQ and non-LGBTQ people that all religions hold anti-LGBTQ views is also important. Such personal and professional exploration affords students the opportunity to move beyond a binary belief that being religious is necessarily antithetical to being LGBTQ and vice versa. This may also offer an important opportunity for students to engage with each other about differences in their beliefs that are rooted in their religious and family upbringing. It also opens the door for students struggling with their identities in areas such as religious beliefs, gender identity, and/or sexual orientation to gain additional perspective and clarity. The in-class viewing of films such as *God and Gays: Bridging the Gap* (Clark & Beck, 2008) and *For the Bible Tells Me So* (Karslake, 2007) and assigned readings from the book *What the Bible Really Says About Homosexuality* (Helminiak, 2000) are examples of methods to move students from a concrete toward a more abstract reasoning approach to religion and LGBTQ people.

Some students may resist such exploration and struggle with psychological views about LGBTQ issues that do not align with their religious, political, or personal beliefs. In these cases, it is important to encourage students to focus on the requirement that they understand the history of LGBTQ psychology to meet the academic course requirements. Learning about and understanding LGBTQ history is not the same as being asked or required to change their beliefs or go against their values. Connecting this to professional development can be an asset to the practical and ethical growth of MHPs in training. The question for MHPs to consider is how and where religion and spirituality help LGBTQ people thrive and how and where they hinder their well-being. It is important for students to gain a personal understanding of how religion may or may not have affected their approach to working with LGBTQ people. Which messages have students consciously or unknowingly adopted that may affect their opinions and their work with LGBTQ clients? Activity 2.2 can be a useful aid for such personal exploration.

Historically, the identity and progression of the LGBTQ community have expanded begrudgingly at times. The addition of letters to the acronym has not always been met with welcoming and affirming inclusion. Indeed, variation in regard to sexual and gender identities has always existed, but historically the LGBTQ community sometimes has downplayed some of these identities. Students may benefit from understanding how the lack of acknowledgment and acceptance from the mainstream community can lead to in-group fighting for limited resources such as acceptance, laws of protection, and so forth. For example, lesbians have historically been slighted and overshadowed by gay men (class, privilege), and people who are bisexual often experience being completely ignored by the community (Rullo, Strassberg, & Miner, 2015). Transgender issues are still seen by some within the LGB community as on the periphery and not truly related to LGB issues (Singh & Burnes, 2010). Not that long ago, many in the LGB movement believed that while acquiring social justice for LGB people in such areas as nondiscrimination laws was important, incorporating transgender rights was seen as too much for middle America to handle; therefore, transgender rights were left out of legislation, presumably to be addressed after LGB rights were won first.

LGBTQ people with multiple sociocultural identities (class, disability, ethnicity, gender, race, religion, etc.) that do not fall within the perceived power norm can also face prejudice and discrimination within the LGBTQ community. Discussion of the segregation of LGBTQ people of color in 1930s New York City and how gender barriers within the LGBTQ community broke down during the AIDS crisis as many lesbians became care providers for gay men who were ill can provide students with a powerful way to learn about the intersections of sociocultural identities.

HISTORICAL ANALYSIS OF *DSM* AND LGBTQ: TEACHING OPPORTUNITIES

The historical notion that homosexuality and transgender identities reflect or are caused by mental illness is important for students to examine. For example, a historical critical analysis of the actions and inactions by gatekeepers of disorder categories related to homosexuality and gender diversity offers students the opportunity to take a more contextual understanding of mental illness in general. Students will benefit from critically examining and reflecting on the steps required for the removal of homosexuality and the more recent advocacy in regard to gender identity in the *DSM*. Class lectures and literature review topics can center on questions such as: When did psychology begin and cease viewing homosexuality as a mental illness and why? What is the recent history and current status of psychology's view of transgender identities and expressions? What is the relationship between the removal of homosexuality from the *DSM* and the inclusion of gender dysphoria? Another useful assignment in a variety of psychology courses such as History and Systems of Psychology or Psychopathology is for students to examine how the various versions of the *DSM* before the inclusion of gender dysphoria were established and what recommendations they have for how future versions of the *DSM* should address gender dysphoria and why.

HISTORICAL UNDERSTANDING OF, AND REACTIONS TO, LGBTQ PEOPLE: TEACHING OPPORTUNITIES

Helping students imagine coming of age and grappling with LGBTQ-related identities and experiences during various zeitgeists is useful in opening a more complicated and thoughtful discussion about the pace of change and the importance of internal and external advocacy efforts. It also allows for the exploration of the social construction of mental illness, as well as how psychological research, politics, religious beliefs, and larger cultural changes in values and behavioral norms all play a role in the process and outcome of developing and revising diagnoses related to sexual orientations and transgender identities. For instance, a careful examination of the early views within psychology toward LGBTQ identities and experiences reveals the ways homosexuality was originally constructed as tied to and reflective of gender variant expressions and identities.

In films in the first half of the 20th century, the code for the character being a gay man was an overly effeminate demeanor and a role as a "sissy" or "pansy" (e.g., actors such as Peter Lorre, Clifton Webb, George Sanders; Eaklor, 2008). Lesbian characters were brazen in their actions for women of the time and/or dressed as men would (e.g., actors such as Katherine Hepburn, Barbara Stanwyck, Greta Garbo, Marlene Dietrich). The first time the word *gay* was used in a movie in reference to a homosexual was in the 1938 movie *Bringing Up Baby*. In the scene, Cary Grant, wearing a women's negligee, was asked why he was wearing such clothes. At this, he jumped up in the air and said, "Because I just went gay all of a sudden." Students watching Vito Russo's classic documentary *The Celluloid Closet* will have a glimpse of how LGBTQ people have been portrayed in movies along the same timeline psychology had its own progression in its view of LGBTQ people. As an exercise, students can hold "case presentations" based on LGBTQ characters, comparing them across the decades and presenting how psychology may have diagnosed and treated the person then compared with now.

Even in courses in which one might not first contemplate addressing historical understandings related to LGBTQ people and psychology, many opportunities exist. For instance, statistics courses can use the quickly changing public opinion poll numbers over the past decade toward LGBTQ-related issues to practice skill building in statistical analysis. Psychology research courses can study the work of Kinsey and Hooker as examples of how psychological research can help change a culture's understanding and beliefs about sociocultural groups and how researchers themselves are at times social justice advocates through their work. Sociocultural psychology courses would benefit from studying historical contexts in which sexuality and gender have changed over time in relation to issues of marginalization, oppression, cultural privilege, and advocacy efforts. Furthermore, such examination may also inform students' understanding of intergenerational differences within and outside the LGBTQ community.

Case Study: A Historical Example of the Mental Health Treatment of LGBTQ People

The change in a matter of decades from mental illness to normalcy in the categorization of LGBTQ people leaves more students assuming that LGBTQ people were always treated by psychology as "normal." Chemical castration, electroshock, and ice pick lobotomies as treatments for LGBTQ people (Milar, 2011) are almost unfathomable for students today to comprehend. Alan Turing's criminalization and court-mandated treatment offer students a glimpse of typical treatment at that time.

Alan Turing is best known for being instrumental in changing the outcome of World War II and is also considered the father of the modern day computer. In 1952, however, Turing found his life completely altered when he was convicted of gross indecency for homosexual acts. He was given the option of incarceration or probation under the court-mandated condition that he receive treatment from an MHP and hormone treatment to cure his homosexuality. He chose to receive mental health treatment and chemical castration. Two years later, Turing committed suicide. The coroner stated, "In a man of his type, one never knows what his mental processes are going to do next" and concluded that Turing had committed suicide "while the balance of his mind was disturbed" (Hodges, 2014, p. 488).

The coroner and others over the years made the assumption that Turing, like the majority of the public during this period, viewed his homosexuality as a deficit. On the contrary, Turing's biographer holds that he was neither ashamed nor did he believe his sexual orientation was in any way a disease or disorder. He chose the mental treatment option to be able to continue working on his experiments. More people have recently hypothesized that he unknowingly inhaled cyanide vapors (a chemical used in his experiments), causing his accidental death (Pease, 2012). Szasz (2009) pointed out, "Even in death, psychiatry and the state stigmatized Turing as mad. The posthumous diagnosis of suicide as mental illness is the ritual degradation ceremony of our therapeutic age" (p. 16). The emphasis on Turing's suicide focuses on his questionable mental health rather than questioning the laws and mental health treatment that Turing and others had to endure against their will because of being LGBTQ.

A recommended assignment (see Activity 2.3) is for students to watch the Academy Award-winning movie *The Imitation Game* (Grossman, Ostrowsky, Schwarzman, & Tyldum, 2014) to experience a time when homosexuality was illegal and mental health treatments devastatingly life altering. Students would then complete a written assignment or participate in an in-class debate using the movie and the selected readings of Szasz (2009) and Hodges (2014) to focus on how different as well as how similar mental health services in Turing's time are to today's.

Conclusion

The current and next generation of MHPs will only benefit from having a historical context and understanding of the impact of psychology in relation to LGBTQ people. As the civil rights advocate William Hastie stated, "History informs us of past mistakes from which we can learn without repeating them. It also inspires us and gives confidence and hope bred of victories already won" (Ware, 1984, p. 144). To support and advocate for LGBTQ individuals, it is our responsibility as MHPs and trainers of MHPs to learn from history to avoid repeating the missteps and sometimes cruel treatment of LGBTQ individuals. We as a profession are moving forward, but we have more work to do in our support of LGBTQ individuals, and understanding the history of LGBTQ psychology is integral to our success.

ACTIVITY 2.1

Sexual Orientation and Gender Identity Measurement Tools: Then and Now

Directions: Students will complete two self-identification activities, one that includes a series of self-identification questions regarding sexual identity and the other regarding gender identity, where the options available to choose from reflect the diverse ways of "measuring," "assessing," and "describing" sexual and gender identity in historical context.

1. Dichotomous model (conventional conflict model of sexuality, 1890s). Circle the statement that is true for you:
   - I am attracted toward people of the same sex.
   - I am attracted toward people of the other sex.
2. Kinsey Scale (late 1940s/early 1950s). Circle the number on the scale below that best represents your psychosexual experiences and responses, where 0 = *exclusively heterosexual* and 6 = *exclusively homosexual*.

0	1	2	3	4	5	6

How do you identify yourself? Check the appropriate box (check only one):
   - Heterosexual
   - Gay/lesbian
   - Bisexual
   - Don't know
3. Bell and Weinberg's (1978) model using the Kinsey Scale.
   (a) Rate yourself from 0 to 6 on the basis of your sexual feelings: _____
   (b) Rate yourself from 0 to 6 on the basis of your sexual behaviors: _____
4. The Shively Scale for Physical/Affectional Preference (Shively & De Cecco, 1977). Rate yourself on both scales below:

Physical Preference

0	1	2	3	4	5	6
Not at all heterosexual			Somewhat heterosexual			Very heterosexual

Affectional Preference

0	1	2	3	4	5	6
Not at all homosexual			Somewhat homosexual			Very homosexual

ACTIVITY 2.1 (*Continued*)

5. Klein Sexual Orientation Grid (KSOG; Klein, Sepekoff, & Wolf, 1985). Rate yourself in the past, in the present, and in the ideal on the following seven components of sexual orientation, using the same scales as above (0–6).

Sexual orientation component	Past	Present	Ideal
Sexual attraction			
Sexual behavior			
Sexual fantasies			
Emotional preferences			
Social preferences			
Self-identification			
Lifestyle			

6. Using a scale of 0 to 6 where 0 = *not at all* and 6 = *very much*, note how much the following statement fits for you: "I find the idea of sex with the same sex appealing" (Laumann, Gagnon, Michael, & Michaels, 1994).
7. Using a scale of 0 to 6 where 0 = *not at all* and 6 = *very much*, note how much each of the following statements fit you:
    (a) I do not typically experience sexual attractions.
    (b) I do not typically experience romantic attractions.
    (c) I am someone who typically experiences romantic attractions.
    (d) I am interested in being in a romantic relationship.
    (e) I am interested in being sexual with another person.
    (f) My sexual attractions are not tied to any one gender identity or gender expression.
    (g) My romantic attractions are not tied to any one gender identity or gender expression.
8. Using your own words, how would you describe your sexual orientation/identity?
9. What, if any, labels do you use to describe your sexual/romantic attractions and/or your sexual orientation/identity to yourself and to others? If you prefer not to use any labels, please explain this preference.

ACTIVITY 2.2

Historical Beginnings of Our Messages About Sexual and Gender Identity

Directions: Fill in various messages you have received about lesbian, gay, bisexual, transgender, queer, and questioning people from the various sources listed below.

Parent(s)/Care provider(s): _____

Sibling(s): _____

Peers as a youth: _____

Teachers/Professors: _____

Religious community: _____

Romantic partner(s): _____

Books: _____

Web: _____

Media: _____

Doctors/Nurses: _____

Classmates: _____

Social networking: _____

Professional training: _____

Work colleagues: _____

Other: _____

Other: _____

ACTIVITY 2.3

"Treating" Homosexuality: Then and Now

Directions: Assign students to learn about how Alan Turing's homosexuality resulted in his arrest, conviction, and court-appointed treatment with a mental health provider (MHP) and hormone treatment for his homosexuality. Students can watch the movie *The Imitation Game* and use two to three additional resources, such as Alan Turing biographies by Szasz (2009) and Hodges (2014) and the movie *The Imitation Game*. Have students either hold an in-class debate or write individual papers focusing on similarities and differences between mental health services today and in Alan Turing's time period.

References

Grossman, N., Ostrowsky, I., & Schwarzman, T. (Producers), & Tyldum, M. (Director). (2014). *The imitation game* [Motion picture]. United States: The Weinstein Company.

Hodges, A. (2014). *Alan Turing: The enigma*. Princeton, NJ: Princeton University Press.

Szasz, T. S. (2009, May). The shame of medicine: The case of Alan Turing. *The Freeman, 59*, 16–17.

References

American Psychiatric Association. (1952). *Diagnostic and statistical manual of mental disorders*. Washington, DC: Author.

American Psychiatric Association. (2013). *Diagnostic and statistical manual of mental disorders* (5th ed.). Washington, DC: Author.

American Psychological Association. (2009). *Report of the APA Task Force on Appropriate Therapeutic Response to Sexual Orientation*. Retrieved from http://www.apa.org/pi/lgbt/resources/therapeutic-response.pdf

American Psychological Association. (2013). *United States of America v. Windsor: Amicus Brief of the American Psychological Association*. Retrieved from http://www.apa.org/about/offices/ogc/amicus/windsor-us.pdf

Bain, K. (2004). *What the best college teachers do*. Cambridge, MA: Harvard University Press.

Beere, C. A. (1990). *Sex and gender issues: A handbook of tests and measures*. New York, NY: Greenwood Press.

Bell, A. P., & Weinberg, M. S. (1978). *Homosexualities: A study of diversity among men and women*. Bloomington: Indiana University Press.

Braitman, W., Brillstein, B., Ehrenzweig, M., Epstein, R., Friedman, J., Grey, B., . . . Tomlin, L. (Producers), & Epstein, R., & Friedman, J. (Directors). (1995). *The celluloid closet* [Motion picture]. United States: Sony Pictures Classics.

Bullough, V. L. (1995). *Science in the bedroom: A history of sex research*. New York, NY: Basic Books.

Bullough, V. L. (2014). *Before Stonewall: Activists for gay and lesbian rights in historical context*. London, England: Routledge.

Burbank, A. (2016, March 17). Vermont vote bans conversion therapy for gay teens. *Burlington Free Press*. Retrieved from http://www.burlingtonfreepress.com/story/news/politics/2016/03/16/vt-senate-votes-ban-conversion-therapy-gay-teens/81786020/

Clark, K. (Producer), & Beck, L. (Director). (2008). *God and gays: Bridging the gap* [Motion picture]. United States: Indican Pictures.

Clarke, V., Ellis, S. J., Peel, E., & Riggs, D. W. (2010). *Lesbian, gay, bisexual, trans, and queer perspectives: An introduction*. http://dx.doi.org/10.1017/CBO9780511810121

Drescher, J. (2014a). Controversies in gender diagnoses. *LGBT Health*, *1*, 10–14. http://dx.doi.org/10.1089/lgbt.2013.1500

Drescher, J. (2014b). Treatment of lesbian, gay, bisexual and transgender patients. In R. E. Hales, S. C. Yudofsky, & L. W. Roberts (Eds.), *The American Psychiatric Publishing textbook of psychiatry* (6th ed.). Arlington, VA: American Psychiatric Press. http://dx.doi.org/10.1176/appi.books.9781585625031.rh37

Drescher J. (2015). Out of *DSM*: Depathologizing homosexuality. *Behavioral Sciences*, *5*, 565–575. http://dx.doi.org/10.3390/bs5040565

Eaklor, V. L. (2008). *Queer America: A GLBT history of the 20th century.* Westport, CT: Greenwood Press.

Faderman, L. (2012). *Odd girls and twilight lovers: A history of lesbian life in 20th-century America.* New York, NY: Cambridge University Press.

Faderman, L. (2015). *The gay revolution: The story of the struggle.* New York, NY: Simon & Schuster.

Gittings, B. (2007). Preface: Show-and-tell. In J. Drescher & J. P. Merlino (Eds.), *American psychiatry and homosexuality: An oral history* (p. xv). Binghamton, NY: Haworth Press.

Griffin, C. (2016). *The path forward on LGBT equality.* Retrieved from http://medium.com/@ChadHGriffin/the-path-forward-on-lgbt-equality-407a73a1e755#.vpdotdnh4

Grossman, N., Ostrowsky, I., & Schwarzman, T. (Producers), & Tyldum, M. (Director). (2014). *The imitation game* [Motion picture]. United States: The Weinstein Company.

Group for the Advancement of Psychiatry. (2012). *The history of psychiatry and homosexuality.* Retrieved from http://www.aglp.org/gap/1_history

Haldeman, D. C. (1994). The practice and ethics of sexual orientation conversion therapy. *Journal of Consulting and Clinical Psychology, 62,* 221–227. http://dx.doi.org/10.1037/0022-006X.62.2.221

Hegarty, P. (2003). Homosexual signs and heterosexual silences: Rorschach research on male homosexuality from 1921 to 1969. *Journal of the History of Homosexuality, 12,* 400–423. http://dx.doi.org/10.1353/sex.2004.0009

Helminiak, D. A. (2000). *What the Bible really says about homosexuality* (Millennium edition). Estancia, NM: Alamo Square Press.

Herek, G. M. (1997–2012). *Facts about homosexuality and mental health.* Retrieved from http://psychology.ucdavis.edu/faculty_sites/rainbow/html/facts_mental_health.html

Herek, G. M. (2014). *Happy 107th birthday, Dr. Evelyn Hooker.* Retrieved from http://www.beyondhomophobia.com/blog

Hodges, A. (2014). *Alan Turing: The enigma.* http://dx.doi.org/10.1515/9781400865123

Hooker, E. (1957). The adjustment of the male overt homosexual. *Journal of Projective Techniques, 21,* 18–31. http://dx.doi.org/10.1080/08853126.1957.10380742

Hooker, E. (1993). Reflections of a 40-year exploration: A scientific view on homosexuality. *American Psychologist, 48,* 450–453. http://dx.doi.org/10.1037/0003-066X.48.4.450

Jarrett, V. (2015). *Petition response: On conversion therapy.* Retrieved from http://www.whitehouse.gov/blog/2015/04/08/petition-response-conversion-therapy

Karslake, D. G. (Producer & Director). (2007). *For the Bible tells me so* [Motion picture]. United States: First Run Features Film.

Katz, J. N. (1978). *Gay American history: Lesbians and gay men in the USA.* New York, NY: Avon Press.

Katz, J. N. (1983). *Gay/lesbian almanac: A new documentary.* New York, NY: Harper & Row.

Kennedy, H. (1997). Karl Heinrich Ulrichs, the first theorist of homosexuality. In V. A. Rosario (Ed.), *Science and homosexualities* (p. 30). New York, NY: Routledge.

Kinsey, A. C., Pomeroy, W. B., & Martin, C. E. (1948). *Sexual behavior in the human male.* Philadelphia, PA: W. B. Saunders.

Kinsey, A. C., Pomeroy, W. B., Martin, C. E., & Gebhard, P. (1953). *Sexual behavior in the human female.* Philadelphia, PA: W. B. Saunders.

Klein, F. (1993). *The bisexual option.* New York, NY: Routledge.

Klein, F., Sepekoff, B., & Wolf, T. J. (1985). Sexual orientation: A multivariable dynamic process. *Journal of Homosexuality, 11,* 35–49. http://dx.doi.org/10.1300/J082v11n01_04

Knauer, N. J. (2000). Homosexuality as contagion: From *The Well of Loneliness* to the Boy Scouts. *Hofstra Law Review, 29,* 401–501.

Laumann, E. O., Gagnon, J. H., Michael, R. T., & Michaels, S. (1994). *The social organization of sexuality: Sexual practices in the United States.* Chicago, IL: University of Chicago Press.

Lawrence v. Texas, 539 U.S. 558, 578 (2003).

Lev, A. I. (2005). Disordering gender identity: Gender identity in the *DSM–IV–TR. Journal of Human Sexuality, 17,* 35–69.

Lev, A. I. (2013). Gender dysphoria: Two steps forward, one step back. *Clinical Social Work Journal, 41,* 288–296. http://dx.doi.org/10.1007/s10615-013-0447-0

Lynn, M., & Dixson, A. D. (Eds.). (2013). *Handbook of critical race theory in education.* New York, NY: Routledge.

Marable, M. (2015). *How capitalism underdeveloped Black America: Problems in race, political economy, and society.* Chicago, IL: Haymarket Press.

Meyer, L. (2016, June 27). License to deny services. *Counseling Today.* Retrieved from http://ct.counseling.org/2016/06/license-deny-services

Milar, K. S. (2011). The myth buster. *Monitor on Psychology, 42*(2). Retrieved from http://www.apa.org/monitor/2011/02/myth-buster.aspx

Morin, S. F. (1977). Heterosexual bias in psychological research on lesbianism and male homosexuality. *American Psychologist, 32,* 629–637. http://dx.doi.org/10.1037/0003-066X.32.8.629

Moss, I. (2014). Ending reparative therapy in minors: An appropriate legislative response. *Family Court Review, 52,* 316–329. http://dx.doi.org/10.1111/fcre.12093

Murphy, T. F. (2003). Redirecting sexual orientation techniques and justifications. In S. LaFont (Ed.), *Constructing sexualities: Readings in sexuality, gender, and culture* (pp. 285–299). Upper Saddle River, NJ: Prentice Hall.

Obergefell v. Hodges, 135 S. Ct. 2584 (2015).

Orel, N. A., & Fruhauf, C. A. (2014). *The lives of LGBT older adults: Understanding challenges and resilience.* Washington, DC: American Psychological Association.

Pease, R. (2012, June 26). Alan Turing: Inquest's suicide verdict "not supportable." *BBC News: Science & Environment.* Retrieved from http://www.bbc.com/news/science-environment-18561092

Reddy, G. (2010). *With respect to sex: Negotiating hijra identity in South India.* Chicago, IL: University of Chicago Press.

Reid, C., & Hawks, H. (Producers), & Hawks, H. (Director). (1938). *Bringing up baby* [Motion picture]. United States: RKO Radio Pictures.

Rousseau, G. (2013). The overlap of discourses of contagion: Economic, sexual, and psychological. In T. Rütten & M. King (Eds.), *Contagionism and contagious diseases: Medicine and literature 1880–1933* (pp. 41–63). http://dx.doi.org/10.1515/9783110306118.41

Rullo, J. E., Strassberg, D. S., & Miner, M. H. (2015). Gender-specificity in sexual interest in bisexual men and women. *Archives of Sexual Behavior, 44,* 1449–1457. http://dx.doi.org/10.1007/s10508-014-0415-y

Shively, M. G., & De Cecco, J. P. (1977). Components of sexual identity. *Journal of Homosexuality, 3,* 41–48. http://dx.doi.org/10.1300/J082v03n01_04

Singh, A. A., & Burnes, T. R. (2010). Shifting the counselor role from gatekeeping to advocacy: Ten strategies for using the ACA Competencies for Counseling Transgender Clients for individual and social change. *Journal for Lesbian, Gay, Bisexual, and Transgender Issues in Counseling, 4,* 241–255.

Spring, J. (2012). *Deculturalization and the struggle for equality: A brief history of the education of dominated cultures in the United States* (7th ed.). New York, NY: McGraw-Hill.

Stein, M. (Ed.). (2004). *Encyclopedia of lesbian, gay, bisexual, and transgender history in America.* New York, NY: Scribner.

Szasz, T. S. (2009). The shame of medicine: The case of Alan Turing. *The Freeman, 59,* 16–17.

Ulrichs, K. (1994). *The riddle of "man-manly" love* (M. Lombardi-Nash, Trans.). Buffalo, NY: Prometheus Books. (Original work published 1864)

United States v. Windsor, 133 S. Ct. 2675, 2682-84 (2013).

Ware, G. (1984). *William Haste: Grace under fire.* Chapel Hill: University of North Carolina Press.

Weitz, K. (1984). What price independence? Social reactions to lesbians, spinsters, widows and nuns. In J. Freedman (Ed.), *Women: A feminist perspective* (3rd ed., pp. 446–456). Palo Alto, CA: Mayfield.

Wiesner-Hanks, M. (2010). *Gender in history: Global perspectives* (2nd ed.). New York, NY: Wiley-Blackwell.

World Health Organization. (2016). *International statistical classification of diseases and related health problems* (10th rev.). Retrieved from http://apps.who.int/classifications/icd10/browse/2016/en

Wundt, W. (1910). *Principles of physiological psychology* (Edward Bradford Titchener, Trans.). New York, NY: Macmillan. (Original work published 1864)

Courtney M. Dunne

Theoretical and Pedagogical Perspectives on Teaching LGBTQ Issues in Psychology

3

P*edagogy* is widely known as the theory and practice of teaching and educating. By using a critical and culturally responsive approach, this chapter addresses theoretical perspectives on teaching lesbian, gay, bisexual, transgender, queer, and questioning (LGBTQ) issues in psychology, with a direct focus on pedagogy. Broadly stated, *critical theory* is a lens through which to understand the oppressive nature of society in an effort to generate a cultural shift aimed at empowerment of those who have been silenced and invisible. In psychology, the most salient LGBTQ issue to be addressed is *perspective*, defined as "a particular attitude toward a way of regarding something; a point of view" (Simpson & Weiner, 1989, Definition 1); engaging in personal reflection to understand perspective allows for culturally responsive teaching. This chapter will help educators examine the attitudes, biases, and core knowledge that compose perspective. It addresses how to teach LGBTQ issues in culturally responsive ways.

This chapter is organized into three sections. The overview addresses relevant key concepts and critical framework

http://dx.doi.org/10.1037/0000015-003
Teaching LGBTQ Psychology: Queering Innovative Pedagogy and Practice, T. R. Burnes and J. L. Stanley (Editors)

for thinking about teaching LGBTQ issues. The second section begins with an examination of current literature and concepts fundamental to understanding and addressing LGBTQ issues in the classroom. After each concept is defined, a subsection addresses how educators might apply it in their teaching. The chapter concludes with a review of the pedagogical approaches necessary for teaching LGBTQ issues using a critical framework.

Framework Overview

Giroux noted that critical pedagogy is not a method but a "political project" (as cited in Tristan, 2013, para. 3) that encourages individuals to think critically about their experience and problems within the social contexts in which they are embedded. It is seen as a range of educational responses to social structures and relations that are inequitable or oppressive. Professionals—specifically, educators—are charged with analyzing, exposing, and challenging the hidden social, cultural, and political processes that are part of knowledge production, including how one's views and assumptions come from a particular cultural and historical formation.

Those who work with critical pedagogy "ask how teachers can affirm the voices of marginalized students, engage them critically, and while at the same time assist them in transforming their communities into sites of struggle and resistance" (McLaren & Hammer, 1989, p. 41). Grounded in critical pedagogy, Kumashiro's (2000) antioppressive approaches to education speak to the urgency of transforming schools through theory and practice so that schools become places of social justice for all people (Lather & Ellsworth, 1996). Kumashiro (2002) described three dominant frameworks for understanding multiple oppressions: a focus on difference, a focus on normalcy, and a focus on intersections. Furthermore, he stated that there are four ways to conceptualize and work against oppression: education that is for the other, educating about the other, educating in such a way as to critique privileging and othering, and educating ultimately to change students and society (Kumashiro, 2002, p. 23). Critical pedagogy works to create positive environments where people can "unpack" their identities with support and affirmation from practitioners, faculty, and peers.

Education for the other focuses on "improving the experiences of the individuals who are *othered* or in some way oppressed by mainstream society" (Kumashiro, 2002, p. 33). Ladson-Billings (1995) argued that individuals have to be able to "recognize, understand, and critique current social inequities" (p. 476). Critical awareness requires learning what society defines as "normal" and understanding that "normal" is a social and contested construct (Birden, 2005). Education should center on the cultural historical realities, past and present constructs of a positive LGBTQ identity, the overlap and intersection of sexual and gender identities, and any other intersecting identities.

To authentically practice culturally responsive pedagogy, one must understand how one's thinking is shaped by one's position and experiences. This presents a particular challenge to a biomedical model because traditionally the role of social factors or individual subjectivity is absent. However, integrating queer content with an examination of social constructs and personal biases is a critical shift in the discipline of psychology. Freire (1998) noted, "The accomplishment of critical consciousness consists in the first place in the learner's capacity to situate herself in her own historicity, for example, to grasp the class, race and sexual aspects of education and social formation" (p. 14). The critical consciousness that Freire referred to includes an awareness that our ideas come from a distinctive set of life experiences and acknowledges that others will have equally valid, albeit different, experiences and ideas (Hinchey, 2004). However, awareness is not enough; developing critical consciousness involves understanding that ideas considered normal versus abnormal and moral versus immoral are a product of our life experiences and not universal law. This begins with understanding the constructs of individual identities and, within this construct, an LGBTQ identity.

CONSTRUCTS OF IDENTITY

Implementing current pedagogical approaches in teaching LGBTQ issues requires an understanding of the historical context and constructs of identity. When we consider identity, we think of "who we are" or "who we have come to be." Yet, the crux of who we are is cultural. Although biological identities (male, female, intersex) are noted at birth, the development of what those identities mean is shaped by cultural and societal forces. Cultural identities are marked by a number of factors (e.g., race, ethnicity, gender, ability, class); however, the real locus of these factors is the notion of difference (Clarke, 2008). It is how we approach difference that determines what kind of educator, practitioner, or leader one will be. So, how have we come to understand difference?

There has been a tendency in modern societies to categorize, medicalize, criminalize, and moralize difference, with varying degrees of salience (Berbrier, 2002). With the advent of the eugenic study of humans in the 19th century, constructions of superiority and inferiority were formed (Davis, 2008). In this context, heterosexuality and gender conformity were the desirable and "normal" traits. Stemming from this concept of normal versus desirable and abnormal versus undesirable, Foucault

(1977, 1978) began to focus on the growing ability of the state to use medicine to dissect, categorize, and control the human body.

Against this background of evolution and eugenics, institutional control and oppression of LGBTQ individuals took shape. In 1952, the medical and scientific community officially defined homosexuality as a mental disorder, when the American Psychiatric Association listed homosexuality as a psychiatric disorder. It was categorized among the sociopathic personality disturbances in the American Psychiatric Association's first official *Diagnostic and Statistical Manual of Mental Disorders* (*DSM–I*; 1952). The stigma associated with a mental health disorder label further perpetuated the institutionalized oppression of LGBTQ people. In the years since the *DSM* was initially published, homosexuality has been classified a variety of ways, all with varying degrees of criticism. In 1973, homosexuality was finally removed from the *DSM–II* (American Psychiatric Association, 1968) as a psychiatric diagnosis; yet, it was not until 1987 that all references to homosexuality were eliminated in the *DSM–III–R* (see Chapter 2 for a more in-depth analysis of these changes).

Similarly, the definition and understanding of gender identity has evolved in the *DSM*. In the fifth and newest edition, *DSM–5* (American Psychiatric Association, 2013), the previous diagnosis of gender identity disorder (GID) is now called *gender dysphoria*. With a new name, the diagnosis also has a new emphasis, focusing on the importance of distress, whereas GID focused on the issue of identity and the incongruity between someone's birth gender and the gender with which he or she identifies. This new emphasis recognizes that the disagreement between birth gender and identity may not necessarily be pathological if it does not cause the individual distress. If a transgender person does not experience distress, he or she may not be diagnosed with gender dysphoria. Although the shift represents progress, the time homosexuality and GID spent as psychological diagnoses increased the pathological stigmatization of LGBTQ individuals and set the backdrop for conversations on identity construction. As such, it becomes the responsibility of educators to transform the conversation—in essence, to queer the conversation.

QUEER PEDAGOGY

Queer pedagogy, grounded in critical theory, introduces ways to challenge biases, assumptions, and customary ways of thinking about traditionally "fixed" categories of sexuality and gender. It challenges us to radically examine and redefine how we think about and conceptualize the act of teaching, our notions and practices of knowledge, and formal and informal curriculum. To queer is to destabilize the social, cultural, and political normatizing structures that work to solidify identities and in doing so skew power toward the "norm" (Whitlock, 2010). Influenced by the work of Butler (1990) and Sedgwick (1990), queer theory challenges the socially constructed heterosexual–homosexual binary and innate power structure and instead offers a more fluid context for sexuality with shifting boundaries and ambivalence, depending on historical, cultural, and social context. Taking a cue from historian Michel Foucault, queer theorists believe sexuality exists on a continuum.

Queer pedagogy assumes a diligence to actively and intentionally model ways that redefine or invoke questions about meanings and concepts that serve to reinforce characterizations of "normal" and perpetuate societal binaries (i.e., normal–abnormal, gay–straight, and male–female). Teaching and infusing queer theory into practice involve actively challenging invisibility to disrupt assumptions and to broaden perspective. For example, assumptions are often made on the basis of appearance. People have an idea in their heads about what a lesbian looks like, and it may take the form of some of the well-known TV personalities with whom we are familiar, such as Ellen DeGeneres or Lea DeLaria (*Orange Is The New Black*). It is more likely, however, that most people do not have a picture of Portia de Rossi (*Ally McBeal*) or Cynthia Nixon (*Sex in the City*) in their minds. Because of this, it is that much more important for LGBTQ educators to come out and call into question one's assumptions and/or presumptions and bring evidence to the diversity in identities. Educators also have to uncover the unearned and unacknowledged privileges that contribute to unconscious oppression (McIntosh, 1998) and teach others how to do the same.

It is important that LGBTQ psychology educators support students—specifically, student trainees—in developing dispositions, knowledge, and skills. Educators have to create professional learning opportunities that intentionally "trouble" teaching practice by looking beyond what is already known. Educators have to experience the discomfort that comes with unknowing what we already know to disrupt assumptions of truth. As such, the relationship of one's own story to one's knowledge becomes the object of inquiry. Grounding teaching in the acknowledgement of assumptions provides a backdrop for a study of generalities, stereotypes, and superficial assessments of "in-ness" and "out-ncss." Educators and practitioners arrive with experience and the question becomes how we use that experience and work with students to access their biases. How can we use the experience of living in multiple "worlds," as most modern adults inevitably do, to encourage both thoughtful and multicultural perspectives to build positive communities and develop cultural identity?

Educators have to foster introspection and dialogue to examine the identities, assumptions, and biases we bring to the classroom. And LGBTQ psychology educators have to dig deeper to participate in a reflexive process. For example, engaging your class in reflective writing allows students to self-engage with their beliefs and assumptions. This is a personal activity in which students can write in journals, perhaps to a prompt about particular dispositions. This type of activity will support a greater understanding of identity constructs, how students understand their own identities, and how they perceive other identities. Expanding on this activity, students can participate in digital storytelling to integrate personal experience and reflection through a variety of media. Directions and resources for digital storytelling can be found in Activity 3.1 at the end of the chapter.

QUEER CONCEPTS

Critical to understanding the continuum and fluidity of queer theory is a basic comprehension of sexual orientation, gender, and gender identity. It is assumed that both students and instructors may not be free of anti-LGBTQ beliefs and, as such, may not want to teach about such important work. The range of microinvalidations and microaggressions by instructors can occur in both LGBTQ topic-related and non-LGBTQ courses. Direct dialogue and immediate remediation for instructors may include mentoring from a colleague, attending diversity workshops, reading articles about LGBTQ individuals, writing personal reflection papers, and increasing opportunities for exposure to LGBTQ people. Whether the course content is LGBTQ laden or not, instructors have a responsibility for creating and modeling an inclusive environment for all students and teaching on the basis of a working knowledge of core vocabulary and concepts affecting the LGBTQ population.

Sexual orientation refers to the physical and/or romantic attraction that one feels toward the same or other gender. Categories of sexual orientation include those who are attracted to the same sex (gay men and lesbians), to members of the other sex (heterosexuals or straight individuals), and to members of both sexes (bisexuals; American Psychological Association, 2012). Consistent with the foundations of queer theory, research has suggested that sexual orientation does not always exist in clearly definable categories and instead occurs on a continuum and/or may present with greater fluidity (Diamond, 2007; Kinsey, Pomeroy, Martin, & Gebhard, 1953; Klein, 1993; Klein, Sepekoff, & Wolf, 1985). Decades ago, *The Kinsey Reports* (Kinsey, Pomeroy, & Martin, 1948; Kinsey et al., 1953) presented research indicating sexuality was more fluid than ever suspected. Kinsey's data disrupted the common assumption that all adults were permanently and exclusively either homosexual or heterosexual and revealed instead the fluidity that belied medical theories about fixed orientations (D'Emilio, 1983).

Kinsey's research also allowed for a deeper understanding of the gender continuum. *Gender identity* refers to a person's innate feelings of one's gender (i.e., male, female or some other gender), which may or may not correspond to the biological sex that was assigned to the person at birth (i.e., on the birth certificate). *Transgender* is the umbrella term used to describe individuals whose gender identity, gender expression, or behavior does not align with the societal norms of the sex they were assigned at birth. *Gender expression*, however, refers to the ways gender is manifested within a given culture (e.g., clothing, communication, physical presentation, behaviors). A person's gender expression may or may not be consistent with socially prescribed gender roles and may or may not reflect their gender identity. It is important to note that sexual orientation, gender identity, and gender expression are exclusive of each other. Given the foundational nature of these concepts, they should be addressed formally and informally in all primary, secondary, and higher education curricula.

Understanding the difference between sexuality and gender is critical for teaching LGBTQ issues. Because the Kinsey Scale (Kinsey et al., 1948) was groundbreaking, it is a useful tool to help move educators' thinking away from the heterosexual–homosexual dichotomy and foster an understanding of queer concepts, thus disrupting the biomedical norm. Developed in 1948, the Kinsey Scale was used to demonstrate that individuals did not always fit into a heterosexual/homosexual binary, that there was a gray area between the two terms. By interviewing people about their sexual history, Kinsey's team developed a seven-point scale, ranging from 0 to 6, with 0 being *exclusively heterosexual* and 6 being *exclusively homosexual*. An additional rating of "X" was used to describe asexuality. Individuals who rate between 1 and 5 experience varying levels of desire for sexual activity with either sex. Sharing the scale and noticing that most individuals fall into Categories 1 to 5 allows for discussion about fluidity versus fixed categories. Discussing what information and what types of questions were used to collect these data will also help educators to reflect on where they might fall on the Kinsey Scale, thus enabling a more reflexive process while learning about sexual and gender fluidity. Such an exercise to use with students is available in Chapter 2 of this volume (Activity 2.1).

A related tool to expand students' minds beyond a binary approach to gender, is the infographic called the *Gender Unicorn* (Trans Student Educational Resources, 2016; a sample activity can be found in Chapter 7). The concepts presented in this tool can aid students in understanding the difference between gender and sexuality as well as the continuum that exists for each. The Gender Unicorn assists students in conceptualizing fluidity and variance regarding gender by providing a depiction of gender, sex assigned at birth, and sexuality that can be used as a simple primer for debunking the gay and straight and male and female binaries.

Related to an expansion from binary to continuum is the need for educators to think deliberately about language choice and use. The language we use often reflects institutional oppression, which shapes the way we view the world. For example, it is common in early education for educators to say, "OK, boys and girls." Such greetings change only slightly through high school and higher education when students are often grouped by "boys and girls" or "ladies and gentlemen." Instead, we have to consider what we are asking and use inclusive nonbinary language. The male–female binary becomes so ingrained that it becomes part of the hidden curriculum in which we passively teach societal norms and expectations. In lieu of "boys and girls," gender-neutral alternatives can be used, including "class," "all," "learners," "students," and so forth. Similarly, educators should avoid grouping students by assumed gender and find alternate ways to group students for activities, such as by favorite color, months in which they were born, and so forth. Another example of expanding our language to be more inclusive is how we refer to our significant others. Avoid the use of gender-specific language such as "boyfriend" and "girlfriend." Instead, educators can use gender-neutral alternatives such as "partner" and "spouse" (see Chapter 6 for greater detail on classroom management that is culturally informed and responsive).

INSTITUTIONAL INVISIBILITY AND POWER

As important as it is to understand gender, sex, and sexuality as they exist separately, it is also necessary to examine them from institutional and intersectional perspectives. The experiences of LGBTQ individuals must be framed within the larger societal context in which heterosexism, homophobia, biphobia, and transphobia are understood as social constructs that perpetuate patriarchy (Herr, 1998) and homogeneity. Understanding the institutional contexts aids in the ability to explore the intersectionality of identities and how they are rendered invisible because of patriarchy and homogeneity. Because schools are social institutions and because LGBTQ individuals do not represent a homogenous group, educators of mental health professionals (MHPs) have to understand and know how to teach issues of intersectionality. Not addressing intersectionality results in greater invisibility.

Homophobia has been described as "terror surrounding feelings of love for members of the same sex and thereby a hatred of those feelings in others" (Lorde, 1984, p. 45). Current research indicates, however, that homophobic and biphobic beliefs are based on disgust-related emotions, not fear (Kimmell, 2005). Similarly, *transphobia* is a reaction of "fear, loathing, and discriminatory treatment of people whose identity or gender presentation (or perceived gender or gender identity) does not 'match' in the societally accepted way, the sex they were assigned at birth" (Lesbian, Gay, Bisexual, Transgender, Queer, Intersex, Asexual Resource Center, 2015, para. 1). Regardless of its underpinning, homophobia, biphobia, and transphobia manifest in many forms, including discrimination, violence, and physical and verbal abuse.

Homophobia, biphobia, and transphobia, although pervasive, serve as merely the mask through which we glimpse a greater systemic issue:

heteronormativity (Farrell, 2004). *Heteronormative discursive practices* are ways in which identity is organized in hierarchical binaries. In this context, man is set up as the opposite (and superior) of women and heterosexual as the opposite (and superior) of homosexual. This belief in the inherent superiority of one form of loving over others and, thereby, the right to dominance (Lorde, 1984) is a root of widespread oppression. Although society is evolving, heteronormative discrimination has been evident in both public and private sectors in the United States.

To disrupt heteronormativity in our practice, we have to examine the ways in which systemic invisibility occurs. Adrienne Rich (1980) called heterosexuality "compulsory" in that our culture assumes everyone to be heterosexual, and society is full of formal and informal messages and enforcements that make it easier to be heterosexual than not. Susan Birden (2005) described what many schools enforce as "compulsory heterosexuality." Schools and other social institutions often teach acceptable gendered conduct in which opposite-gender love is presented as the only viable option, whereas the value of same-gender relationships is omitted entirely, denounced, or denigrated. For example, according to the 2013 National School Climate Survey, only 18.5% of LGBTQ students are taught positive representations of LGBTQ history, people, and events (Kosciw, Greytak, Palmer, & Boesen, 2014). As social institutions that reflect cultural values and norms, schools sanctioning an environment that neglects the lives of LGBTQ students and dismissing the legitimacy of these individuals will have a minimized contribution to learning (Walters & Hayes, 1998). There remains a push for homogeneity, where conformity to cultural and societal norms is valued, and nonconformity leads to invisibility.

Academic institutions are a reflection of our larger society, facing the same social issues, pressures, and prejudices. Although colleges and universities have made significant strides in the past decade, creating more welcoming, supportive, and safe environments in which to address LGBTQ concerns and issues, much work remains to be done. Campus Pride's 2010 National Climate Survey documented the experiences of nearly 6,000 university students, faculty, staff, and administrators across the United States who identify as LGBTQ. Key findings from the report indicated more than half of LGBTQ students of every race, color, and ethnicity report harassment, isolation, and fear on campus, with transgender and nonconforming students most likely to experience blatant oppression and hostility (Rankin, Weber, Blumenfeld, & Frazer, 2010). Therefore, colleges and universities are failing to provide the environment that research suggests is critical for learning and scholarship. For example, fewer than 7% of accredited U.S. institutions of higher education offer institutional support for LGBTQ constituents in the form of policies; of these, only 13% include sexual identity policy protections, and 6% include gender identity policy protections (Rankin et al., 2010).

Similarly, although the availability of LGBTQ resources and programs (e.g., safe space/ally programming, LGBTQ faculty advisors, LGBTQ centers) has increased, the percentage of institutions that use them remains unclear. To challenge invisibility, conversations about LGBTQ needs must be brought to the forefront. Universities have to promote new thinking about course offerings and course content that teaches students about contemporary LGBTQ scholarship and cultural issues. This involves having ample opportunities for faculty discussion and professional development to support and enhance the shared concepts and language relevant to LGBTQ issues. Similarly, mentorship of teaching fellows and adjunct instructors that align with the principles of social justice and diversity are also important.

Students need a mechanism for exploring institutional invisibility and power and yet, historically, they have not been taught to examine their individual and social group identities and the power or privileges that each identity either gives or denies them. Cox and Devine (2015) argued that understanding the content, process, and structure of cognitions related to social groups is important because these cognitions form the building blocks of prejudice, discrimination, and oppression. They stressed the important responsibility MHPs have to understand how it was learned, how it is activated, and how to change this.

Understanding the cognitive mechanisms and structure of stereotypes supports a critical antioppressive and culturally responsive approach. It is through this approach that we can assess what has been denied and unacknowledged—what is invisible. So, we are charged with the task of making the invisible visible. To foster this learning, students with intersecting identities have to see themselves within an educational context—their lives, their histories. Safe and meaningful conversations, such as those that encourage open discussion about identities and experiences that do not assume gender, sexuality, race, ability, and so forth, should be pervasive for students to create relationships, make comparisons, and start challenging their understanding and oppressions. One way to do this is to ask students to locate themselves as members of different communities or identity groups and then examine the power (or lack thereof) that comes with each group affiliation. "White Privilege: Unpacking the Invisible Knapsack" (McIntosh, 1998) is a groundbreaking article that all educators should read, become familiar with, and use within the educational setting. McIntosh (1992), a Caucasian female, created a list of all the privileges she is afforded because of her race. It included things such as, "I can be sure that my children will be given curricular materials that testify to the existence of their race" and "I do not have to educate my children to be aware of systemic racism for their own daily protection" (pp. 166–167).

Although McIntosh's (1992) article examined the social construct of race, there are certain privileges afforded other identity groups that society has held as the norm. We can ask students to examine heterosexual and cisgender (a person who does not identify as transgender) privilege. Some of the privileges may include (a) being certain that curricular materials will testify to the existence and validity of their sexual orientation, gender identity, and family structure; (b) having job security and not worrying about being terminated on the basis of gender identity or sexual orientation; and (c) not having to worry about having a safe and accessible bathroom or locker room to use. These affordances can be used as discussion points, and students can use them to think about their own privileges and that of others.

In terms of identifying what is visible, students can also participate in an institutional scavenger hunt. By exploring the academic environment and community (in addition to home environments and communities), students can search for heteronormative or cisgender messages in addition to antioppressive messages. The messages may be in print, in action, or in spoken word. The scavenger hunt is the starting point for a discussion of how privilege and societal norms are visible components of our daily environment. For a full description of this activity, see Activity 3.2 at the end of the chapter.

INTERSECTIONALITY

Institutional structures, such as schools, often perpetuate homogeneity. Yet, homogeneity neglects individuality and intersectionality. The idea of *intersectionality*, originally used by Crenshaw (1989), conceptualized the ways in which different forms of social inequality, oppression, and discrimination interact and overlap in multidimensional ways. Because a person's identity is composed of a multitude of facets and dimensions that intersect in complicated ways, it is argued that educators should analyze the intersectional aspects of identity and deconstruct the associated assumptions and privileges that perpetuate invisibility and injustice (Sharp, 2009). Intersectionality is also a critical lens for bringing awareness and social justice to overcome invisibility by deconstructing issues of power and privilege.

To be critical and transformative, antioppressive practices have to focus on intersecting identities and how the intersection is different from one subordinate identity. A thorough understanding of oppressions includes an examination of how some groups and identities are othered, whereas others are privileged. This is done by focusing on what constitutes the societal "norm" and the otherness that exists in opposition to the norm. It has been argued that classrooms, even university classrooms, are reflective of society or are even more conservative than society (Applebaum, 2003). Regardless, critical theorists agree that schools, like society, constitute cultures of power, with the ability to both transmit and transform institutional oppression (Applebaum, 2003; Delpit, 1995). Using cultural norms, values, and beliefs, schools assist in the development of a hetero-normative perspective on teaching and learning (MacGillivray, 2004).

To address intersectionality, educators are challenged to explore social justice on a deeper level. This means emphasizing ethical values, care, and respect. Educators may encounter contested values, beliefs, and behaviors of their students that they may or may not recognize and accept. As stated earlier and emphasized throughout this chapter, educators have to understand who they are and their views on the sources of historical, social, and cultural inequities and privileges (Darling-Hammond, 2005; Ladson-Billings, 2005).

Educators have an obligation to teach students that their opinions matter by creating opportunities for all voices to be heard. They have to be taught, such as through role playing, how to participate in a discussion to encourage a free-flowing exchange of ideas. However, bell hooks (1994) warned that one way of knowing and thinking should not be replaced with another. Students ought to be taught that there are multiple ways of knowing, thinking, and being. As educators, we have a duty to use questioning as a tool to help students make connections between ideas. In addition, educators have the responsibility to consistently ask whose voice is not being heard and what is left unsaid. One way to help educators and students unpack their own identities and make sense of those around them is through a visual movement activity called *I-dentify*. This activity allows students to move in and out of a circle if they identify with a specific affinity group (i.e., being a child of LGBT parents, being a member of a religious group other than Christianity). I-dentify gives "voice" to a person's identity through movement and without words. This activity is explained more fully in Activity 3.3.

Also, educators have to think critically about the curriculum and materials used in the classroom. Does the narrative represent the diverse group? Educators have to consider what revisions have to be made to include greater diversity in ethnicity, language, ability, sexuality, gender, socioeconomic status, and religion. Do the content and methodology reflect 21st-century teaching and learning? Specifically, integrating web-based learning modules would increase visibility and accessibility while simultaneously allowing for differentiation of learning styles.

In genuinely integrated ways, instruction benefits from including diverse family structures and relationships. Curricular materials should accurately represent the existence and contribution of people who are LGBTQ. The challenge here, however, is to be aware enough that the adaptations are not stereotypical, that they truly reflect the tapestry of our diverse society. For example, when students in a family therapy course think about diverse family structures such as a two-mom family or two-dad family, speculations can be made that one mom assumes a feminine role and one a masculine role. Similar assumptions may be made for two-dad families. In reality, having two parents of the same sex does not necessarily equate with societal expectations and assumptions of gender norms, roles, and expression.

INTERSECTIONAL INVISIBILITY

Intersectionality, a product of rich diversity, sometimes may lead to polarizing conflicts as individuals navigate the cultural and social dimensions of their life. In regard to simultaneous intersectionality, Purdie-Vaughns and Eibach (2008) hypothesized that possessing multiple subordinate-group identities renders a person "invisible" relative to those with single subordinate-group identities. They argued that because people with multiple subordinate-group identities do not fit the prototypes of their respective dominant identity groups, they experience *intersectional invisibility* or "the general failure to fully recognize people with intersecting identities as members of their constituent groups" (Purdie-Vaughns & Eibach, 2008, p. 378). For instance, people who identify as deaf and lesbian may experience intersectional invisibility because they do not completely fit the prototype of the deaf identity group or the LGBTQ identity group. The deaf group sees them as outsiders because they are not heterosexual, and the LGBTQ group sees them as outsiders because they are not hearing. As practitioners, it is critical that we reflect and examine the intersectionalities in the groups we are working with to determine whether intersectional invisibility exists and what needs would benefit from being addressed. At certain times, specific dimensions of identity may be more salient than at others, but at no time is anyone without multiple identities.

Addressing intersectional invisibility requires an inclusive curriculum that has positive representations of LGBTQ people, access to resources related to an LGBTQ identity, and openness about intersecting identities. A holistic approach to an inclusive environment is looking at all aspects of difference for positive representations to be woven throughout daily activities, university and school life, curriculum, and instruction. Inclusion of people, events, and histories with intersecting identities helps to reduce prejudice and intolerance. Emily Style (1996) introduced the idea of curriculum as a means to provide students with windows and mirrors. The curriculum serves as a mirror when it reflects individuals and their experiences back to themselves. The curriculum also serves as a window that introduces and provides opportunities to understand the experiences and perspectives of those who possess different identities. As such, educators must examine and challenge the institutional structures, particularly curriculum, that perpetuate invisibility in order to work toward positive social change for those experiencing intersectional invisibility. To aid students in understanding intersectionalities, educators have to provide opportunities to dissect their own intersections. A foundational way to present intersectionalities is through the use of Venn diagrams. Venn diagrams are visual ways to see the interconnectedness or relationship of two or more concepts. They allow one to see the differences and overlaps and, thus, appeal to visual learners. Figure 3.1 is an example of a 23-year-old graduate student in a counseling psychology program who, for a course assignment, created a Venn diagram in which she dissected components of her identity or institutional oppressions that may lead to intersectional invisibility. Intersectionality is not always neat; in fact, it is messy. The following excerpt from a recent case study looks at three young women who experienced intersectionality and, at times, intersectional invisibility.

Dunne (2013) interviewed three adolescents, Tori, Lexi, and Danni, who identified as deaf, lesbian persons of color. All three students made references to gender nonconformity by identifying as tomboys. The results indicated that their nonconformity to the social expectations of gender affected their understanding of sexuality. The intersection between gender and sexuality was informed by a patriarchal heteronormative society. In this instance, the dominant notion of biological sex depended on the heterosexual assumption that the only possible configuration is male or female "opposite sexes." Gender is achieved or constructed through a process whereby males and females become men and women, attaining different and distinct traits based on sex (Ingraham, 1994).

Tori, Lexi, and Danni all struggled with the complex intersections of sex, gender, and sexuality. In conversation, Tori quickly explained that she identified as female and as a lesbian. Then she made the following comment: "I am a woman, but I feel like I have to be a man because I am attracted to and want to date women. I think that is how I need to feel because I like women." This was Tori's way of normalizing her attraction to the same sex. Lexi commented that she felt more comfortable as a boy (i.e., wearing boys' clothes) but continued to identify as female. Danni reported that her family suspected she would identify as lesbian on the basis of her clothing (i.e., it was designed for boys) and her "tomboy attitude." These examples demonstrate the ways in which our under-

FIGURE 3.1

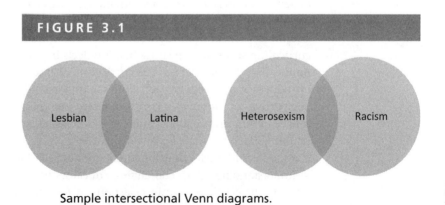

Sample intersectional Venn diagrams.

standing of sex, gender, gender expression, and sexuality intersect and are sometimes confounding for the person as well as others.

Tori, Lexi, and Danni's understandings of sex, gender, and sexuality were intertwined, reflecting societal pressure to fit neatly into the expectations of the world. Gender, a core aspect of identity, is a socially constructed concept, and these adolescents were socially encouraged to recognize the differences between women and men—and live within them, rather than unearth new definitions of identity and power that are more suitable to their own personalities, experiences, and lives.

This case study speaks to the need to explicitly teach the concepts discussed in this chapter: assumptions, perspective, bias, stereotyping, sexuality, gender, gender identity, and so forth. By using some of the examples from the chapter, educators can help students fully examine intersectionality. By engaging in reflexive practices, educators can assist learners in challenging their automatic assumptions regarding these socially constructed binaries (i.e., male/female, heterosexual/LGBTQ). Using an intersectional pedagogical approach may strengthen the understandings of the matrix of oppression as related to a multitude of social inequalities.

Conclusion

Critical theorists study the phenomena of privilege and oppression in social institutions in hopes of transforming these institutions and emancipating the oppressed (Morrow & Brown, 1994). Arguably, schools should be places where knowledge is formed for the purpose of democratic empowerment and resistance, as opposed to conformity and assimilation (Freire, 1970; hooks, 2003). Academic institutions (of all levels) contribute to homophobia, transphobia, and heterosexism by maintaining heteronormative and cisgender privilege through the oppression of LGBTQ individuals. As such, educators have to examine their participation in education that maintains hegemonic social structures, while simultaneously working to create inclusive antioppressive learning environments. Because of this multiplicity of oppressions, educators and MHPs are challenged to deconstruct power relations that uphold intersectional invisibility in the academic and work environments.

If we expect to create antioppressive environments, it seems reasonable to argue that as educators, we have to challenge institutional values and norms to deconstruct the power and privilege that fosters inequities. To maintain and develop ongoing dialogue that fosters reflexive teaching and learning, schools have to be committed to ongoing professional development for all faculty, administrators, and staff. Practitioners have to be able to turn theory into practice connections and have the space to do so. School administrators must encourage faculty and staff to make the invisible visible. The environment must be equally safe for staff and students, and diversity, in every form, must be celebrated.

To understand LGBTQ issues and teach students how to live pragmatically and immediately in their current environment, educators must consider how to retool themselves to meet the complex challenges of intersectionalities. The reality is that our environments are bursting with intersectionalities that are often invisible, overlooked, or not addressed. Teaching LGBTQ issues in psychology involves purposefully addressing intersectional diversity (e.g., cultural, racial, ethnic, sexual, gender, ability, linguistic) to empower students with the knowledge, skills, and attitudes that will help them transform the world and enhance their realities.

ACTIVITY 3.1

Digital Storytelling

Directions: *Digital storytelling* is a form of digital media production that allows people to share a story or present an idea. The media may include animation, video, stills, audio only, or any other forms of non-physical media. Share information on digital storytelling, perhaps by showing students an example of a personally created digital story or one already found at one of the links provided. As a class, group, or individual activity, have participants produce a digital story on a topic related to LGBTQ issues in psychology. Examples might include a "coming out" story, issues of privilege and bias in therapy, forms of LGBTQ oppression, addressing the intersection of identities in psychological research, how individuals understand, describe, and express their gender expansive identity, and so forth.

Goal: The goal of this activity is to share a personal narrative or the understanding of a specific topic related to LGBTQ issues and/or anti-oppressive education.

Educator Instructions:

The eight steps for digital storytelling include the following.

1. Start with an idea.
2. Research, explore, and learn.
3. Write a script.
4. Develop a storyboard plan.
5. Gather and create images, audio, and video.
6. Put it all together.
7. Share.
8. Reflect and offer feedback.

Materials:

- Computer access with overhead projector and screen
- Storyboard graphic (found at the websites provided)
- Laptops and Wi-Fi access for each participant

Resources:

http://www.digitalstorytelling.coe.uh.edu/index.cfm
http://www.samanthamorra.com/category/digitalstorytelling/
http://www.schrockguide.net/digital-storytelling.html

ACTIVITY 3.2

Institutional Scavenger Hunt

Directions: Split the students into groups of four (or use another grouping method of your choice). Use one class period to allow the groups to go throughout the building, student center, residence halls, campus, and so forth. Instruct the groups to collect environmental evidence in the school that demonstrates both oppressive and anti-oppressive practices, specifically heteronormative or cisgender examples, as well as positive messages regarding sociocultural identities. Take photos where relevant. Examples may include posters or flyers advertising school functions or overheard conversations (remind students that all names must be not be used). Students could also make an inventory of the institution's online presence, capturing screen images or writing descriptions of any online oppressive or antioppressive images or messages. At the next class, student groups present the information they uncovered demonstrating oppressive and anti-oppressive practices. The presentations should include visuals, such as photos, PowerPoint, charts, and so forth. Each group should explain why they believe certain practices are oppressive or antioppressive or positive and what steps could be taken to encourage more antioppressive and positive sociocultural messages and practices around campus. Students may also do this activity outside the classroom and in their communities; students can bring back their findings to present to the class or upload them to a shared online folder for the class to view and discuss.

Goal: The goal of this activity is for students to identify, observe, and analyze what type of messages (oppressive vs. anti-oppressive) fill our academic and social environment, specifically what may be viewed as heteronormative and cisgender.

Materials:

■ At least one notepad and writing utensil per group
■ Camera for each group (i.e., student cell phone with camera)
■ Internet access

ACTIVITY 3.3

I-dentify!

Directions: Present an overview to the class. "It's important to consider all of our characteristics, internal and external, that make us individuals. When we think about identity, most people think about 'visible' characteristics such as race and gender. Yet, one's sex and gender expression or gender identity may not all align in the way that society perceives as the norm. We have to challenge ourselves to examine the 'invisible' characteristics such as ability, social class, language, and sexual orientation."

Goal: This activity provides a way to explore diversity in the classroom, despite a homogeneous surface. Participants will connect with their own identities, recognize and openly address issues of difference, and start to think consciously about building genuine relationships and maintaining an anti-oppressive environment and safe space.

This activity will include moving around while being silent in order to observe what is happening and how we feel followed by a discussion. Participants create a large circle using the perimeter walls of the room and leave equal space between the center of the circle and the walls. Participants should be facing the center of the room. The instructor will state a phrase and remain stationary. Participants will move to the center of the room inside the circle depending on whether or not they "I-dentify" with the category and, thus, reveal a component of their individual identity.

(continued)

ACTIVITY 3.3 (Continued)

Ensure that participants know that this is a safe space and they can choose not to reveal parts of themselves by not moving for certain categories. Discuss confidentiality with the entire group, emphasizing the importance of maintaining confidentiality as a means to maintain a safe environment. Share that not moving does not mean one is choosing to identify or not identify with a statement, but simply making the decision not to choose.

To better understand the activity, here is an example. The instructor says, "If you are a woman, I-dentify!" All individuals who identify as a woman would move into the circle, noticing who moved and who did not. The educator instructs participants to return to their original location after each "I-dentifying" movement is completed. At the end of the movement activity, regroup and discuss what participants noticed and felt. Discussion points are listed next. Ask participants to write a reflection paper about this experience and what emotions were evoked for them.

Do you I-dentify?

1. You are a woman.
2. You are of a faith tradition other than Christianity.
3. You are a member of a club at school.
4. You are an only child.
5. You are African American, Black, or of African descent.
6. You have your own car.
7. You feel that educators and students at school do not understand you.
8. You are Latino/Latina, Chicano/Chicana, or Mestizo/Mestiza or identify another way with a Spanish-speaking or Latin or South American culture.
9. Your parents are divorced.
10. You are a man.
11. You have at least one parent with a college degree.
12. Your family unit does not consist of a mother and a father.
13. You are Caucasian.
14. You have a supportive family.
15. You or someone you love (family or friends) is lesbian, gay, bisexual, queer, or transgender.
16. You or your family has worried at some point how they would pay the bills.
17. You have lived in one house your entire life.
18. You or someone you love has a disability.
19. A language other than English is used in your home.
20. You received a scholarship to attend school.
21. You have experienced bullying.
22. You identify as Native American.
23. You have two working parents.
24. You can use public restrooms without fear of verbal abuse, physical intimidation, or arrest.

Discussion Questions

The following questions may be used for the group discussion as well as for the reflection paper:

- Did you ever feel pressure to move with the group? During which questions? Why do you think you felt this way?
- Did you ever feel vulnerable during this activity?
- Were you ever afraid to move into the circle? Do you think others felt this way?
- Was there a time when you felt pride about one or two of the identities in the exercise? If yes, when and why? If no, why not?
- Were you surprised by which participants moved for different statements? Do you think this is significant? Why?

References

American Psychiatric Association. (1952). *Diagnostic and statistical manual of mental disorders*. Washington, DC: Author.

American Psychiatric Association. (1968). *Diagnostic and statistical manual of mental disorders* (2nd ed.). Washington, DC: Author.

American Psychiatric Association. (1987). *Diagnostic and statistical manual of mental disorders* (3rd ed., rev.). Washington, DC: Author.

American Psychiatric Association. (2013). *Diagnostic and statistical manual of mental disorders* (5th ed.). Washington, DC: Author.

American Psychological Association. (2012). Guidelines for psychological practice with lesbian, gay, and bisexual clients. *American Psychologist, 67*, 10–42. http://dx.doi.org/10.1037/a0024659

Applebaum, B. (2003). Social justice, democratic education, and the silencing of the words that wound. *Journal of Moral Education, 32*, 151–162. http://dx.doi.org/10.1080/0305724032000072924

Berbrier, M. (2002). Disempowering minorities: A critique of Wilkinson's "task for social scientists and practitioners." *Journal of Sociology and Social Welfare, 29*(2), 3–19.

Birden, S. (2005). *Rethinking sexual identity in education*. Lanham, MD: Rowman & Littlefield.

Butler, J. (1990). *Gender trouble: Feminism and the subversion of identity*. New York, NY: Routledge.

Clarke, S. (2008). Culture and identity. In T. Bennett & J. Frow (Eds.), *The Sage handbook of cultural analysis* (pp. 510–529). http://dx.doi.org/10.4135/9781848608443.n25

Cox, W. T. L., & Devine, P. G. (2015). Stereotypes possess heterogeneous directionality: A theoretical and empirical exploration of stereotype structure and content. *PLoS ONE, 10*(3), e0122292. http://dx.doi.org/10.1371/journal.pone.0122292

Crenshaw, K. (1989). Demarginalizing the intersection of race and sex: A Black feminist critique of antidiscrimination doctrine, feminist theory, and antiracist politics. *University of Chicago Legal Forum, 140*, 139–167.

Darling-Hammond, L. (2005). New standards and old inequalities: School reform and the education of African American students. In J. E. King (Ed.), *Black education: A transformative research and action agenda for the new century* (pp. 197–223). Mahwah, NJ: Erlbaum.

Davis, L. (2008). Postdeafness. In H. Bauman (Ed.), *Open your eyes: Deaf studies talking* (pp. 314–326). Minneapolis: University of Minnesota Press.

Delpit, L. (1995). *Other people's children: Cultural conflict in the classroom*. New York, NY: The New York Press.

D'Emilio, J. (1983). *Sexual politics, sexual communities: The making of a homosexual minority in the United States, 1940–1970* (2nd ed.). Chicago, IL: The University of Chicago Press.

Diamond, L. M. (2007). A dynamical systems approach to the development and expression of female same-sex sexuality. *Perspectives on Psychological Science, 2,* 142–161. http://dx.doi.org/10.1111/j.1745-6916.2007.00034.x

Dunne, C. (2013). *Deaf/LGBTQ intersectional invisibility in schools: The lived experiences of deaf lesbian students of color at a school for the deaf* (Unpublished doctoral dissertation). University of Pennsylvania, Philadelphia.

Farrell, K. (Ed.). (2004). *Interrupting heteronormativity.* Syracuse, NY: The Graduate School of Syracuse University.

Foucault, M. (1977). *Discipline and punish: The birth of the prison* (R. Hurley, Trans.). Harmondsworth, England: Penguin.

Foucault, M. (1978). *The history of sexuality: An introduction* (R. Hurley, Trans.). Harmondsworth, England: Penguin.

Freire, P. (1970). *Pedagogy of the oppressed* (M. B. Ramos, Trans.). New York, NY: Continuum International.

Freire, P. (1998). *Pedagogy of freedom.* New York, NY: Rowman & Littlefield.

Herr, K. (1998). Learning lessons from school: Homophobia, heterosexism, and the construction of failure. *Journal of Gay & Lesbian Social Services, 7,* 51–64. http://dx.doi.org/10.1300/J041v07n04_04

Hinchey, P. (2004). *Becoming a critical educator: Defining a classroom identity, designing a critical pedagogy.* New York, NY: Peter Lang.

hooks, b. (1994). *Teaching to transgress: Education as the practice of freedom.* London, England: Routledge.

hooks, b. (2003). *Teaching community: A pedagogy of hope.* New York, NY: Routledge.

Ingraham, C. (1994). The heterosexual imaginary: Feminist sociology and theories of gender. *Sociological Theory, 12,* 203–219. http://dx.doi.org/10.2307/201865

Kimmell, M. (2005). *The gender of desire: Essays on male sexuality.* Albany: State University of New York Press.

Kinsey, A. C., Pomeroy, W. B., & Martin, C. E. (1948). *Sexual behavior in the human male.* Philadelphia, PA: Saunders.

Kinsey, A. C., Pomeroy, W. B., Martin, C. E., & Gebhard, P. H. (1953). *Sexual behavior in the human female.* Philadelphia, PA: Saunders.

Klein, F. (1993). *The bisexual option* (2nd ed.). New York, NY: Harrington Park.

Klein, F., Sepekoff, B., & Wolf, T. J. (1985). Sexual orientation: A multivariable dynamic process. *Journal of Homosexuality, 11,* 35–49. http://dx.doi.org/10.1300/J082v11n01_04

Kosciw, J. G., Greytak, E. A., Palmer, N. A., & Boesen, M. J. (2014). *The 2013 National School Climate Survey: The experiences of lesbian, gay, bisexual, and transgender youth in our nation's schools.* New York, NY: GLSEN.

Kumashiro, K. K. (2000). Toward a theory of antioppressive education. *Review of Educational Research, 70*, 25–53. http://dx.doi.org/10.3102/00346543070001025

Kumashiro, K. K. (2002). *Troubling education: "Queer" activism and antioppressive pedagogy*. New York, NY: Routledge.

Ladson-Billings, G. (1995). Toward a theory of culturally relevant pedagogy. *American Educational Research Journal, 32*, 465–491. http://dx.doi.org/10.3102/00028312032003465

Ladson-Billings, G. (2005). Is the team all right? Diversity and teacher education. *Journal of Teacher Education, 56*, 229–234. http://dx.doi.org/10.1177/0022487105275917

Lather, P., & Ellsworth, E. (1996). Situated pedagogies: Classroom practices in postmodern times. *Theory into Practice, 35*, 70–71. http://dx.doi.org/10.1080/00405849609543704

Lesbian, Gay, Bisexual, Transgender, Queer, Intersex, Asexual Resource Center. (2015). *Words that hurt*. Retrieved from http://lgbtqia.ucdavis.edu/educated/words.html

Lorde, A. (1984). *Sister outsider*. Berkeley, CA: Crossing Press.

MacGillivray, I. (2004). *Sexual orientation and school policy: A practical guide for teachers, administrators, and community activists*. Lanham, MD: Rowman & Littlefield.

McIntosh, P. (1992). White privilege and male privilege: A personal account coming to see correspondence through work in women's studies. In M. Anderson & P. H. Collins (Eds.), *Race, class, and gender* (pp. 76–87). Belmont, CA: Wadsworth.

McIntosh, P. (1998). White privilege: Unpacking the invisible knapsack. In P. S. Rothenberg (Ed.), *Race, class, and gender in the United States: An integrated study* (4th ed., pp. 165–169). New York, NY: St. Martin's Press.

McLaren, P., & Hammer, R. (1989). Critical pedagogy and the postmodern challenge: Toward a critical postmodernist pedagogy of liberation. *Educational Foundations, 3*, 29–62.

Morrow, R., & Brown, D. (1994). *Critical theory and methodology*. Thousand Oaks, CA: Sage.

Purdie-Vaughns, V., & Eibach, R. P. (2008). Intersectional invisibility: The distinctive advantages and disadvantages of multiple subordinate-group identities. *Sex Roles, 59*, 377–391. http://dx.doi.org/10.1007/s11199-008-9424-4

Rankin, S., Weber, G., Blumenfeld, W., & Frazer, S. (2010). *2010 state of higher education for lesbian, gay, bisexual, and transgender people*. Charlotte, NC: Campus Pride.

Rich, A. (1980). Compulsory heterosexuality and lesbian existence. *Signs: Journal of Women in Culture and Society, 5*, 631–660. http://dx.doi.org/10.1086/493756

Sedgwick, E. K. (1990). *Epistemology of the closet*. Berkeley: University of California Press.

Sharp, M. (2009). Deconstructing silos. In J. W. Koschoreck & A. K. Tooms (Eds.), *Sexuality matters: Paradigms and policies for educational leaders* (pp. 103–121). Lanham, MD: Rowman & Littlefield.

Simpson, J. A., & Weiner, E. S. (Eds.). (1989). *The Oxford English dictionary*. Oxford, England: Clarendon Press.

Style, E. (1996). Curriculum as window and mirror. *Social Science Record, 33*(2), 21–28.

Trans Student Educational Resources. (2016). *The gender unicorn*. Retrieved from http://www.transstudent.org/gender

Tristan, J. M. B. (2013, February 6). Henry Giroux: The necessity of critical pedagogy in dark times. *Truthout*. Retrieved from http://www.truth-out.org/news/item/14331-a-critical-interview-with-henry-giroux

Walters, A. S., & Hayes, D. M. (1998). Homophobia within schools: Challenging the culturally sanctioned dismissal of gay students and colleagues. *Journal of Homosexuality, 35*, 1–23. http://dx.doi.org/10.1300/J082v35n02_01

Whitlock, R. U. (2010). Getting queer: Teacher education, gender studies, and the cross-disciplinary quest for queer pedagogies. *Issues in Teacher Education, 19*, 81–104.

Jeanne L. Stanley

Teaching Ethics in Relation to LGBTQ Issues in Psychology

4

Vignette 1. I know I have been working with him for 3 months on career counseling, but I had no idea he's bisexual. I do not feel comfortable helping him around his boyfriend issues. What do you want me to do? I told you that I want to refer him because that is what is best for him. I don't think bisexuality is real. People say that because they don't want to admit they are really homosexual.

Vignette 2. Isn't teaching about homosexuality and transgender as "normal" in reality more your agenda and, quite frankly, that of liberal-based, national professional associations? I do not feel I have to learn about a lifestyle that I do not agree with. It would be like in the future, when I am a professor, requiring my students to read and learn how to do therapy to cure these people. I think we have a right not to have to read and follow everything we believe is not ethical. After all, if the ethics codes say that we are to be honest with our clients, then I assume we are also required to be honest with you. I, therefore, assume this won't affect my grade because I am being honest

http://dx.doi.org/10.1037/0000015-004
Teaching LGBTQ Psychology: Queering Innovative Pedagogy and Practice, T. R. Burnes and J. L. Stanley (Editors)

with you. The First Amendment grounds us on being able to speak our opinion in class.

Vignette 3. Dr. Grove, I did not come to classes last weekend because the classes for my clinical psychology program were held at the college's Queer Student Campus Resource Center. My religion does not condone homosexuality, so I did not feel comfortable walking into the center. Hey, I'm proud to be a straight guy with strong religious values and a love for psychology, but I really can't support a lifestyle that is not in line with my moral beliefs. I know you will understand because you support diversity, including religious diversity.

These three examples exemplify the discrepancy between one's personal beliefs and one's professional obligations as a mental health provider (MHP). Such conflicts have played out over the last few decades inside classrooms, faculty meetings, community mental health centers, and supervision offices, as well as courtrooms and legislative hearings. The discrepancy speaks to the importance of instructing educators and supervisors who work with MHPs on how to address situations in which a student's or clinical trainee's personal worldviews collide with professional standards for supporting and affirming people who are lesbian, gay, bisexual, transgender, queer, or questioning (LGBTQ).

The purpose of this chapter is to assist educators in addressing ethical issues when teaching LGBTQ psychology. As LGBTQ visibility and rights have increased (i.e., marriage equality, nondiscrimination laws at the state and federal levels), resistance has surfaced from mental health trainees, educators, and providers who do not agree with the 1973 removal of homosexuality as a mental illness or the more recent change that replaced gender identity disorder with gender dysphoria in the fifth edition of the *Diagnostic and Statistical Manual of Mental Disorders* (*DSM–5*; American Psychiatric Association, 2013). In particular, affirming diverse sexual orientations and gender identities has moved to the forefront of ethical debates for MHPs. Discord between one's personal worldview and that of the mental health professions has evolved from ethical debates contained within the classroom into lawsuits and legislation that threaten to trump professional standards and disrupt the provision of services to LGBTQ individuals.

This chapter begins with an overview of professional ethics codes and guidelines relevant to working with LGBTQ people. Recognizing that knowledge of ethics codes, in and of itself, does not provide clear steps to resolve dilemmas such as those in the vignettes, the next section discusses how ethics codes can be used to address potential challenges in training MHPs to work effectively with LGBTQ and other diverse clientele. A strengths-based approach to assist trainees and providers in moving toward an ethical and affirmative stance in working with LGBTQ individuals is presented. Recommendations for educational activities are included at the end of the chapter.

American Psychological Association Ethics Codes: Principles, Standards, Guidelines, and Statements

The following discussion of the *Ethical Principles of Psychologists and Code of Conduct* (American Psychological Association [APA], 2010; hereafter referred to as the Ethics Code) as well as other guidelines published by APA and other professional associations such as the American Counseling Association (ACA) provides educators with the relevant resources for shaping their curriculum. These ethics codes and guidelines address the education and training of MHPs and prescribe how MHPs work with the public. The APA's Ethics Code has several principles and standards relevant to supporting LGBTQ individuals.

It is crucial that students gain a thorough understanding of two specific sections of the APA Ethics Code relevant to their respective professions as they learn about LGBTQ psychology. First, the General (or aspirational) Principles of the APA Ethics Code, which offer a moral foundation for psychological practice aiming to inspire psychologists to higher levels of care and assist them in ethical decision making, provide an excellent foundation for instruction. MHPs who "understand the moral principles behind the Ethics Code will have criteria by which to determine whether their actions are reasonable or appropriate" (Knapp & Vandecreek, 2004, p. 247). Second, the Ethical Standards (Code of Conduct) are used by both the APA Ethics Office and by state boards as disciplinary criteria for psychologists (Knapp & Vandecreek, 2004) and "may also serve an educational purpose" (Knapp & Vandecreek, 2004, p. 248) for training MHPs. Academic coursework and supervision provide abundant opportunities for MHP trainees to gain an understanding of the relevant principles and standards so as to be able to apply them when working with LGBTQ individuals.

PRINCIPLES

The three main principles of the APA Ethics Code relevant for providers working with LGBTQ populations are Principles A, D, and E. Principle A: Beneficence and Nonmaleficence states first and foremost that psychologists strive to be beneficial and to do no harm while they "seek to safeguard the welfare and rights of those with whom they interact." Principle D: Justice states, "fairness and justice entitle all persons access to and benefit from the contributions of psychology." Justice "may also refer to fair or equal treatment" (Knapp & Vandecreek, 2004, p. 249), including that of gender and sexual orientation. Principle E: Respect for People's Rights and Dignity addresses how psychologists work to eliminate bias in their career by becoming aware of and respecting differences regarding sociocultural identity factors, including gender and sexual orientation. This principle implies that psychologists do not condone or participate in prejudicial activities such as sexual orientation change efforts (SOCE) including conversion therapy or professional training that is prejudicial in content against LGBTQ individuals.

STANDARDS

The three main Code of Ethics standards that directly relate to supporting and affirming LGBTQ individuals are Standards 2, 3, and 7. Standard 2: Competence calls for psychologists to work only with the areas and populations in which they have education, training, supervision, consultation, and professional experience. This standard clearly states that psychologists are responsible for gaining knowledge and understanding factors associated with LGBTQ individuals or for making appropriate referrals. All three vignettes at the beginning of this chapter are examples of students struggling with competence in regard to gaining knowledge, skills, and personal understanding to work with LGBTQ clients. In Vignette 1, a clinical trainee wants to refer a client because she is influenced by her personal beliefs. She does not want to work with a person who is bisexual. The issue of personal beliefs serving as a potential loophole in working with diverse clients is addressed later in this chapter.

Standard 3: Human Relations states that in their professional role, psychologists may not discriminate, harass, demean, or sexually harass others (i.e., clients, students, supervisees, colleagues) on the basis of sociocultural factors, including gender, gender identity, or sexual orientation. Standard 3 is of particular importance because of the increase in "religious freedom" bills and "conscience clause" legislation, discussed later in this chapter.

Standard 7: Education and Training has gained a great deal of attention in the last few years because of LGBTQ issues, lawsuits, and legislative wrangling. At its core, Standard 7 requires educational and training programs "to provide appropriate knowledge and experiences necessary to train competent and ethical professionals." Vignette 2 exemplifies such a struggle: A professor and the program are charged with providing appropriate knowledge in regard to working with LGBTQ individuals, but the student does not want to learn or engage in the material. Standard 7 also states that education and training programs have to be transparent, ensuring that they provide clear, accurate, and up-to-date descriptions of their programs. Program materials should provide prospective and current students with the program's description, goals, objectives, content areas, required courses, and requirements to complete the program.

In Vignette 3, a graduate program has written requirements for students in regard to both required class attendance and the expectation that students will gain a range of competencies in learning how to work with socioculturally diverse clients. These requirements are also stated in the course syllabi. The student in the vignette, however, informed the professor after the classes had been held that for religious reasons, he would not go into a classroom housed in the Queer Student Campus Resource Center on the college's campus. When such actions are taken by students, educators and trainers have to keep in mind that "when students can 'opt out' of essential parts of the education and training because of their beliefs, the result is, by definition, inadequate training" (Hancock, 2014, p. 6).

GUIDELINES AND STATEMENTS FOR PRACTICE, EDUCATION, AND TRAINING

The *Guidelines on Multicultural Education, Training, Research, Practice, and Organizational Change for Psychologists* (herein referred to as the Multicultural Guidelines; APA, 2003) summarize the knowledge and skills required of the profession for supporting historically marginalized or disfranchised groups, including social group identity or membership such as LGBTQ individuals. These documents are viewed as aspirational and are to be used in tandem with APA Ethical Standards.

APA has also approved additional multiple practice guidelines relevant to LGBTQ individuals (for a full listing, see APA, 2011a). APA adopted the *Resolution on Appropriate Therapeutic Responses to Sexual Orientation* in 1998, which was then expanded in 2009 on the basis of an APA task force outcome that found SOCE unlikely to be successful and, more concerning, harmful to individuals. The APA went further and called for the end of SOCE by MHPs by adopting the *Resolution on Appropriate Responses to Sexual Orientation Distress and Change Efforts* (APA, 2009, Appendix A). Other national and international mental health organizations have similar guidelines and statements supporting LGBTQ individuals; these organizations include but are not limited to the American Psychiatric Association, American Medical Association, American Academy of Pediatrics, American Association for Marriage and Family Therapy, American School Counselor Association, and Pan American Health Organization. The *Practice Guidelines for LGB Clients* (APA, 2011b) and the *Guidelines for Psychological Practice With Transgender and Gender Nonconforming People* (APA, 2015b) are discussed in more detail later in the chapter.

The *Guidelines and Principles for Accreditation of Programs in Professional Psychology* (G & P; APA, 2006) address the training of psychologists (the application of education). Most relevant to this discussion are Domains A and G of the G & P. Domain A: Eligibility states that "the program engages in actions that indicate respect for and understanding of cultural and individual diversity" (APA, 2006, p. 6) as reflected in its recruitment and retention policies for faculty and students, curriculum and field placements, nondiscriminatory policies and operating conditions, and avoidance of actions that restrict program access on grounds irrelevant to success. Gender identity and sexual orientation are both specifically included within the G & P's definition of cultural and individual diversity. Further, Domain G: Public Disclosures is similar to Standard 7 of the APA Ethics Code, which calls for programs to be transparent by accurately and completely describing themselves. Education and training sites can refer to the useful work of the APA's Education Directorate (APA, 2013) that developed the document "Professional Psychologist Competencies to Serve a Diverse Public." In addition, APA's Board of Educational Affairs created a beneficial flowchart (APA Education Directorate, 2013) to assist programs in developing plans, expectations, and policies for conflict resolution in instances when a trainee's personal beliefs are in conflict with the profession's ethical competencies.

RELATED ETHICS CODES AND STANDARDS

The ACA Ethics Code (ACA, 2014) specifically includes the following nondiscrimination statement (C.5): "Counselors do not condone or engage in discrimination against prospective or current clients, students, employees, supervisees, or research participants based on . . . gender, gender identity, sexual orientation" (p. 9). The code also states that counselors have to be aware of and avoid imposing their personal values and beliefs or discriminating against their clients.

The Association of Lesbian, Gay, Bisexual, and Transgender Issues in Counseling (ALGBTIC), a division of ACA, created and maintains the *Competencies for Counseling Lesbian, Gay, Bisexual, Queer, Questioning, Intersex, and Ally Individuals* (ALGBTIC LGBQQIA Competencies Taskforce, 2013). An entire section of the document addresses the ethical practice of competent counselors working with LGBTQ clients. Professionals are directed to use ethical decision-making models that take into account LGBTQ individuals when facing ethical conundrums. Counselors are encouraged to seek supervision and/or consultation with a professional or a colleague who is well-trained and experienced in working with LGBTQ individuals "when their personal values conflict with counselors' professional obligations related to LGBTQ (lesbian, gay, bisexual, queer, questioning) individuals about creating a course of action that promotes the dignity and welfare of LGBQQ individuals" (ALGBTIC LGBQQIA Competencies Taskforce, 2013,

p. 16). In this document, ACA also takes a clear stance on the "serious ethical concerns" (ALGBTIC LGBQQIA Competencies Taskforce, 2013, p. 5) regarding the ineffective and harmful approaches of SOCE "which attempt to alter, 'repair' or 'convert' individuals' affectional orientation/gender identity/expression" (ALGBTIC LGBQQIA Competencies Taskforce, 2013, p. 14).

ACA (2010) also addressed ethical issues in regard to gender expansive and transgender (GET) people in a series of competencies for counseling with transgender clients. The American School Counselor Association (ASCA) provides guidance in supporting LGBTQ youth in schools. The ASCA's national model sets standards for school counselors to advocate for marginalized students, including GET students (ASCA, 2014; Singh & Burnes, 2009). Integrally important standards for training medical and mental health professionals working with GET people are the World Professional Association for Transgender Health *Standards of Care* (SOC; Coleman et al., 2012). The SOC states that the "treatment aimed at trying to change a person's gender identity and expression to become more congruent with sex assigned at birth . . . is no longer considered ethical" (Coleman et al., 2012, p. 186). Professionals who are untrained and inexperienced in practice with GET individuals can feel confused; indeed, their inexperience may lead to worse consequences, including serious ethical and legal breaches of care. The *Guidelines for Psychological Practice With Transgender and Gender Nonconforming People* (APA, 2015b) assist psychologists to "address the unique challenges and strengths of transgender and gender non-conforming people, ethical and legal issues, lifespan considerations, research, education and training, healthcare, and advocacy" (p. 2).

Other MHP organizations in social work, family therapy, psychiatric–mental health nursing, and related fields also have ethics codes and standards in place to inform and guide MHPs to effectively support rather than discriminate against LGBTQ individuals. Awareness and understanding of the codes and guidelines is important; however, difficulties inevitably arise.

Best-Laid Plans: Program Policy, Legal, and Legislative Challenges to Ethics Codes

It is important to resist assuming that instruction in the ethics codes provides everyone who is exposed to them with a simple and uniform decision-making algorithm to follow when faced with ethical conundrums. As with any codes or laws, interpretation can lead to gray areas that sometimes leave providers facing ethical challenges. Furthermore, loopholes related to ethics codes may lead to confusion. Such gray areas are evident in relation to work with LGBTQ people and, therefore, must be addressed in the classroom so that trainees have a grasp of their professional ethical responsibilities.

RELIGIOUS EXEMPTION ARGUMENT

Program and training site administrators and trainees who disagree with and choose not to follow APA's ethical guidelines regarding supporting and affirming LGBTQ individuals could until recently use a "religious exemption" to circumvent ethics codes, as exemplified in Vignette 3. Approved in 1996, Footnote 4 of APA's (2006) G & P allowed institutions with a religious affiliation or purpose to override ethical standards in regard to cultural diversity and direct their admissions and hiring decisions to be in alignment with their religious affiliation and/or purpose.

Footnote 4 left a void in LGBTQ rights and protection for students, staff, and faculty in admission or retention decisions made on the basis of religious teaching regarding homosexuality. In 2014, Biaggio documented six APA-accredited doctoral programs in religious institutions that overtly condemned homosexual conduct and held either expectations or requirements for students and faculty to refrain from such behavior, thereby creating and maintaining a repressive environment for LGBTQ individuals. Such programs were also able to use Footnote 4 to justify why they did not have to teach ethics codes or coursework about supporting LGBTQ people. Furthermore, they could choose to support or, at best, take a neutral stance toward SOCE. Footnote 4 was also used within religious institutions constraining educators from being able to teach about the healthy and positive aspects of LGBTQ identities.

Advocates for the removal of Footnote 4 equated it to a discriminatory pattern of treatment, noting that trainees and psychologists cannot refuse to treat groups of people (e.g., Jewish, Black, Muslim, LGBTQ people) on the basis of the MHP's beliefs and values (Bieschke & Mintz, 2012). Although many within APA opposed the inclusion of Footnote 4 in the G & P, in 2002, APA's Committee on Accreditation unanimously voted not to remove Footnote 4. Their decision to maintain the "religious exemption" came in response to the U.S. Department of Education (DOE) position "that if the footnote was removed, it (DOE) would be forced to consider revoking APA's recognition as an accrediting body" (Smith, 2002, p. 16).

After years of social justice advocacy by individuals and groups within APA, such as the American Psychological Association of Graduate Students–Committee on Sexual Orientation and Gender Diversity, Footnote 4 has been removed from the new Standards of Accreditation

(SoA) for Health Service Psychology (APA, 2015c). In its place, the SoA set as a precedent "serving a diverse public" (APA, 2013, "Preparing Professional Psychologists," para. 5) and addressed the issue as follows:

> Some trainees possess worldviews, values or religious beliefs that conflict with serving specific subgroups within the public. For example, they may experience strong negative reactions toward clients/patients who are of a particular sexual orientation, religious tradition, age or disability status. (para. 3)

The SoA holds the stance that "training programs address conflicts between trainees' worldviews, beliefs or religious values and professional psychology's commitment to offering culturally responsive psychological services to all members of the public, especially to those from traditionally marginalized groups" (APA, 2013, "Preparing Professional Psychologists," para. 2). On the programmatic level, the SoA supports the education and training of students in both secular and faith-based settings and states clearly that "compelling pedagogical interests require that each program prepare graduates to navigate cultural and individual differences in research and practice, including those that may produce value conflicts or other tensions arising from the intersection of different areas of diversity" (APA, 2015c, p. 9).

COMMUNITY LIFESTYLE STATEMENTS

Some institutions still require students, staff, and faculty to sign "community lifestyle statements" that serve to subvert LGBTQ individuals' or others' LGBTQ identities. For example, at the time of this writing, a university that has an APA-accredited doctoral psychology program maintains the following:

> Our lifestyle excludes immoral practices and calls us to transformed living as we "offer [our] bodies as living sacrifices" to God (Romans 12:1–2). In regard to sexual morality, we believe that only marriage between a man and a woman is God's intention for the joyful fulfillment of sexual intimacy. . . . Sexual behaviors outside of this context are inconsistent with God's teaching. (George Fox University, 2015, para. 5)

Biaggio (2014) found programs that stated in writing that students could not partake in "homosexual behavior [and] all forms of physical intimacy that give expression to homosexual feelings" and that "all members of its community—students, faculty, administrators/managers, staff, and trustees—. . . abstain from what it holds to be unbiblical sexual practices . . . [including] homosexual forms of explicit sexual conduct or such behavior will result in disciplinary action" (p. 1). Such statements can have the effect of censuring a student from openly identifying as LGBTQ, a faculty member being open about their committed relationship with someone of the same sex, or a heterosexual ally supporting the LGBTQ rights by attending a Gay Pride event.

Religious exemption and community lifestyle statements are useful teaching topics when training about LGBTQ ethical issues, and MHP educators may consider raising the following questions with students to generate discussion: (a) What happens when students who were sure they could "suppress" their sexual and/or gender identity realize during the program that doing so is not possible and decide to "come out" at the end of their coursework and prior to their internship and dissertation? (b) What does it mean for students who self-identified as heterosexual and signed the community lifestyle statement but, during the program, begin for the first time to understand their gender and/or sexual identity as different than that before entering the program? (c) From the perspectives of APA, mental health training programs in religious-based institutions, and LGBTQ students/staff/faculty in such programs, how and why did Footnote 4 stand for over 20 years? (d) What should heterosexual allies who are expected to refrain from supporting the LGBTQ "lifestyle" do if they want to attend a same-sex wedding or present at a conference on supporting and affirming LGBTQ clients? Such discussion in the classroom will encourage reflection and guidance when conflicts arise for an MHP in regard to their beliefs and sociocultural identities and their profession's ethical standards.

STUDENTS, PROGRAMS, TRAINING, AND THE COURTS

Conflict between students' personal beliefs and actions or inactions in their training and client care within their educational institutions have escalated into legal disputes. Educators can use examples, such as the vignettes at the beginning of the chapter, as teaching tools in class for discussing and working through such conundrums. Students may also learn about and discuss recent court cases in which students sued their educational institutions after they were dismissed from their programs for not meeting the program's requirements for becoming multiculturally competent providers where LGBTQ individuals are involved (Hancock, 2014). Three such cases, all involving MHPs-in-training, involve key areas of these debates: *Ward v. Wilbanks*, 2010; *Ward v. Polite*, 2012; and *Keeton v. Anderson-Wiley*, 2010. These court cases are relevant for teaching MHPs and should be included in coursework because they give a view of how legal and ethical concerns can collide in regard to the competency of MHPs when working with LGBTQ individuals.

In the two Ward cases, Ms. Ward was a graduate student in the counseling master's program at Eastern Michigan State University.

After being assigned a gay male client who had previously received counseling regarding his same-sex relationship, Ward asked her supervisor whether she could refer the client because she could not support his same-sex behavior. Ward argued that she followed the ethical guidelines by referring a client she felt she could not support. The program countered that Ward chose to follow her personal beliefs that were discriminatory in practice and, therefore, inconsistent with the requirements of the program and the profession (Haldeman & Rasbury, 2014). The program offered her the following choices: to take part in a remedial program, voluntarily leave the program, or request a formal hearing. Ward chose the formal hearing and was dismissed from the program. After suing the university and after two court cases, an out-of-court settlement agreement was reached between and the student and the university.

The Keeton case involved a graduate student in counseling from Augusta State University. In her courses, Ms. Keeton asserted that if she were to work with LGBTQ clients, she would express her views of the immoralities of their same-sex behavior and then either use SOCE or refer the client to a practitioner who practiced SOCE to rectify the clients' behavior. The program faculty expressed their concern to the student and asked her to complete a remediation program because of the deficits in her multicultural competency in working with LGBTQ clients. She refused remediation and then sued, claiming that the remediation plan violated her First Amendment rights. The court rejected Keeton's claim on the grounds that the program did not ask her to alter her personal religious beliefs but to not use her beliefs to discriminate against clients. Keeton's proposed actions were in direct conflict with the ACA Ethics Code because she planned to not only impose her values on clients but also to discriminate against them on the basis of their sexual orientation.

Administrators of educational programs for MHPs have become concerned that lawsuits and legislation will trump program requirements, even though such requirements are based on professional ethics codes and standards. Professors, program directors, and administrators may wonder whether they should strictly follow their profession's ethics codes and risk lawsuits from students whose personal beliefs toward diverse groups are in direct contention with what is best for the students' clients.

The court in the Keeton case cited the 1988 U.S. Supreme Court decision in *Hazelwood School District v. Kuhlmeier*, finding in favor of the educational institution, citing "if there is a legitimate educational concern involved, free speech can be regulated by the educational institution" (Hancock, 2014, p. 6). Students' personal values as counselors may not outweigh their ethical obligations to the client, and the program, therefore, has to intervene to prevent harm to the client (Hancock, 2014). Bieschke and Mintz (2012) aptly argued that the core issue in these cases is one of the competences of the trainee in following the ethical requirements of their profession. Although such cases have not yet specifically involved psychologists or psychologists-in-training, similar cases are likely to follow.

LEGISLATION AFFECTING EDUCATION AND TRAINING OF MENTAL HEALTH PROVIDERS

In response to such legal cases, politicians have recently become more involved in efforts to regulate the education, training, service provision, and discipline of MHPs. Legislation has surfaced with the goal of "protecting" students and MHPs and religiously based educational institutions' rights to the point that their moral obligations supersede that of LGBTQ clients' access to care. Under such names as "conscience clauses," "religious freedom bills," and "religious liberty bills," the outcome of such legislation is that politicians, rather than educational institutions and professional organizations, establish the parameters of competence for training and the provision of services.

Examples of laws that directly affect graduate programs' education and training of MHPs include Arizona's law HB 2565 (State of Arizona, Senate Bill 1365, 2012), which specifies that a university cannot discipline or discriminate against a student in an MHP program if the student "refuses to counsel a client about goals that conflict with the student's sincerely held religious belief if the student consults with the supervising instructor or professor to determine the proper course of action to avoid harm to the client" (APA, 2015a, para. 3). Opponents to such bills refer to them as "First Do Harm" bills because such bills give "counseling students the ability to refuse patients service based on . . . their sexual orientation" (Equality Michigan, 2012, para. 1–2). Caldwell (2016) noted that such laws make it become "much harder for the training program to take *any* action against a student who states a religiously-based intent to discriminate, or who actually does discriminate in their work" (para. 5).

Legislation has expanded to protect the service provision of MHPs who, because of their personal beliefs (i.e., religious beliefs), do not want to counsel LGBTQ individuals. In 2016, Tennessee passed Bill 1556, known as the "Therapist Bill," which states,

> (a) No counselor or therapist providing counseling or therapy services shall be required to counsel or serve a client as to goals, outcomes, or behaviors that conflict with the sincerely held principles of the counselor or therapist; provided, that

the counselor or therapist coordinates a referral of the client to another counselor or therapist who will provide the counseling or therapy.

(b) The refusal to provide counseling or therapy services as described in subsection (a) shall not be the basis for:

    (1) A civil cause of action;

    (2) Criminal prosecution. (LegiScan, 2016, para. 1)

LGBTQ individuals are not recognized as a protected class by federal laws. Therefore, even if legislation is written that does not apply to the denial of services to individuals covered under federal law, the legislation essentially makes permissible discrimination against LGBTQ clients on the basis of personal beliefs, religious beliefs, or matters of conscience.

MHPs, however, are also held to the standards of their profession. They may not ignore their professional ethics codes that specifically state they may not discriminate because their personal beliefs are not in line with those of their clients. APA's (2010) Standard 3.01 (Unfair Discrimination) clearly states, "In their work-related activities, psychologists do not engage in unfair discrimination based on age, gender, gender identity, race, ethnicity, culture, national origin, religion, sexual orientation, disability, socioeconomic status or any basis proscribed by law." ACA's (2014) ethical code A.11.b., Values Within Termination and Referral, is also clear:

Counselors refrain from referring prospective and current clients based solely on the counselor's personally held values, attitudes, beliefs, and behaviors. Counselors respect the diversity of clients and seek training in areas in which they are at risk of imposing their values onto clients, especially when the counselor's values are inconsistent with the client's goals or are discriminatory in nature.

The politician who sponsored Tennessee's Bill 1556 stated that it was created in direct response to the Ward and Eastern Michigan State University cases because ACA's 2014 ethics codes "overstepped their authority and elevated their code above the First Amendment" (Sher, 2016, para. 7). ACA countered to no avail, stating the bill was "an unprecedented attack on the American Counseling Association's Code of Ethics. . . . an unwanted and unnecessary blow to the counseling profession and those who benefit from the services of a professional counselor" (ACA, 2016, para. 5).

Legislators are thereby taking on the role of dictating what MHPs can and cannot be disciplined for. Many of these types of legislation are in direct conflict with state licensing boards that use the ethics codes and standards of national organizations, such as the ACA and APA, to regulate licensees. Take, for example, Arizona's law SB 1365, which specifically prohibits the denial, suspension, or revocation of a person's professional license for

> declining to provide any service that violates the person's sincerely held religious beliefs, expressing sincerely held religious beliefs in any context, as long as services provided otherwise meet the current standard of care or practice for the profession, providing faith-based services that otherwise meet the current standard of care or practice for the profession, making business-related decisions in accordance with sincerely held religious beliefs, including employment decisions, client selection decisions and financial decisions. (Rudow, 2013, para. 19)

National MHP associations such as the ACA and APA's Committee on LGBTQ Concerns are actively addressing such legislation. If such laws continue to pass in states, national associations' nondiscriminatory statements and ethics codes will be at risk of relinquishing power. Bieschke and Mintz (2012) noted that without action in the form of clearly articulated training standards and ethics codes, the mental health professions are "dangerously close to losing both our professional autonomy in setting the standards for our profession and the academic freedom to determine the appropriate training for our students" (p. 203).

This kind of legislation is more likely to increase rather than decrease in the coming years. Following the 2015 ruling by the U.S. Supreme Court in favor of same-sex marriage across the nation, there was a significant uptick in antigay legislation throughout the United States. In just the first 4 months of 2016, nearly 200 anti-LGBTQ bills were introduced in 34 states compared with 115 bills during all of 2015 (Human Rights Campaign, 2016).

The bottom line is that LGBTQ clients' access to care is strongly at risk because of such legislation. As Caldwell (2016) aptly pointed out,

> When religious therapists are empowered by law to discriminate as they see fit, and when licensing boards have their power to discipline such actions largely scaled back, the ultimate outcome is that more therapists will choose to turn away gay and lesbian clients rather than developing the competency needed to effectively work with them. That's a particular problem in rural areas where mental health providers are few, and for non-English speakers whose choices of competent providers may be very limited even in a large city. (para. 7)

It is essential for MHP educators to remain up-to-date on the range of local, state, and national regulations that can hinder their ability to educate about supporting and affirming LGBTQ individuals. Educators have to help MHP students expand in and engage with diversity issues and thereby increase their competency of care for a much broader base of clients (Grey, 2014). It is, therefore, important for educators to provide readings, activities, and assignments that give students experience in learning how to keep continuously up-to-date on the sociopolitical contexts affecting their profession throughout their career. In addition, MHP educators have to advocate actively through their place of employment, state and national level professional associations, and directly through local, state, and federal legislation to support all clients being equally able to receive services from MHPs.

Strengths-Based Approaches to Teaching Ethics in LGBTQ Psychology

MHP educators can curtail future discrimination by counselors in our profession by taking a strengths-based approach to teaching about LGBTQ psychology. Gurung (2012) aptly stated that there are four foundational areas in which ethics are instrumental in the role of teaching psychology: (a) ethical considerations for classroom pedagogy or course design (see Chapter 3 of this volume for a more detailed discussion), (b) the use of pedagogical research, (c) conducting pedagogical research (both [b] and [c] are addressed in Chapter 10 of this volume), and (d) faculty–student interactions. Faculty–student interactions regarding ethics are well suited for educators to incorporate an empowerment model with a strengths-based approach. The goal of such a model is to provide trainees with the essential knowledge and skills necessary to be ethical and competent MHPs who possess professional diversity competencies in terms of (a) demographic competency and (b) dynamic worldview inclusivity (Bieschke & Mintz, 2012). *Demographic competency* refers to MHPs having the knowledge and skills to work with clients who are demographically different from themselves. *Dynamic worldview inclusivity* is having the capacity to hold one's own values while working with and valuing those whose worldviews differ from one's own. Being able to have the competence to work with those who challenge our belief system and expand our viewpoints is the basis for Principle E: Respect for People's Rights and Dignity of the APA Ethics Code and is instrumental in being able to empower our clients rather than unconsciously or consciously hinder them. For instance, as more religious bodies and institutions are opening dialogue and providing pockets of acceptance and potential sources of support for LGBTQ individuals, MHP educators also have to be open-minded to the range of sociocultural identities of students, including religious and spiritual identities.

Educators are encouraged to take a strengths-based approach to teaching ethics in LGBTQ psychology given that the history of psychology has not always been supportive and for many years took a deficit, pathologizing stance toward people who were LGBTQ (see Chapter 2 of this volume for a more detailed description). The following strengths-based approach that an instructor can adopt while training MHPs encompasses five areas: (a) patience; (b) developmental process: empathy and understanding of the learning process reminds us to be both patient with the learner and aware of the developmental processes of the learner—just as when a client comes out in regard to their sexual and/or gender identity and goes through a series of processes, learners move through similar processes as they move forward in their multicultural competency; (c) modeling: rather than taking a deficit approach toward a student who is struggling to gain an inclusive and dynamic worldview, professors and supervisors should model holding one's value system in check and maintaining a supportive role for the client; (d) tap into the existing strengths of the learner: instead of ignoring the needed areas of growth, use the trainee's strengths to move forward—LGBTQ psychology educators can help trainees learn how a therapist's empathic abilities can tap into the client's perspective rather than letting value judgments cloud one's abilities; and (e) prevention: potential trainees and programs alike benefit from programs having written value statements that clearly state the "expectations for trainees, trainers, and the training environment [that are] intended to foster the development of trainees' competences to provide services to individuals that represent a challenge to trainees' worldviews" (Bieschke & Mintz, 2012, p. 196).

In regard to prevention, APA (2015a) requires programs to have written policies in place that specifically address students' expectations regarding learning course material, conduct with clients, involvement in supervision, referral processes, and procedures involved in formal disciplinary review hearings. Such written policies would have been useful for the program and the student in Vignette 3. The five areas of this strengths-based approach may also be identified and discussed throughout the course to assist students' learning process. If remediation is recommended or required, it is also important to keep this strengths-based model in mind. The goal is to expand the multicultural self-awareness, knowledge, and skills of students, staff, and faculty and increase their ability to support a range of sociocultural identities, including those of people who are LGBTQ.

The SoA (APA, 2015c) also offers educators and trainers useful information about how to effectively work with students who, because of personal beliefs, may find it difficult to support LGBTQ clients. Because a developmental approach is at the foundation of professional growth for students in various mental health professions, it is increasingly significant for supervisors and instructors in resolving situations such as those in the opening vignettes:

Trainers take a developmental approach to trainee skill and competency acquisition and support individual trainees in the process of developing competencies to work with diverse populations. Trainers respect the right of trainees to maintain their personal belief systems while acquiring such professional competencies. Trainers also model the process of personal introspection; the exploration of personal beliefs, attitudes and values; and the development of cognitive flexibility required to serve a wide diversity of clients/patients. Training to work with diverse clients/patients is integral to the curriculum, and consists of both didactic coursework and practical training. (APA, 2013, para. 3)

Teaching ethics in relation to LGBTQ issues in psychology is best done across a range of courses and supervision opportunities. The content integrates well into program foundation courses such as ethics and law, history, and professional development. Furthermore, the material is integral in stand-alone LGBTQ psychology courses as well. The content transposes well across the various disciplines of mental health such as psychology, counseling, social work, nursing, and psychiatry. All share the same goals of MHPs being culturally competent and leading with their professional practices rather than their personal values. Regardless of the specific discipline, mental health educators and supervisors alike have to be aware and continually make the effort to address relevant LGBTQ and ethical content throughout the program for students.

At this time, a strengths-based perspective in teaching professional ethics and affirming practices toward LGBTQ people is not globally accepted. Fears and realities of the negative consequences related to supporting LGBTQ people are evident in many countries. It is, therefore, imperative to educate students about both demographic competency and dynamic worldview inclusivity, as described earlier. Depending on the political, religious, and cultural landscape at the time, this may happen in incrementally small ways through such teaching moments as "what if" questions and scenarios that expand a student's understanding and support of LGBTQ individuals. Again, at its foundation is the ability to teach and encourage MHPs to be cognizant of their own values and beliefs while simultaneously working with and valuing those whose worldviews differ from their own.

Activities for Teaching Ethics in LGBTQ Psychology

Educators are in a unique position to provide learning opportunities for sociocultural competency so that trainees become aware of their own values while using dynamic worldview inclusivity in their work with clients. Engaging students' learning through assignments in which they work through ethical conundrums around demographic differences (i.e., gender and sexual identities) prepares them for dynamic world-view inclusivity. Activities and experiential exercises in courses convert the theoretical into application and experience, thereby solidifying learning. Multicultural competency, consisting of the MHP gaining awareness, knowledge, and skills, is best learned through integrating experiential learning opportunities that require both personal and professional growth experiences (Sue, Bingham, Porché-Burke, & Vasquez, 1999), and such activities are in line with APA's (2003) Multicultural Guidelines. Gonsiorek (2014) also noted that gaining exposure to "judicious pedagogy is a powerful tool for transforming potential conflict about these issues into valuable learning" (p. 115).

Activity 4.1, Ethical Conundrums and Decision-Making Group Presentation in Context, is an example of such an assignment. It is a useful activity involving a class presentation by students following the course lecture and readings. The goal is to assist students in better understanding the range of potential ethical complexities and decision-making processes experienced by MHPs in training when working with GET clients. Activity 4.2, Mock Trial, is also best done after students have had exposure to the relevant course material through readings, lectures, and discussion. This activity is useful in bringing the course content to a more direct and layered understanding of MHPs' training regarding LGBTQ individuals. Activity 4.3, Policies and Processes Consultant, is a useful activity best assigned in the later portion of a course when the course material, lectures, and discussions can be combined to assist students in their learning. All three activities could be easily modified to work with online courses as well.

Conclusion

The discussion in this chapter of codes, standards, legislation, and program procedures highlighted progress as well as remaining areas of needed growth with respect to ethics in teaching LGBTQ psychology. Students, practitioners, supervisors, and educators in the fields of mental health have to be made aware that despite the progress surrounding LGBTQ rights, LGBTQ people still experience minority stress. The increased minority stressors (e.g., stigmatization, prejudicial and discriminatory events, expectations for rejection, concealing one's identities, internalized homophobia, ameliorative coping processes) for LGBTQ individuals account for the higher rates of mental health concerns compared with those of heterosexuals (Cochran, Sullivan, & Mays,

2003; Meyer, 2003; Newcomb & Mustanski, 2010). More recent work has also found similar outcomes for GET individuals (Kosciw, Greytak, Palmer, & Boesen, 2014). This chain of stigma-related stressors through social/interpersonal, emotional, and cognitive channels increases an LGBTQ individual's mental health needs and results in a higher prevalence of LGBTQ individuals seeking mental health services. As part of one's ethical and legal obligations related to multicultural competence, MHP trainees and practitioners must learn that, in light of the impact of stigma-related stress, they should refrain from actions that may further add to an LGBTQ person's stress in the form of perceived prejudice, discrimination, or rejection.

Ethics are central to the provision of mental health services, research, and education. The positive steps forward in the last half of the century involving the *DSM* and the ethical guidelines of MHP organizations have led to increased support and affirmation of LGBTQ individuals. It is critical for MHP educators to consider the various stages of an MHP's professional development and work with students to empower their ability to support LGBTQ individuals. Valuing and holding varying worldviews, even those opposed to one's own, is core to the profession, and this must be conveyed throughout the training of MHPs. When one elects to be an MHP, one cannot opt out of obtaining competency or worldview inclusivity by choosing to not learn, not attend class, or not work with people who do not align with one's personal beliefs. Students and MHPs alike must place the needs of their clients first by learning and maintaining cultural competency and leading with their professional rather than personal values and beliefs.

ACTIVITY 4.1

Ethical Conundrums and Decision-Making Group Presentation in Context

Directions: Four groups will create a 10-minute presentation for an undergraduate or graduate psychology course about potential ethical complexities and decision-making processes relevant to counseling and clinical trainees working with gender expansive and/or transgender individuals. Presenters should be sure to address demographic competencies (i.e., the ability and knowledge to work with diverse client demographics) and dynamic worldview inclusivity (i.e., the capacity to work with and value those whose worldviews differs from one's own) and include both prevention and intervention recommendations. The four groups of presenters will differ on the basis of the site in which they have their field placement (if trainee) or work (if community members or licensed practitioners):

(a) a community mental health center,
(b) a university counseling center,
(c) a Veterans Affairs medical center, or
(d) a public high school.

ACTIVITY 4.2

Mock Trial

Directions: A mock trial format will be used to discuss and debate one of three cases relevant to LGBTQ clients and ethical issues related to the provision of services by mental health providers (MHPs) in training. The three cases involved are

(a) *Keeton v. Anderson-Wiley* (2010),
(b) *Ward v. Wilbanks* (2010), and
(c) *Ward v. Polite* (2012).

Students will be randomly assigned to one the following teams for the mock trial.
Defense Team for the MHP students Keeton and Ward Team Members:

1. Keeton in her own defense,
2. Ward in her own defense,
3. mental health expert witness(es), or
4. defense lawyer(s).

Defense Team for the Universities Team Members:

1. student's professor or supervisor, and
2. defense lawyer(s).

The teams will meet ahead of the debate to prepare their side. Read professional readings and resources individually before meeting as a group to plan your side of the debate. Prepare a total of three key points for your case. Each group will have up to 5 minutes to present each point. A timer will be used to keep the time equal for the groups, and the group will lose points each time they go over the 5-minute limit. After each point, the other group will then have up to 2 minutes to respond in support of their case.

Note. This is not an assignment for law students but for MHPs in training to critically address issues relevant to training counselors and cultural competency in working with LGBTQ individuals.

ACTIVITY 4.3

Policies and Processes Consultant

Directions: Facilitators should tell learners that they have been hired by a university to create and implement policies and processes for successfully preparing professional mental health practitioners to serve a diverse public. The university is contracting with you because in the past 4 years, they have had three different situations (two involving students and one with a university seminar supervisor) in which there were personal conflicts based on religious and/or moral beliefs that kept those involved from being able to counsel LGBTQ individuals. No policies or processes are currently in place regarding professional competence and personal conflict with a trainee or employee's beliefs about LGBTQ individuals. The university would like you to use

▪ the American Psychological Association Education Directorate flowchart (2013),
▪ relevant national association statements and recommendations, and
▪ journal articles to create and support your recommendations.

Be sure to also create a value statement after reviewing at least three to five other existing value statements. Write a four- to five-page report to the university's or center's trustees or board of directors clearly stating and justifying your recommendations. Include your recommended value statement.

References

ALGBTIC LGBQQIA Competencies Taskforce. (2013). Association for Lesbian, Gay, Bisexual, and Transgender Issues in Counseling competencies for counseling with lesbian, gay, bisexual, queer, questioning, intersex, and ally individuals. *Journal of LGBT Issues in Counseling, 7,* 2–43. http://dx.doi.org/10.1080/15538605.2013.755444

American Counseling Association. (2010). Competencies for counseling with transgender clients. *Journal of LGBT Issues in Counseling, 4,* 135–159. http://dx.doi.org/10.1080/15538605.2010.524839

American Counseling Association. (2014). *ACA code of ethics.* Retrieved from http://www.counseling.org/docs/ethics/2014-aca-code-of-ethics.pdf?sfvrsn=4

American Counseling Association. (2016). *Tennessee advances bill that tells counselors to discriminate.* Retrieved from http://www.counseling.org/news/updates/2016/03/24/tennessee-advances-bill-that-tells-counselors-to-discriminate

American Psychiatric Association. (2013). *Diagnostic and statistical manual of mental disorders* (5th ed.). Arlington, VA: Author.

American Psychological Association. (1998). Resolution on appropriate therapeutic responses to sexual orientation. *American Psychologist, 53,* 934–935.

American Psychological Association. (2003). Guidelines on multicultural education, training, research, practice, and organizational change for psychologists. *American Psychologist, 58,* 377–402. http://dx.doi.org/10.1037/0003-066X.58.5.377

American Psychological Association. (2006). *Guidelines and principles for accreditation of programs in professional psychology (G & P).* Retrieved from http://www.apa.org/ed/accreditation/about/policies/guiding-principles.pdf

American Psychological Association. (2009). *Report of the American Psychological Association Task Force on appropriate therapeutic responses to sexual orientation.* Retrieved from http://www.apa.org/pi/lgbt/resources/therapeutic-response.pdf

American Psychological Association. (2010). *Ethical principles of psychologists and code of conduct (2002, Amended June 1, 2010).* Retrieved from http://apa.org/ethics/code/index.aspx

American Psychological Association. (2011a). *APA policy statements on lesbian, gay, bisexual, and transgender concerns.* Retrieved from http://www.apa.org/about/policy/booklet.pdf

American Psychological Association. (2011b). *Practice guidelines for LGB clients.* Retrieved from http://www.apa.org/pi/lgbt/resources/guidelines.aspx

American Psychological Association. (2013). *Preparing professional psychologists to serve a diverse public.* Retrieved from http://www.apa.org/ed/graduate/diversity-preparation.aspx

American Psychological Association. (2015a). *The "conscience clause" in professional training.* Retrieved from http://www.apa.org/ed/graduate/conscience-clause-brief.aspx

American Psychological Association. (2015b). Guidelines for psychological practice with transgender and gender nonconforming people. *American Psychologist, 70,* 832–864. http://dx.doi.org/10.1037/a0039906

American Psychological Association. (2015c). *Standards of accreditation for health service psychology.* Retrieved from http://www.apa.org/ed/accreditation/about/policies/standards-of-accreditation.pdf

American Psychological Association Education Directorate. (2013). *Preparing professional psychologists to serve a diverse public: Addressing conflicts between professional competence and trainee beliefs.* Retrieved from http://www.apa.org/pi/lgbt/resources/policy/diversity-preparation.pdf

American School Counselor Association. (2014). *The school counselor and LGBTQ youth.* Retrieved from http://www.schoolcounselor.org/asca/media/asca/PositionStatements/PS_LGBTQ.pdf

Biaggio, M. (2014). Do some APA-accredited programs undermine training to serve clients of diverse sexual orientations? *Psychology of Sexual Orientation and Gender Diversity, 1,* 93–95. http://dx.doi.org/10.1037/sgd0000027

Bieschke, K. J., & Mintz, L. B. (2012). Counseling psychology model training values statement addressing diversity: History, current use, and future directions. *Training and Education in Professional Psychology, 6,* 196–203. http://dx.doi.org/10.1037/a0030810

Caldwell, B. (2016, February 23). *How this year's religious freedom bills would impact therapists.* Retrieved from http://www.psychotherapynotes.com/how-this-years-religious-freedom-bills-would-impact-therapists/

Cochran, S. D., Sullivan, J. G., & Mays, V. M. (2003). Prevalence of mental disorders, psychological distress, and mental health services use among lesbian, gay, and bisexual adults in the United States. *Journal of Consulting and Clinical Psychology, 71,* 53–61. http://dx.doi.org/10.1037/0022-006X.71.1.53

Coleman, E., Bockting, W., Botzer, M., Cohen-Kettenis, P., DeCuypere, G., Feldman, J., . . . Zucker, K. (2012). Standards of care for the health of transsexual, transgender, and gender nonconforming people, version 7. *International Journal of Transgenderism, 13,* 165–232. http://dx.doi.org/10.1080/15532739.2011.700873

Equality Michigan. (2012). *Michigan house to vote on "first do harm" counseling bill today! Tell your legislator to vote "NO" on House Bill 5040.* Retrieved from http://www.equalitymi.org/media-center/news/michigan-house-vote-first-do-harm-counseling-bill-today-tell-your-legislator-vote

George Fox University. (2015). *Community lifestyle statement*. Retrieved from http://www.georgefox.edu/offices/hr/lifestyle-statement.html

Gonsiorek, J. C. (2014). A few wider angle perspectives on Hancock. *Psychology of Sexual Orientation and Gender Diversity, 1*, 114–116. http://dx.doi.org/10.1037/sgd0000042

Grey, M. J. (2014). Discerning a political context in religious-exemption legislation. *Psychology of Sexual Orientation and Gender Diversity, 1*, 310–312. http://dx.doi.org/10.1037/sgd0000068

Gurung, R. A. R. (2012). Consuming scholarship of teaching and learning: Using evidence-based pedagogy ethically. In R. E. Landrum & M. A. McCarthy (Eds.), *Teaching ethically: Challenges and opportunities* (pp. 67–76). http://dx.doi.org/10.1037/13496-006

Haldeman, D. C., & Rasbury, R. L. (2014). Multicultural training and student beliefs in cultural context. *Psychology of Sexual Orientation and Gender Diversity, 1*, 289–292. http://dx.doi.org/10.1037/sgd0000076

Hancock, K. (2014). Student beliefs, multiculturalism, and client welfare. *Psychology of Sexual Orientation and Gender Diversity, 1*, 4–9. http://dx.doi.org/10.1037/sgd0000021

Hazelwood School District v. Kuhlmeier, 484 U.S. 260 (1988).

Human Rights Campaign. (2016). *HRC legal director answers members' questions on anti-LGBT state bills* [Audio podcast]. Retrieved from http://soundcloud.com/humanrightscampaign/listen-hrc-legal-director-answers-members-questions-on-anti-lgbt-state-bills

Keeton v. Anderson-Wiley, 733 F. Supp. 2d 1368 (S.D. Ga. 2010).

Knapp, S., & Vandecreek, L. (2004). A principle-based analysis of the 2002 American Psychological Association Ethics Code. *Psychotherapy: Theory, Research, Practice, Training, 41*, 247–254. http://dx.doi.org/10.1037/0033-3204.41.3.247

Kosciw, J. G., Greytak, E. A., Palmer, N. A., & Boesen, M. J. (2014). *The 2013 National School Climate Survey: The experiences of lesbian, gay, bisexual and transgender youth in our nation's schools*. New York, NY: GLSEN.

LegiScan. (2016). *Tennessee Senate Bill 1556 (in recess)*. Retrieved from http://legiscan.com/TN/text/SB1556/2015

Meyer, I. H. (2003). Prejudice, social stress, and mental health in lesbian, gay, and bisexual populations: Conceptual issues and research evidence. *Psychological Bulletin, 129*, 674–697. http://dx.doi.org/10.1037/0033-2909.129.5.674

Newcomb, M. E., & Mustanski, B. (2010). Internalized homophobia and internalizing mental health problems: A meta-analytic review. *Clinical Psychology Review, 30*, 1019–1029. http://dx.doi.org/10.1016/j.cpr.2010.07.003

Rudow, H. (2013, January). Resolution of EMU case confirms ACA Code of Ethics, counseling profession's stance against client discrimination.

Counseling Today. Retrieved from http://ct.counseling.org/2013/01/resolution-of-emu-case-confirms-aca-code-of-ethics-counseling-professions-stance-against-client-discrimination/

Sher, A. (2016, April 6). Bill that would allow therapists to reject gay clients passes Tennessee House. *Times Free Press*. Retrieved from http://www.timesfreepress.com/news/politics/state/story/2016/apr/06/bill-allow-therapists-reject-gay-clients-passes-tennessee-house/359114/

Singh, A. A., & Burnes, T. R. (2009). Creating developmentally appropriate, safe counseling environments for transgender youth: The critical role of school counselors. *Journal of LGBT Issues in Counseling, 3*, 215–234. http://dx.doi.org/10.1080/15538600903379457

Smith, D. (2002, January). Accreditation committee decides to keep religious exemption. *Monitor on Psychology, 33*(1). Retrieved from http://www.apa.org/monitor/jan02/exemption.aspx

State of Arizona, S.B. 1365. (2012). Retrieved from http://www.azleg.gov/legtext/50leg/2r/bills/sb1365c.pdf

Sue, D. W., Bingham, R. P., Porché-Burke, L., & Vasquez, M. (1999). The diversification of psychology: A multicultural revolution. *American Psychologist, 54*, 1061–1069. http://dx.doi.org/10.1037/0003-066X.54.12.1061

Ward v. Polite, 667 F.3d 727 (6th Cir. 2012).

Ward v. Wilbanks, No. 09-11237 (E.D. Mich. 2010).

Anneliese A. Singh and Kim Lee Hughes

Integrating Resilience and Social Justice Pedagogical Strategies When Teaching About Sexual Orientation and Gender Diversity

5

Teaching lesbian, gay, bisexual, transgender, queer (LGBTQ) psychology often focuses on understanding the sexual orientations and gender identities of LGBTQ people. However, because LGBTQ people experience societal oppression that influences their well-being, instructors should also use pedagogical strategies that explore LGBTQ experiences of resilience to oppression. Further, we recommend that instructors also focus on the important role of social justice when working with LGBTQ people.

Instructors may begin by defining resilience and social justice in general terms. For instance, Masten (2001) defined *resilience* as the ability people have to move through and cope with adverse life experiences. In addition, Hartling (2005) asserted the importance of collective and community resilience as major influences on positive health outcomes. Understanding individual resilience to oppression can help guide mental health practitioner (MHP) interventions when

http://dx.doi.org/10.1037/0000015-005
Teaching LGBTQ Psychology: Queering Innovative Pedagogy and Practice, T. R. Burnes and J. L. Stanley (Editors)

working with LGBTQ people who experience societal heterosexism. Because LGBTQ people often develop peer and social networks that help buffer them from minority stress, discrimination, and violence (Meyer, 2003), understanding collective and community resilience is likewise a vital component of learning holistically about LGBTQ people and their needs.

Instructors teaching LGBTQ psychology may then define social justice as both processes and actions that they may engage in to reduce societal barriers, increase access to needed resources to decrease inequities, and address issues of privilege and oppression in clinical interventions (Singh & Salazar, 2010). Social justice and resilience are interrelated constructs; the more injustice that LGBTQ people experience, the more they may develop resilience or experience threats to their resilience. In this chapter, we review the literature undergirding LGBTQ psychology teaching strategies, explore resilience and social justice related to gender diversity and sexual orientation, provide case examples of didactic and experiential strategies, and share approaches to integrating online content into LGBTQ psychology teaching.

Exploring Resilience and Social Justice in LGBTQ Psychology Literature

Scholars assert the importance of designing pedagogical strategies so that advocacy and social justice are more integrated into course curricula (Kassan, Fellner, Jones, Palandra, & Wilson, 2015; Mallinckrodt, Miles, & Levy, 2014; Singh, 2010; Whitman & Bidell, 2014). Instructors can achieve this integration of social justice into their curricula and graduate programming through an emphasis on several foci, including ethics and decision making (Ametrano, 2014; Whitman & Bidell, 2014), self-awareness and greater understanding of self in relation to privilege and oppression (Kassan et al., 2015; Singh, 2010), and the incorporation of actual outreach and service elements into various required courses to provide service learning opportunities (Mallinckrodt et al., 2014). In each of these foci, instructors in LGBTQ psychology should rely less on traditional pedagogical strategies of didactic, hierarchical teaching to incorporate advocacy and service.

Embedding advocacy and service into the LGBTQ psychology curriculum allows students to engage in self-reflection and increase their awareness about privilege and oppression related to LGBTQ people and communities. This approach can be informed by the scientist–practitioner–advocate model (Mallinckrodt et al., 2014), which asserts that MHPs should be trained to integrate advocacy into their research and clinical practices. Integrating the scientist–practitioner–advocate model into LGBTQ psychology courses may also enhance graduate students' professional sense of purpose and direction. Such a model closely integrates these three areas of scientist, practitioner, and advocate within a course, rather than separating these identities out or focusing solely on a scientist–practitioner model. For instance, course discussions would continuously endeavor to review research with a focus on applications to both practice and advocacy and vice versa.

The scientist–practitioner–advocate model (Mallinckrodt et al., 2014), also known as a collaborative model, can also help instructors develop LGBTQ psychology curricula guiding graduate trainees to base their practice on psychological research and professional ethical standards, as opposed to personal disposition and belief (Whitman & Bidell, 2014) informed by anti-LGBTQ stances. A collaborative model is particularly important when teaching about resilience and social justice approaches related to gender identity, gender expression, and sexual orientation to students who may have limited or prejudiced perspectives about gender and sexual diversity because of their religious beliefs (Bowers, Minichiello, & Plummer, 2010). This collaborative model can help develop a learning environment in which these students may share perspectives, and even lack of knowledge, that they may have about LGBTQ people, which is critical for examining stereotypical notions of what it means to be LGBTQ. When designing LGBTQ psychology curricula exploring resilience and social justice, instructors can ground their pedagogical strategies in research suggesting that increased interpersonal contact with the LGBTQ community leads to less anti-LGBTQ prejudice in graduate students because the students develop empathy regarding their identities of privilege and oppression (Bidell, 2012; Satcher & Schumacker, 2009; Whitman & Bidell, 2014).

Addressing Distinct Groups Within the LGBTQ Umbrella

Instructors who use social justice and resilience pedagogical strategies in teaching LGBTQ psychology should be mindful to differentiate these approaches according to the distinct group—lesbian, gay, bisexual, transgender, and/or queer—as opposed to grouping all subgroups into one category. Members of the LGBTQ community are often categorized as a unit; yet, members of the various communities may not experience their intersectionality in the same ways (Bauerband & Galupo, 2014; Warner & Shields, 2013; Worthen, 2013). For example, the group distinctions between sexual orientation and gender identities are important because transgender persons generally have to disclose their status, whereas individuals do not have to disclose their sexual orientation (Bauerband & Galupo, 2014).

Intersectionality does not only refer to the interplay between gender identity, gender expression, and sexual orientation but also plays an important role when considering issues of race and ethnicity as related to gender identity, gender expression, and sexual orientation (Veenstra, 2013). Identity is relational in nature, and LGBTQ persons find validation, which may increase identity salience, in connection to others who share their identities (Singh, 2013). Specifically, the interplay between discrimination and race/ethnicity, gender identity, gender expression, and sexual orientation may predict political activism (Swank & Fahs, 2013) and promote resistance strategies (Singh, 2013). The salience of one identity over another may be informed by contextual factors, including racism (Bowleg, 2013; Singh, 2013), heterosexism (Bauerband & Galupo, 2014), and sexism (Babbitt, 2013), which cause social stress and can negatively affect mental health and wellness (Meyer, 2003; Testa, Habarth, Peta, Balsam, & Bockting, 2015). As such, MHPs are agents of change when they teach about gender identity, gender expression, and sexual orientation in LGBTQ psychology by addressing each distinct group within the LGBTQ umbrella (García-Ramírez, Balcázar, & De Freitas, 2014).

It is important for instructors to be mindful that having a global perspective on the intersections that influence LGBTQ people's lives is important. For example, LGBTQ people can have diverse experiences of immigration, acculturation, and international experiences outside a U.S. context—or that influence their experience of a U.S. context. An example is designing an entire course dedicated to intersectionality and social identity development for LGBTQ individuals, as opposed to dedicating one segment of a cross-cultural mental health course to LGBTQ topics. If instructors do not have the freedom to develop an entire course in this manner, one can endeavor to integrate an intersectional perspective within existing courses so that LGBTQ people are not solely and narrowly viewed within their gender and sexual orientation identities. In this way, LGBTQ psychology instructors can devote significant attention to each distinct group under the LGBTQ umbrella and delve more critically into issues of gender identity, gender expression, and sexual orientation.

Case Examples Exploring Resilience and Social Justice in LGBTQ Pedagogy

Just as self-reflection on gender identity, gender expression, and sexual orientation is a foundational component of exploring resilience and social justice, case examples or vignettes can also be an essential way of bringing LGBTQ learning "to life" for students, supervisees, and clients when teaching LGBTQ psychology. In designing a strong case vignette exploring LGBTQ experiences of resilience and social justice, it is important to ensure that the case explores (a) intersectionality, (b) individual experiences of societal oppression, and (c) individual and community sources of resilience. Two case vignettes are explored next, and questions for discussion are also included.

CASE 1: SONALI QUESTIONS HER SEXUAL ORIENTATION

Sonali is an 18-year-old South Asian woman living in Sri Lanka. She sought counseling on the basis of a friend's advice at her university counseling center. Her parents are Muslim, and Sonali wears a traditional hijab and identifies as "religious." She identified her religion as very important to her in managing her stress. In her first semester of college, Sonali met another Muslim, South Asian woman to whom she felt sexual attraction. As Sonali presents for counseling, she questions her sexual orientation, expresses fears about disclosing this information to her friends, and says that she "can never tell" her family about her doubts.

When LGBTQ psychology instructors use an international LGBTQ case, such as Sonali's, the timing of when the case is presented is important to consider. Because the case of Sonali entails an understanding of multiple identities and specific resilience and social justice concerns related to sexual orientation, gender identity, gender expression, and religion (among others), LGBTQ psychology instructors can spend the first part of class defining constructs such as intersectionality, multiple identities, and multiplicative experiences of stress and resilience that LGBTQ people have. In the case of Sonali specifically, there is also the issue of attempting to understand international counseling resources and approaches (in Sri Lanka for Sonali) and the ways that LGBTQ identities are experienced in those countries without assuming the United States has "better" or more LGBTQ-affirming services than other countries (this may be true, but not always). After the class has an understanding of these constructs, instructors can use questions such as the following to explore how MHPs might work with this client in exploring resilience and social justice: (a) What are the potential experiences of social injustice to explore with Sonali? (b) What are the potential sources of resilience to explore with Sonali? (c) How will you explore Sonali's doubts about her sexual orientation related to resilience and social justice from an intersectional perspective? and (d) What are the potential advocacy strategies (e.g., teaching self-advocacy skills, connecting the personal experiences Sonali has to larger systemic change) you may have to consider?

CASE 2: HELPING JUAN GET ACCESS TO CARE

Juan is a 45-year-old Chicano, transgender man who presents in your office with concerns about "getting on hormones." He wants to begin hormone therapy but needs a letter of referral from an MHP and does not have insurance to cover this medical care. Juan would like to engage in social and medical transition but expresses concern about whether he can afford the change of his name assigned at birth and other identity documents, as well as accessing top surgery in a year. He is seeing you on a reduced fee scale.

LGBTQ psychology instructors can use an example case such as the one of Juan to guide students to consider underexplored identities (e.g., social class) when working with LGBTQ clients and the power differential that often exists and shapes the counseling experience for LGBTQ people. Once students have a strong understanding that the intersectionality of many identities for LGBTQ people can lead to multiple experiences of both stress and resilience regarding mental health, this type of case can be used at the beginning or end of an LGBTQ psychology class. Instructors could use a case example at the beginning of class to challenge students to use constructs they know to identify ways to navigate issues of power, privilege, and societal barriers that LGBTQ people face that may or may not be anticipated by a helping professional. The case of Juan could also be used at the end of class to integrate class learning about the social justice and resilience barriers that LGBTQ people face when accessing counseling.

When exploring Juan's case from a resilience and social justice perspective, LGBTQ psychology instructors can address the financial concerns impinging on Juan's health care access and opportunities for advocacy: (a) What are the major barriers to trans care that Juan faces? (b) What is your role as an MHP related to advocacy in working with Juan? (c) How will you balance exploring resilience while also addressing barriers to trans care when working with Juan? and (d) What are the potential advocacy strategies (e.g., coordinating transgender-affirmative health care, advocating for transgender-affirmative policies within your counseling office or at a legislative level) you may have to consider?

Teaching Strategies Related to Resilience and Social Justice

The foundation of LGBTQ psychology pedagogy exploring resilience and social justice should begin with ongoing self-reflection on instructor gender and sexual orientation journeys before the beginning of a course. In this self-reflection, instructors can assess their static or fluid notions of sexual orientation, gender identity, and gender expression. This instructor self-reflection can then be shared with students at the outset of the course as a way to spark and cultivate curiosity about how they might develop their gender identity, gender expression, and sexual orientation and make decisions about how those features intersect with their personal and professional identities. For instance, instructors can ask the following: (a) What were your earliest memories of your gender identity, gender expression, and sexual orientation? (b) What were the messages you received about your gender identity, gender expression, and sexual orientation? (c) Who gave you these messages about gender identity, gender expression, and sexual orientation? and (d) How did these messages influence your overall development and experiences of your gender identity, gender expression, and sexual orientation?

Once this self-reflection is initiated at the beginning of the course, instructors can define constructs of resilience and social justice and then repeat the questions integrating these constructs (e.g., When you think about your earliest memories of your gender identity, gender expression, and sexual orientation, what were the sources of resilience and issues of social justice for you?). The resilience and social justice framework of this self-reflection intentionally and simultaneously identifies both the societal threats to well-being and the development of resilience to these oppressions. For instance, someone who is now an instructor may have received negative messages about being a "tomboy" growing up. This experience may have decreased their self-esteem, but this person may have also been able to develop peer support with other gender nonconforming children. In this self-reflection, identifying the societal oppressions related to social justice (e.g., sexism in this example) and the resilience strategies developed (e.g., social support) should also be balanced with the continuing threats to (e.g., lack of family support, media messages) or supports of (e.g., presence of family support) resilience. Once a thorough and ongoing self-reflection on gender identity, gender expression, and sexual orientation related to resilience and social justice is explored, this self-reflection would help instructors understand how to guide students and clients in their own self-reflection in these areas and provide concrete, easy-to-understand examples that instructors can share with their students.

As previously described, instructors can use case examples to support trainees in learning about LGBTQ social justice concerns and the development of potential resilience. Further, MHPs can assist students as they explore the meaning of their identities and the ways that those identities may challenge their professional identity. In working with LGBTQ students and clients, graduate students must develop the skills needed to navigate aspects of their own belief systems (i.e., religious beliefs, beliefs about class, beliefs about gender expression) that may interfere with the ethical codes of their profession (Ametrano, 2014; Remley & Herlihy, 2010; Whitman & Bidell, 2014). Therefore, MHPs have the charge to develop curricula that support students' professional and personal development and to help students reconcile their personal values with their professional values (Ametrano, 2014).

BALANCING DIDACTIC AND EXPERIENTIAL TEACHING STRATEGIES

Instructors who teach LGBTQ psychology should be intentional when infusing programs and courses with a social justice focus by incorporating both didactic and experiential teaching strategies as each best fits the content, drawing from global LGBTQ perspectives that are helpful (Kassan et al., 2015). For example, it may be difficult to teach students about empathy for "difference" without an experiential component (Whitman & Bidell, 2014). At the same time, information about ethical principles, theories, profession-specific codes of ethics, and legal issues has to be taught didactically (Ametrano, 2014). These more traditional didactic approaches can include elements of social justice and resilience by including a wider variety of theoretical and critical perspectives (e.g., liberation psychology, relational cultural theory, intersectionality). A combination of didactic and experiential teaching strategies grounded in social justice and resilience theory, when well crafted, may challenge students to assess their stereotypes and biases about the communities they serve (Singh, 2010). It is an opportunity also to reflect on how LGBTQ identities are experienced around the world.

Empathy is rarely gained in a vacuum, even in an LGBTQ psychology classroom. One way that students develop empathy regarding difference is engaging with diverse populations in the classroom and the field. Instructors can support students' development by offering multiple opportunities to engage in concepts beyond their textbooks, which may include multimedia presentations (e.g., movies), interactive activities (e.g., the privilege walk), panel discussions, and field trips, as well as advocacy projects that are interwoven into the course curricula that explore resilience and social justice for LGBTQ people. In sum, instructors may find that they foster greater learning outcomes when they incorporate students' lived experiences and experiential activities.

USING DIDACTIC STRATEGIES TO TEACH ABOUT GENDER DIVERSITY AND SEXUAL ORIENTATION

Didactic strategies in teaching about gender diversity and sexual orientation may be especially effective in LGBTQ psychology courses that occur near the beginning of a graduate program and/or at the beginning of any course (Ametrano, 2014; Singh, 2010). The purpose of didactic teaching strategies is to impart knowledge, which may include a discussion of assigned readings about gender diversity and sexual orientation and/or an assigned writing task about the student's experiences with the LGBTQ community before entering a mental health program of study. For instance, instructors can provide an assignment that invites graduate students to reflect on their own intersectionality and ways that their identities of privilege and oppression have shaped their understandings of LGBTQ people and communities (Singh, 2010). As a course progresses, the instructor can include information about the ethics code of a particular mental health profession, such as that of the American Psychological Association (APA; 2010), so that students may have the opportunity to explore ethical decision making (Ametrano, 2014; Remley & Herlihy, 2010) and the social justice barriers that may be implicit when working with the LGBTQ community.

Beyond lectures and papers, there are intergroup facilitation strategies that LGBTQ psychology instructors can use in the classroom setting. There are feminist approaches, which tend to focus on collaboration, that may allow the instructor to pose questions about ideas that students can explore and discuss (Singh, 2010) related to how students have benefitted in LGBTQ liberation movements (e.g., freedom to explore sex and sexuality). This may be effective once students have begun to grapple with theoretical and ethical concepts and have engaged in consciousness-raising activities. It may be helpful to break students up into small groups for discussion. The instructor can note themes discussed and share those small group themes with the class instead of presenting information in a lecture format (Ametrano, 2014). Didactic approaches may be important for students to master the traditional role of practitioner while embracing the new mandate to advocate (Mallinckrodt et al., 2014).

EXPERIENTIAL TEACHING STRATEGIES USING SELF-REFLECTION AND MOVEMENT

Experiential teaching strategies may allow instructors to bring issues of social justice to light for students (Singh, 2010). When done well, experiential teaching strategies on issues related to gender identity, gender expression, and sexual orientation can facilitate broader MHP student understanding of their biases, assumptions, beliefs, and hopes for the LGBTQ community (Kassan et al., 2015; Mallinckrodt et al., 2014; Singh,

2010). Incorporating experiential teaching strategies, such as journaling and free writing about personal awareness, into issues of social justice can expose students to expanded perspectives (Singh, 2010). The process of infusing more experiential teaching strategies into the education of MHP students puts the instructor in the role of learner–collaborator and of advocate, as opposed to the director of student outcomes (Ametrano, 2014; Mallinckrodt et al., 2014).

When using experiential teaching strategies regarding issues of gender identity, gender expression, and sexual orientation it is important to construct a learning environment that empowers students to explore issues of privilege and oppression and their personal experiences as being both privileged and oppressed (Singh, 2010). Inside the classroom, instructors can use expressive arts to help graduate students explore their salient identities. Singh (2010) suggested teaching social justice advocacy using an expressive arts exercise based on the metaphor of a quilt. The exercise challenges the graduate student to contextualize specific social justice issues, such as racism, ableism, sexism, and classism, in relation to the metaphor of the quilt by creatively piecing together a representation of their lived experiences of three distinct isms (2010). Specifically, the student is encouraged to reflect on the role particular isms have played in their lived experiences and present that creatively to their classmates. The student may select multiple books, photographs, musical selections, or any other relevant symbol to piece together a "quilt" that is representative of their self-exploration of their identities of privilege and oppression. An expressive arts approach like the quilt metaphor exercise may allow graduate students to develop greater self-awareness of issues of gender identity, gender expression, and sexual orientation.

Experiential teaching strategies can also include activities such as panel discussions with members of the LGBTQ community inside the classroom (Whitman & Bidell, 2014), as well as having students partner with LGBTQ community organizations on advocacy and social justice projects (Kassan et al., 2015; Mallinckrodt et al., 2014). These community organizations might also be internationally focused, whether housed in the United States (e.g., OutRight Action International) or another country (e.g., India Gat Pride). Depending on what the instructor ascertains students need most, it also might be more helpful to have a panel of MHPs who are LGBTQ advocates to model how MHPs may build resilience and advocacy into LGBTQ counseling interventions. A focus on infusing experiential teaching strategies in mental health graduate programs may assist students in moving beyond mastering facts and diagnostic codes about gender identity, gender expression, and sexual identity to understanding their own values and behaviors and motivate students to become social change agents (Ametrano, 2014; Remley & Herlihy, 2010; Singh, 2010). Thus, such strategies may also help bridge the gap between LGBTQ-affirmative ethics codes and practices and issues of anti-LGBTQ religious conservatism in the profession (Bowers et al., 2010; Whitman & Bidell, 2014).

INTEGRATING ONLINE CONTENT IN TEACHING RESILIENCE AND SOCIAL JUSTICE

Integrating online content offers new and innovative ways to teach about gender identity, gender expression, and sexual orientation in a constructivist community (Bryant & Bates, 2015). In addition to static content, online interaction in various forms lends itself to teaching resilience and social justice and can reach far beyond social media hashtags and efforts to counter Internet "trolls." For example, students in an LGBTQ psychology course might develop and deliver Webinar workshops for teens or parents of teens on how to recognize and cope with online bullying while promoting healthy online practices through the use of role-plays and resource sharing.

As more MHP training programs offer online course options, the ability to use technology in ways that engage students in social justice issues depends on the connection the instructor can make with the students in the virtual environment (Joyner, Fuller, Holzweiss, Henderson, & Young, 2014). There are several components that promote student satisfaction and facilitate connection to the instructor. Current literature describes four elements as fundamental to student satisfaction and retention in online learning: effective and timely communication, the perception of instructor accessibility, useful online tools and resources, and instructor feedback that exceeds grading and evaluation (Bailie, 2015; Bryant & Bates, 2015; Cole, Shelley, & Swartz, 2013; Joyner et al., 2014).

Incorporating these four elements effectively may allow instructors to grapple with topics of gender identity, gender expression, and sexual orientation in an online learning environment (Bryant & Bates, 2015). Although the online learning environment may present pedagogical challenges, it is possible to establish good rapport with graduate students even if there are limited course meetings (Joyner et al., 2014). Instructors can foster connection with graduate students by establishing a course homepage, by facilitating active discussion boards, by sending timely, personalized e-mail to graduate students, and by offering virtual office hours (Joyner et al., 2014). In addition, the homepage may have a section on up-to-date and useful resources for MHP trainees (i.e., links to the APA and American Counseling Association ethics codes, links to national MHPs LGBTQ-supportive organizations, and professional articles). Moreover, graduate students reported enjoying the convenience of online courses while simultaneously citing a desire for more interaction with the instructor and other students (Cole et al., 2013). The desire for more interaction can be addressed by developing hybrid courses in mental health graduate programs, even if the students only meet once in the duration of the course (Cole et al., 2013).

Research about online learning environments showed that graduate students wanted more proactive interactions with their instructors through constructive feedback and guidance that moved beyond perfunctory phone calls and reactionary grading evaluations; students wanted their instructors to act as consultants and collaborators (Bailie, 2015; Bryant & Bates, 2015; Joyner et al., 2014). Consultation and collaboration may be particularly important for instructors in mental health graduate programs to incorporate when teaching about issues of gender identity, gender expression, and sexual orientation in an online environment. The unique and fresh approach of online learning environments may offer students new insights into complex issues related to privilege and oppression in mental health graduate programs. At the same time, new approaches offer distinct challenges to LGBTQ psychology instructors, which should be undertaken with continuing education and professional support from colleagues and administrators. Continuing education on LGBTQ considerations can be sought across disciplines of psychology, counseling, social work, and other helping professions. This continuing education can also be in person or online, including staying current on LGBTQ resilience and wellness-based literature and approaches to practice and advocacy.

Teaching Activities Exploring LGBTQ Resilience and Social Justice

It is important to note that instructors can draw on their own lives and experiences in exploring resilience and social justice to adapt these teaching strategies. Further, instructors can explore how these constructs influence their LGBTQ students' and clients' lives. In processing each activity, it is important to explore the intersectionality of various specific LGBTQ identities under the LGBTQ umbrella and the intersection of gender identity, gender expression, and sexual orientation, as well as any emotions and "aha" moments that arise and connect these clearly to resilience, social justice, and effectively serving LGBTQ clients.

ACTIVITY 5.1. MY RESILIENCE JOURNEY: EXPLORING SUPPORTS AND BARRIERS

Activity 5.1 is an example of an exercise for self-exploration of MHP resilience, intersectionality, and social justice. Once students have reflected on their own resilience journeys, it can be helpful to help them identify how to explore resilience and issues of social justice with their clients. In Activity 5.2, LGBTQ psychology instructors teach students how to develop resilience plans with LGBTQ clients. This can be a good activity to use at the end of a teaching unit on multiple experiences of stress and resilience for LGBTQ clients.

ACTIVITY 5.2. DEVELOPING RESILIENCE PLANS WITH LGBTQ CLIENTS

Exploring the potential intersections within each of the questions is also important as follow-up probes to these questions. After processing this activity with the class, the LGBTQ psychology instructor can then ask how this activity might be used in individual counseling in one or multiple sessions or as homework between sessions. Instructors can also explore how this activity might have to be adjusted for the multiple identities of LGBTQ clients in the group.

Conclusion

In this chapter, we described the importance of including the constructs of resilience and social justice in LGBTQ psychology courses. Didactic, experiential, and online teaching examples of LGBTQ pedagogy integrating resilience and social justice explorations with LGBTQ clients were provided. LGBTQ psychology instructors should carefully consider issues of timing and processing the learning from these teaching activities and should continuously embed multiple and intersecting identities for LGBTQ clients into their discussions of resilience and social justice. Instructors teaching LGBTQ psychology from a resilience and social justice perspective develop commitments to stay abreast of the current scholarship in these areas and can organize peer instructor support groups and consultation opportunities to provide accountability for teaching LGBTQ psychology from a more holistic perspective. Some of these peer supports might even come from international sources, so instructors can think broadly about how to enliven and enrich their access to sources of supportive LGBTQ pedagogy and help maintain a global perspective in their teaching. Instructors can also endeavor to participate in grassroots and direct action supporting LGBTQ rights from an intersectional and advocacy perspective as a way to support LGBTQ resilience and social justice outside the classroom and provide students with opportunities to learn social justice change skills.

ACTIVITY 5.1

My Resilience Journey: Exploring Supports and Barriers

Directions: In this activity, learners are given or take out a blank piece of paper. Then, learners draw a curvy line from the left side of the paper to the right. They should then draw an X on the left side of the line and write *Start*; then, they should draw an X on the right side of the line and write *Now*. Instructors should tell learners to imagine this line representing their life from birth to this moment of "now." Each learner should take a moment to think about all of the people, experiences, and events in their respective lives that have helped them understand and feel good about their gender identity, gender expression, and sexual orientation. Students should then write these down along the line, and mark these with a plus ("+") sign. This is their resilience.

Learners should then take a moment to think about all of the people, experiences, and events in their respective lives that were barriers or threats to feeling good about their gender identity, gender expression, and sexual orientation. Students should then write these down along the line, and mark these with a minus ("−") sign. These are the threats to their resilience and represent social justice concerns. LGBTQ psychology instructors can then divide the class into dyads so the students may explore their own resilience journeys related to gender identity, gender expression, and sexual orientation, as well as hear a different type of journey from their own. Specific processing questions for the dyads can include the following:

▪ What was your experience developing your resilience journey?
▪ Did anything surprise you or challenge you about your resilience journey?
▪ If a mental health professional was working with you at various points in your resilience journey, what interventions would have been helpful for him or her to use related to your gender identity, gender expression, and sexual orientation?

ACTIVITY 5.2

Developing Resilience Plans With LGBTQ Clients

Directions: Instructors ask for volunteers to play the role of fictional "clients" in a group counseling session using a fishbowl method. The instructor plays the role of the "group counselor," and the remainder of the class sits in a circle outside the "fishbowl" containing the group members. As the group counselor, the instructor first explains to the client what resilience is: "*Resilience* is our ability to bounce back from tough times." Then, the group counselor asks clients to write on a sheet of paper answers to the following questions:

1. As an LGBTQ person, what helps me get through hard times?
2. As an LGBTQ person, what are the challenges I face in getting through hard times?
3. As an LGBTQ person, what do I need to thrive and feel good about myself and my life?
4. How have I internalized negative beliefs about myself?
5. How does society have to change to support me more as an LGBTQ person?

Once clients have completed the list, the group counselor asks clients to circle the three most important resilience supports and the three most challenging resilience threats. The group counselor then asks clients to turn the page over and write how they can integrate the three resilience supports into their life more and what they need to shift in their life or what support they need to buffer themselves from the resilience threats.

References

American Psychological Association. (2010). *Ethical principles of psychologists and code of conduct (2002, Amended June 1, 2010)*. Retrieved from http://www.apa.org/ethics/code/index.aspx

Ametrano, I. M. (2014). Teaching ethical decision making: Helping students reconcile personal and professional values. *Journal of Counseling & Development, 92*, 154–161. http://dx.doi.org/10.1002/j.1556-6676.2014.00143.x

Babbitt, L. G. (2013). An intersectional approach to Black/White interracial interactions: The roles of gender and sexual orientation. *Sex Roles, 68*, 791–802. http://dx.doi.org/10.1007/s11199-011-0104-4

Bailie, J. L. (2015). Online graduate instruction: What faculty consider reasonable in relation to what students expect. *Journal of Online Learning & Teaching, 11*, 42–54.

Bauerband, L. A., & Galupo, M. P. (2014). The Gender Identity Reflection and Rumination scale: Development and psychometric evaluation. *Journal of Counseling & Development, 92*, 219–231. http://dx.doi.org/10.1002/j.1556-6676.2014.00151.x

Bidell, M. P. (2012). Examining school counseling students' multicultural and sexual orientation competencies through a cross-specialization comparison. *Journal of Counseling & Development, 90*, 200–207. http://dx.doi.org/10.1111/j.1556-6676.2012.00025.x

Bowers, R., Minichiello, V., & Plummer, D. (2010). Religious attitudes, homophobia, and professional counseling. *Journal of LGBT Issues in Counseling, 4*, 70–91. http://dx.doi.org/10.1080/15538605.2010.481961

Bowleg, L. (2013). "Once you've blended the cake, you can't take the parts back to the main ingredients": Black gay and bisexual men's descriptions and experiences of intersectionality. *Sex Roles, 68*, 754–767. http://dx.doi.org/10.1007/s11199-012-0152-4

Bryant, J., & Bates, A. J. (2015). Creating a constructivist online instructional environment. *TechTrends, 59*, 17–22. http://dx.doi.org/10.1007/s11528-015-0834-1

Cole, M. T., Shelley, D. J., & Swartz, L. B. (2013). Academic integrity and student satisfaction in an online environment. In H. Yang & S. Wang (Eds.), *Cases on online learning communities and beyond: Investigations and applications* (pp. 1–19). http://dx.doi.org/10.4018/978-1-4666-1936-4.ch001

García-Ramírez, M., Balcázar, F., & de Freitas, C. (2014). Community psychology contributions to the study of social inequalities, well-being and social justice. *Psychosocial Intervention, 23*, 79–81. http://dx.doi.org/10.1016/j.psi.2014.07.009

Hartling, L. (2005). Fostering resilience throughout our lives: New relational possibilities. In D. Comstock (Ed.), *Diversity in development: Critical contexts that shape our lives and relationships*. Pacific Grove, CA: Thomson/ Wadsworth.

Joyner, S. A., Fuller, M. B., Holzweiss, P. C., Henderson, S., & Young, R. (2014). The importance of student-instructor connections in graduate level online courses. *MERLOT Journal of Online Learning and Teaching, 10*, 436–445.

Kassan, A., Fellner, K. D., Jones, M. I., Palandra, A. L., & Wilson, L. J. (2015). (Re)considering novice supervisor development through a social justice lens: An experiential account. *Training and Education in Professional Psychology, 9*, 52–60. http://dx.doi.org/10.1037/tep0000041

Mallinckrodt, B., Miles, J. R., & Levy, J. J. (2014). The scientist–practitioner–advocate model: Addressing contemporary training needs for social justice advocacy. *Training and Education in Professional Psychology, 8*, 303–311. http://dx.doi.org/10.1037/tep0000045

Masten, A. S. (2001). Ordinary magic. Resilience processes in development. *American Psychologist, 56*, 227–238. http://dx.doi.org/10.1037/0003-066X.56.3.227

Meyer, I. H. (2003). Prejudice, social stress, and mental health in lesbian, gay, and bisexual populations: Conceptual issues and research evidence. *Psychological Bulletin, 129*, 674–697. http://dx.doi.org/10.1037/0033-2909.129.5.674

Remley, T. P., & Herlihy, B. (2010). *Ethical, legal, and professional issues in counseling* (3rd ed.). Upper Saddle River, NJ: Pearson Education.

Satcher, J., & Schumacker, R. (2009). Predictors of modern homonegativity among professional counselors. *Journal of LGBT Issues in Counseling, 3*, 21–36. http://dx.doi.org/10.1080/15538600902754452

Singh, A. A. (2010). Teaching social justice advocacy: Using the metaphor of a quilt. *Psychology of Women Quarterly, 34*, 550–553.

Singh, A. A. (2013). Transgender youth of color and resilience: Negotiating oppression and finding support. *Sex Roles, 68*, 690–702. http://dx.doi.org/10.1007/s11199-012-0149-z

Singh, A. A., & Salazar, C. F. (2010). The roots of social justice in group work. *Journal for Specialists in Group Work, 35*, 97–104. http://dx.doi.org/10.1080/01933921003706048

Swank, E., & Fahs, B. (2013). An intersectional analysis of gender and race for sexual minorities who engage in gay and lesbian rights activism. *Sex Roles, 68*, 660–674. http://dx.doi.org/10.1007/s11199-012-0168-9

Testa, R. J., Habarth, J., Peta, J., Balsam, K., & Bockting, W. (2015). Development of the Gender Minority Stress and Resilience Measure. *Psychology of Sexual Orientation and Gender Diversity, 2*, 65–77. http://dx.doi.org/10.1037/sgd0000081

Veenstra, G. (2013). The gendered nature of discriminatory experiences by race, class, and sexuality: A comparison of intersectionality theory and the subordinate male target hypothesis. *Sex Roles, 68*, 646–659. http://dx.doi.org/10.1007/s11199-012-0243-2

Warner, L. R., & Shields, S. A. (2013). The intersections of sexuality, gender, and race: Identity research at the crossroads. *Sex Roles, 68,* 803–810. http://dx.doi.org/10.1007/s11199-013-0281-4

Whitman, J. S., & Bidell, M. P. (2014). Affirmative lesbian, gay, and bisexual counselor education and religious beliefs: How do we bridge the gap? *Journal of Counseling and Development, 92,* 162–169. http://dx.doi.org/10.1002/j.1556-6676.2014.00144.x

Worthen, M. G. (2013). An argument for separate analyses of attitudes toward lesbian, gay, bisexual men, bisexual women, MtF and FtM transgender individuals. *Sex Roles, 68,* 703–723. http://dx.doi.org/10.1007/s11199-012-0155-1

Carlton W. Parks and Theodore R. Burnes

Engaging Culturally Informed Classroom and Behavior Management Techniques in LGBTQ Psychology Learning Environments

6

A s the global population becomes more and more socioculturally diverse, it is increasingly incumbent on instructors at the
undergraduate and graduate levels to expand their classroom
course content and classroom behavior management techniques to better reflect these various diverse voices, including
lesbian, gay, bisexual, transgender, queer, and/or questioning
(LGBTQ) and gender diverse voices (Banks & Banks, 2012).
Specifically, there is an increasing necessity for students to produce thoughtful and high-quality oral and written work, to
engage in critical thinking, and to work collaboratively toward
common goals in a small group of diverse professionals (both
domestically and internationally). Scholars (e.g., Burnes,
2013) have additionally noted the importance of addressing
classroom dialogue and dynamics in graduate classrooms in
which diversity and multiculturalism are being addressed. In
particular, instructors are being called to address the dynamics
of marginalization and oppression that occur in learning spaces
when educating trainees in the helping professions about
diverse populations (Case, 2007; Case et al., 2008).

http://dx.doi.org/10.1037/0000015-006
Teaching LGBTQ Psychology: Queering Innovative Pedagogy and Practice, T. R. Burnes
and J. L. Stanley (Editors)

By paying direct attention to these classroom dynamics and behaviors during graduate-level training, mental health professionals (MHPs) who are also educators are preparing graduate-level professionals-in-training to become culturally informed leaders in their respective domains of specialty. Close attention to such dynamics leads to an emerging goal of ensuring the classroom materials and views being presented in graduate-level coursework are reflective of the realities of LGBTQ populations and gender diversity that exists both nationally and internationally. This chapter provides a road map for psychology instructors as they systematically incorporate material related to LGBTQ individuals and communities into their required readings and classroom discussions. All suggestions in the road map are grounded in the framework of multicultural education (e.g., Banks & Banks, 2012; Howe & Lisi, 2014) and our experience in the classroom.

Why Is Classroom and Behavior Management Important?

The importance of grounding one's teaching strategy in a theoretical framework that celebrates culture and diversity cannot be overstated (Giroux & McLaren, 2014); such a framework must also guide the instructor in creating an environment that can challenge learners to explore diversity issues while feeling safe and connected in a learning space. Specifically, engaging in *classroom management* is defined as creating and curating positive learning environments for learners through the development of learning activities both inside and outside the classroom (e.g., class activities, readings, films) and assessment and accountability structures (e.g., assessment of learning through assignments or exams, guidelines for behavior in the classroom). *Behavior management*, in contrast, is the application of designed classroom experiences through enforcement of constructed policies and goals and processing situations that emerge during learning (e.g., inappropriate dynamics that threaten the learning environments). The instructor can use a combination of classroom management and behavior management to provide not only positive learning processes and outcomes for everyone in a learning community but also extensive, practical materials on problem solving to build individual behavior change plans for learners as appropriate (Jones & Jones, 2015).

Scholars (e.g., Bieschke & Mintz, 2012; Burnes & Singh, 2010) have noted the importance of using classroom management strategies in psychology education that originate from a multicultural framework that also embraces social justice themes. Thus, the pedagogical strategies presented in this chapter are grounded in multicultural education perspectives (e.g., Banks & Banks, 2012; Howe & Lisi, 2014; Shade, Kelly, & Oberg, 1998), as well as multicultural feminist perspectives (hooks, 1994, 2000). Both of these perspectives reflect (a) the realities of the phenomenological experiences of oppressed populations; (b) the limited economic, social, and political realities and choices facing marginalized and stigmatized populations; and (c) the need for professional advocates within our society to assist these populations in the equalization of power. Further, the respective literature in these various subdisciplines of education has also begun to present and scholastically legitimize how individuals with multiple and intersecting minority identities resulting in multiple oppressions often face disproportionate stressors (e.g., hate crimes, unemployment).

The literature focusing on classroom management in learning environments is often based on traditional, didactic classroom settings and has yet to catch up with the growing multicultural literature focusing on racial, gender, and sexual orientation microaggressions in traditional classrooms (e.g., Sue, 2010; Sue & Sue, 2013). One key theme that is considered is the instructor's keen appreciation and awareness of the prevalent cognitive–affective linkages that exist whenever affect-laden material such as LGBTQ psychology is being explored in a classroom context. Some work focusing on classroom management within college classrooms has addressed this reality (e.g., Browning & Kain, 2000; Weimer & Cassidy, 2013). Such topics may evoke feelings of fear and anxiety and challenge students' existing belief systems. Similarly, working with affect-laden material can increase the likelihood for instructors to use unprofessional behaviors, thus creating unsafe classroom environments.

In the literature on the role of instructors in implementing classroom management skills, there is little research reflecting the need for awareness and appreciation of LGBTQ individuals' mental health and well-being or the classroom processes needed for teaching LGBTQ psychology. Notably, Case and Lewis (2012) suggested that instructors' preparation in and use of an intersectionality-focused framework to talk about LGBTQ issues in the classroom provides better classroom outcomes. With such a small body of work from which to draw, the need for instructors to adapt traditional classroom management strategies and make them more applicable to teaching LGBTQ psychology becomes paramount.

Setting Clear Boundaries

Scholars have suggested the need to create safe classroom environments with clear boundaries before and during the first class. Depending on the setting, some students may bring emotionally charged personal opinions about gender and sexuality into the classroom. Thus, instructors should create strong ground rules for classroom discussions; inviting students to cocreate means to keep each other accountable within that community. Initially, behavior guidelines may focus on the "dos and don'ts" of classroom discussions, including the use of gender pronouns. Instructors can model inclusion for persons of various gender identities and expressions. Moreover, instructors in all settings should model ways to show respect, curiosity, and humility when building knowledge in a community.

Online instruction can raise additional concerns for instructors. Specifically, side conversations (i.e., interactions between a dyad or a triad of students that are kept separate from everyone else) can be a real challenge for instructors to process accurately and interpret when class discussions are occurring online. This process raises the need for some "on-the-ground" class sessions with the students so that the instructor has a better sense of classroom interactions. In addition, there has to be classroom etiquette and rules that are tailored to online instructional formats particularly for those instances (e.g., when students bring in ambiguous documents that become the center of classroom discussions). Such etiquette and rules should be posted in an online forum, embedded into the syllabus, assigned as required reading for the first assignments in the course, and referred to routinely by the instructor.

Choosing Material to Inform Class Discussions

After the initial creation of a safe learning environment, instructors' strategic selection of readings becomes a component of classroom management.

CURATED DAILY DIGESTS

A useful initial step in the process of orienting those in the course to the day-to-day issues relevant to LGBTQ individuals is for instructors to set search tools in browsers on the Internet to send to their computer related daily or digest versions of articles that are related to their course content. An early assignment in a course may involve students also following daily Internet searches. Further, students may use a variety of article and event collection sources and various online search engines, such as Twitter, Google Scholar, or ResearchGate, to find appropriate sources for these assignments. Further, students may use hashtags to link articles with certain Twitter feeds to create electronic networks of information that is useful to the classroom process. Such searching provides both faculty and students with a catalyst for current, informed classroom dialogues.

TOOLS TO GUIDE RESPECTFUL DIALOGUE

As part of classroom management, the instructor must also explicitly note the importance of students' holding and listening to perspectives different from their own, even if students may not agree with such alternative perspectives. Supplemental textbooks that can be of value in assisting students to embrace the range of perspectives associated with any classroom dialogue are those in the series *Taking Sides: Clashing Views* (e.g., McKee & Taverner, 2013; Schroeder, 2015), an edited series of volumes focusing on controversial topics. Such a text will allow students to become well informed so they can participate in balanced classroom dialogues taking into account multiple sides of any controversial topic related to LGBTQ psychology. The ultimate goal here is for classroom dialogues to be grounded in empirical data instead of only on students' positive and/or negative affective reactions to sensitive topics or their autobiographical experiences. Having these dialogues grounded in data can help to decrease the frequency with which microaggressions can occur in difficult dialogues in a particular course (Sue & Sue, 2013).

STUDYING FILMS

Films that explore LGBTQ and gender diversity topics can also inform class discussion (e.g., *Transamerica*; Macy & Tucker, 2005) and learning activities (e.g., *Boys Don't Cry*; Kaplan, Koffler, & Pierce, 1999). The successful use of films as a teaching intervention within a course depends heavily on systematic planning during course development. As student learning outcomes, course assignments, and required readings are being developed, the selection of the films or film clips can be made as a way to measure and assess student learning while providing material for the classroom process. Instructors should pay attention to the direct connections between the course content, required readings, and the films. Instructors should preview films in their entirety before choosing to include the film as a part of any course.

Students can be instructed to be prepared to discuss these films along a number of dimensions once the students have learned about the class ground rules. The instructor can articulate the roles and functions of the film(s) with relative ease when questioned by students from the first day and throughout the remainder of the course. The decision whether to require the viewing of the film in its entirety or specific film segments should be made before the first day of class. In addition, the instructor should create an alternative assignment in case a student does not feel comfortable watching the film(s) in question (e.g., trauma histories if the film is explicit or violent). Students need adequate exposure during the course to topics and issues related to films shown in class so that they have little difficulty processing and understanding what is occurring during the film and its relationship to the course content. Similarly, they must be provided with the prominent themes in the films that are directly related to the course content before viewing the film. We have found that students benefit enormously when this level of preparation has occurred before they view these films.

Another way for students to better process films with LGBTQ and/or gender diversity story lines is to consider 10 to 15 discussion questions while viewing the film. The students are made aware of the discussion questions early in the course, so they are prepared to discuss them following the film. These questions address the film's themes and the relationship between the themes and the course content. As part of their reflection when watching such films, MHP trainees should reflect on the current state of MHPs' empirical applied knowledge and the current professional standards of providing culturally informed services to LGBTQ and gender diverse populations. Finally, trainees' affective responses to the film and their biases, myths, and stereotypes can be openly discussed and the classroom guidelines followed with great care and attention. Instructors should plan adequate time to discuss the film; if there is insufficient time to discuss a film when the film ends, the instructor should block time at the beginning of the next class to discuss the film and possibly send students questions for reflection using e-mail or an electronic classroom aid (e.g., Blackboard, Moodle).

Allowing Silent Voices to Be Heard

After selecting appropriate diverse readings and learning activities, instructors should consider how to allow "silent voices" to be heard in classroom discussions. The classroom discussions must be a safe place to voice all views, even unpopular ones that might upset some of the class (Case, 2007; Case et al., 2008). Individuals who have one or more socially oppressed identities may have unique perspectives that differ from those of students who have one or more socially privileged identities. Further, there may be multiple individuals from one particular socially oppressed group who have very different experiences from each other because of their respective combinations of identities and life experiences (Cole, 2009). Such deconstruction of identities within the context of classroom discourse and process are more likely to result in students being open to participating in classroom discussions in the future.

Although every student has a unique combination of privileged and oppressed identities, those students who have multiple marginalized identities (resulting in multiple oppressions) and who may be reluctant to share their experiences should be carefully monitored by course instructors. For example, a Caucasian bisexual male student and an African American gay male student may both be in a cross-cultural psychology class. As they learn about certain perspectives on the mental health of LGBTQ individuals, they may have different reactions, critiques, and understandings of the course material. The African American gay male student may feel silenced if his perspective does not match the information expressed in the learning materials, particularly if he does not feel supported by the instructor in sharing alternative viewpoints. Such differing perspectives should be honored and be part of the catalyst for discussions that value all learners.

To account for such silent voices, the instructor should continually monitor classroom discussion guidelines to ensure that all students have an overall positive classroom experience when these discussions occur. The time allotted for classroom discussions, as well as the intensity of the classroom dialogue topics, are selected on the basis of how well these dialogues have been experienced in the immediate past by all the students. A great deal of monitoring and, at times, flexibility are also essential for the instructor. Students typically do not enjoy being placed on display in a classroom to represent their marginalized group. Instead, they prefer to filter their attitudes and beliefs concerning a marginalized or stigmatized group through their required readings or other classroom experiences. Instructors can, therefore, model how to speak unequivocally on a topic while keeping their comments grounded in empirical data.

Interacting With Invited Speakers

Instructors who wish to invite speakers or community panels as part of their class should pay special attention to the development of questions to ensure that students avoid asking idiosyncratic personal questions of their guests or panelists, instead grounding questions in the course materials and previous classroom dialogues. Likewise, it is useful to assist the panelists by preparing them beforehand regarding (a) the students with whom they will be interacting, including their developmental statuses with respect to their exposure to LGBTQ studies and materials, and (b) the classroom dialogues that have occurred to date and how students' affective responses were expressed. In addition, instructors may prepare the panelists about the possible kinds of questions they will receive from students and the course content reviewed thus far. This level of preparation should reduce the likelihood of "awkward" silences between the students and the panelists between questions.

Another tip when using panel discussions is to choose circumscribed themes instead of being too broad and expansive. Capping the number of panelists at five can also help streamline the conversation. In our experience, we have found that limiting both the theme and number of speakers results in a more comprehensive discussion of the topic rather than a superficial and scattered discussion.

Using Diary Logs to Support the Classroom Process

The use of diary logs is an invaluable strategy for supporting the classroom process. Instructors benefit from requesting diary logs on a weekly basis concerning the phenomenological experiences of students in the course as LGBTQ topics are incorporated into the classroom dialogues. Such logs and journal entries are ways for students to let the instructor know what they are thinking and feeling about the course, the material, and the classroom process. Moreover, diary logs are a place where students' myths, biases, stereotypes, and attitudes about LGBTQ populations are expressed without the possibility of retribution. The ultimate goal here is for students to have a place to expand their awareness, appreciation, and ownership of their myths, stereotypes, and biases about the course material and/or classroom process. Through feedback on the logs, the instructor can guide students in how to acquire the skills to maintain a professional demeanor that does not permit these biases, stereotypes, and myths to sabotage their ability to engage in ethical and culturally sensitive professional conduct in the classroom and their future career.

The instructor never evaluates or grades diary logs. Also, the instructor does not initiate a discussion with students concerning the thematic content of their diary logs. Rather, the value of such a log is that it permits the instructor to have a pulse on each student and how each student is experiencing the course, which is invaluable in classroom dialogues and future course planning. The diary log can offer the instructor a barometer of when to discuss issues during both the didactic portion of the course and also the experiential training components (e.g., classroom dialogues).

Facilitating Difficult Classroom Dialogues

Although instructors may do all that they can to create safety in a classroom space, difficulties may still emerge as students react to course material. Further, it may be difficult for learners to understand their own reactions; therefore, learners may use a learning space (e.g., classroom dialogue, group reflection time in a psychoeducational workshop) to express controversy that mirrors their own feelings. In dialogues in which topics are sensitive and evoke affective responses from students, voices of students with one or more marginalized identities must be welcomed and encouraged by the classroom members, even when they are controversial and may upset a sizeable number of classroom members (e.g., dialogues highlighting students with multiple minority identities resulting in multiple oppressions). Such responses can be similar to responses from students in non-LGBTQ psychology courses. Problematic behavior may range in affect, cognition, tone and pitch of voice, or problematic overt behavior (Jones & Jones, 2015).

Instructors teaching LGBTQ psychology are encouraged to view the documentary film *Race in the Classroom: The Multiplicity of Experience* (Derek Bok Center, 1992). This film does an excellent job of illustrating classroom dialogues that have gotten out of control and become counterproductive to the learning process particularly when they involve sensitive topics in an ethnically and culturally diverse university classroom. Instructors should make sure that, as the discussion begins to generate heated and/or affective responses, they remind students of the classroom ground rules, ensuring that students are using appropriate language and gently confronting stereotypes by asking questions (e.g., "Are you sure that all lesbian women have that experience, even if they come from different ethnic groups?" "Would all transgender men agree with that statement?").

If particularly problematic, instructors can stop the process and ask people to take a few minutes to breathe, have a break, or write things down so that they can filter some of their feelings on paper before articulating them out loud in a respectful way. Specifically, it might be helpful for instructors to remind students to use "I" statements to reflect their feelings instead of criticizing other students. Also, it is important for instructors to heavily facilitate such conversation and reflections ("So, I heard her say that she feels upset when you use those words. What are your reactions to that? And, as you respond, can you respond to her directly? Also, what are other students' thoughts about how what's happening here in our learning environment is tied to the film?").

Professional Development Activities

The various classroom and behavior management strategies discussed in this chapter exemplify the necessity for instructors to have a keen understanding of LGBTQ issues and to be able to facilitate classroom discourse in a way that infuses humility and respect into student learning. Thus, it is incumbent on instructors to continually engage in professional development activities to strengthen their teaching skills and their expertise on certain topics.

CONTINUING EDUCATION

Instructors' enrollment in continuing education courses, workshops, and professional development training in multicultural psychology, LGBTQ studies, gender studies, ethnic studies, social work, and sociology is critical. Such continuing education only expands instructors' horizons and prepares them for the new realities with respect to LGBTQ and gender expansive and transgender (GET) populations (e.g., intersectionality, multicultural issues, cohort influences, gender issues, sexology, sociology). Because the field of LGBTQ psychology is relatively young and the world is rapidly evolving, LGBTQ psychology education must be seen as a lifelong process, and instructors will, therefore, have to update their knowledge continually and expand their understanding. Such professional development activities permit the instructor to embark on a multidisciplinary study of teaching LGBTQ psychology that provides them with additional support and expertise. Moreover, when added to international knowledge and travel experiences, increased interactions with ethnically and culturally diverse LGBTQ and GET populations from around the globe yield a more international perspective of LGBTQ psychology.

EXPERT TEACHERS

An expert teacher's consultation with a novice instructor, starting with the course development process and ending with course completion and evaluation, is typically an eye-opening experience and can provide all parties in the consultation relationship with valuable learning. This structure provides an optimal intensive training experience for novice instructors to benefit from expert teachers through teaching assistantships and coteaching experiences. It is also useful for the expert teacher to consider and verbalize the ways and whys they teach LGBTQ psychology.

Training in small group facilitation skills for instructors and teaching assistants helps them become more effective as small group facilitators in a university classroom and community setting. Such training empowers instructors to deal more effectively with conflict in a small group context and provides students with instructors who are capable of being more active group facilitators during classroom dialogues (Burnes & Ross, 2010). Being an inadequate small group facilitator can potentially sabotage a classroom discussion and, subsequently, a classroom learning environment. Such training can be invaluable, particularly when novice instructors perceive themselves as being uncomfortable and ill-equipped to deal effectively when it comes to a range of LGBTQ topics.

SMALL GROUP INTROSPECTIVE WORK

Experiential small group training for instructors, teaching assistants, and graders focusing on their own intercultural processes with diverse groups is another invaluable training experience. Such a group can meet throughout the duration of a course and typically serves as a "consultation" or "peer supervision" group. The size of the group should be no larger than six to eight instructors, and the term of the group should be for a minimum of 8 weeks. The goal is for instructors, teaching assistants, and graders to create a safe space in which to discuss their personal journeys regarding their biases, myths, stereotypes, and so forth, and how they may have or have negatively affected their professional demeanor in the teaching profession, including in their work with their professional colleagues. Agreed-on ground rules in such a group are also important. It is a unique experience for teaching personnel who have never engaged in such an interaction to open themselves up to their colleagues and allow their colleagues to see them from a different perspective. This becomes a valuable experience for novice instructors as well as seasoned instructors.

An important aspect of this experiential small group diversity training is the exploration of the instances in one's life when instructors perceived themselves as "being oppressed" and the phenomenological experiences associated with that reality. Likewise, a discussion of the instances in their lives when instructors perceived themselves as "being the oppressor" of someone they know and the phenomenological experiences associated with that reality is also important. Both instances may account for times inside and outside the classroom. A safe arena is essential for instructors to explore fully, cognitively and affectively, how these experiences (i.e., affect-laden autobiographical memories) can be processed openly. These instructors will be vulnerable within a supportive environment, and such an experience can truly be a healing experience. Such small group experiences for instructors have the power to rejuvenate and empower them to go back into the classroom and dramatically change the classroom experiences for future cohorts of students.

Conclusion

It is becoming critically important that we create culturally rich classroom experiences that simulate the global world that MHPs will be joining in the 21st century. Thus, the linkage between the university environment and the needs of the workplace, particularly with respect to diversity, cannot be underestimated. Increasingly, there are pressures on universities to provide culturally informed learning environments that incorporate the realities of their future professional world. Thus, instructors are reworking their curriculum and degree program structures to adapt to the increasing pressures and demands of teaching future MHPs to work effectively in interdisciplinary health care teams in a variety of contexts.

In this chapter, we have indicated that MHPs are not only called to learn to teach in a variety of more structured ways but also that they need a model of learning to teach that assesses their ability to negotiate environments that contain multiple perspectives about diversity (even when these perspectives are different from and adversarial toward each other). Specifically, teaching apprenticeship modules designed for MHPs learning to teach LGBTQ psychology have to (a) establish long-term relationships with a variety of different settings in which teaching occurs, (b) identify examples of how difficult dialogues have been successfully addressed in these environments and use these examples in various apprenticeship models to train future educators, and (c) incorporate the assessment of the ability of MHP educators-in-training to navigate and negotiate challenging dialogues in learning environments during teaching experiences. These experiences will allow scholars, in turn, to update and modify research, training, and practice initiatives focused on classroom management and behavior management.

Instructors are paying more attention to having their classroom materials and discussions reflect the globally diverse society that currently exists, so they model the 21st-century professional with respect to thoughts, attitudes, and behaviors along a number of dimensions, including acceptance of ethnically and culturally diverse LGBTQ and gender diverse populations. Learners involved in a variety of different settings, including the university level and community settings, will have to begin to think more globally than locally when contemplating their professional goals and career trajectories. One of the major transitions for university graduates entering the workforce will be their ability to think more critically "on their feet" to process more efficiently incoming stimuli, specifically, incoming stimuli that have to be filtered or processed through a cross-cultural lens because they often involve individuals who are culturally different from themselves. Therefore, their training has to provide professionals-in-training with an opportunity to create a structure that assists learners in engaging in small group dialogues with individuals who are culturally different from themselves using a professional demeanor that keeps in check their biases, assumptions, stereotypes, myths, and so forth. LGBTQ psychology classroom training experiences and internship experiences within work environments and training in community settings must reflect such opportunities. Such experiences will be invaluable to future cohorts of professionals-in-training seeking to make a smooth transition between the university environment and the workplace.

References

Banks, J. A., & Banks, C. A. M. (2012). *Multicultural education: Issues and perspectives* (8th ed.). Hoboken, NJ: Wiley.

Bieschke, K. J., & Mintz, L. B. (2012). Counseling psychology model training values statement addressing diversity: History, current use, and future directions. *Training and Education in Professional Psychology, 6*, 196–203. http://dx.doi.org/10.1037/a0030810

Browning, C., & Kain, C. (2000). Teaching lesbian, gay, and bisexual psychology contemporary strategies. In B. Greene & G. L. Croom (Eds.), *Education, research, practice in lesbian, gay, bisexual, and transgendered psychology: A resource manual* (pp. 46–58). http://dx.doi.org/10.4135/9781452233697.n2

Burnes, T. R. (2013, January). Does the teacher really know? Investigating instructor competence in cross-cultural psychology courses. In T. R. Burnes (Chair), *Transforming multicultural psychology: Engagement, renewal, and action across generations.* Symposium conducted at the National Multicultural Conference and Summit, Houston, TX.

Burnes, T. R., & Ross, K. (2010). Applying social justice to oppression and marginalization in group process: Interventions and strategies for group counselors. *Journal for Specialists in Group Work, 35*, 169–176. http://dx.doi.org/10.1080/01933921003706014

Burnes, T. R., & Singh, A. A. (2010). Integrating social justice into the practicum experience for psychology trainees: Starting earlier. *Training and Education in Professional Psychology, 4*, 153–162. http://dx.doi.org/10.1037/a0019385

Case, K. A. (2007). Raising White privilege awareness and reducing racial prejudice: Assessing diversity course effectiveness. *Teaching of Psychology*, *34*, 231–235. http://dx.doi.org/10.1080/00986280701700250

Case, K. A., Bartsch, R., McEnery, L., Hall, S., Hermann, A., & Foster, D. (2008). Establishing a comfortable classroom from day one: Student perceptions of the reciprocal interview. *College Teaching*, *56*, 210–214. http://dx.doi.org/10.3200/CTCH.56.4.210-214

Case, K. A., & Lewis, M. K. (2012). Teaching intersectional LGBT psychology: Reflections from historically Black- and Hispanic-serving universities. *Psychology & Sexuality*, *3*, 260–276. http://dx.doi.org/10.1080/19419899.2012.700030

Cole, E. R. (2009). Intersectionality and research in psychology. *American Psychologist*, *64*, 170–180. http://dx.doi.org/10.1037/a0014564

Derek Bok Center for Teaching and Learning, Harvard University (Producer). (1992). *Race in the classroom: The multiplicity of experience* [Motion picture]. Retrieved from http://www.fas.harvard.edu/~bok_cen/vids/prev2/race.html

Giroux, H. A., & McLaren, P. (2014). *Between borders: Pedagogy and the politics of cultural studies*. New York, NY: Routledge.

hooks, b. (1994). *Teaching to transgress: Education as the practice of freedom*. New York, NY: Routledge.

hooks, b. (2000). *Feminism is for everybody: Passionate politics*. Boston, MA: South End Press.

Howe, W. A., & Lisi, P. L. (2014). *Becoming a multicultural educator: Developing awareness, gaining skills, and taking action*. Thousand Oaks, CA: Sage.

Jones, V., & Jones, L. (2015). *Comprehensive classroom management: Creating communities and solving problems* (11th ed.). New York, NY: Pearson-Prentice Hall.

Kaplan, C., & Koffler, P. (Producers), & Pierce, K. (Director). (1999). *Boys don't cry* [Motion Picture]. USA: Fox Searchlight.

Macy, W. H. (Producer) & Tucker, D. (Director). (2005). *Transamerica* [Motion picture]. USA: Harvey Weinstein and Bob Weinstein.

McKee, R., & Taverner, W. (2013). *Taking sides: Clashing views in human sexuality* (13th ed.). Dubuque, IA: McGraw Hill.

Schroeder, E. (2015). *Taking sides: Clashing views in gender* (7th ed.). New York, NY: McGraw-Hill.

Shade, B. J., Kelly, C., & Oberg, M. (1998). *Creating culturally responsive classrooms*. Washington, DC: American Psychological Association.

Sue, D. W. (2010). *Microaggressions in everyday life: Race, gender, and sexual orientation*. Hoboken, NJ: Wiley.

Sue, D. W., & Sue, D. (2013). *Counseling the culturally diverse: Theory and practice* (6th ed.). New York, NY: Wiley.

Weimer, M., & Cassidy, A. (2013). *Teaching strategies for college classrooms*. Madison, WI: Magna.

Theodore R. Burnes and Paul N. T. Hovanesian

Psychoeducational Groups in LGBTQ Psychology

7

P sychoeducational groups provide education as a form of treatment "not only because of the knowledge acquired in the process but also because of the perceptions that may be changed as a result" (Gladding, 2011, p. 11). There are various forms of psychoeducation commonly incorporated into the practice of mental health providers (MHPs), including prevention psychoeducational groups, workshops, and in-service training. In many forms, psychoeducation is based on combinations of educational information (Yalom & Leszcz, 2005), acquisition of adaptive coping skills through training and immersion exercises, and prevention of specified problems through group member interactions regarding life difficulties (Horne, Levitt, & Wheeler, 2014). The term *psychoeducation* refers to a modality of mental health service delivery focused on promoting education, awareness of resources, and adaptive coping skills regarding specified psychological and social difficulties, as well as life stressors (American Group Psychotherapy Association

http://dx.doi.org/10.1037/0000015-007
Teaching LGBTQ Psychology: Queering Innovative Pedagogy and Practice, T. R. Burnes and J. L. Stanley (Editors)

[AGPA], 2007; Mason, Vazquez, & Mason, 2014; Yalom & Leszcz, 2005). Psychoeducation is documented as a therapeutic approach that teaches clients practical and positive skills to improve a range of psychological issues (Conyne, 2010). Conducting psychoeducation in a group format can help individuals learn skills from other members and from facilitators in a guided format that promotes resilience and well-being. This chapter highlights elements of psychoeducation group design and theory we feel are most relevant to professionals who use psychoeducation as an instruction method within a framework of lesbian, gay, bisexual, transgender, queer, and/or questioning (LGBTQ) psychology.

Graduate students and preservice professionals who plan to lead psychoeducation groups can benefit from taking part in such a group as part of their training. With the need for such training comes the important idea that pedagogy as a psychoeducational endeavor is two-fold in nature: Successfully imparting information in a psychoeducation group combines a purposeful rationale derived from research and the promotion of personal and collective wellness and change. Further, examining the manifestation of psychological stressors, as well as personal resiliency and strengths, is at the forefront of psychoeducation group design to best address the implementation of intervention services (Rasmussen & Lavish, 2014). To increase efficacy, "a culture-centered perspective giving credence to group and individual characteristics" (Conyne, 2010, p. 38) ought to be taken into account to promote ethical and comprehensive services. Modeling how a psychoeducation group works (and in some cases, does not work) can be a powerful way to prepare students who will provide this service to others.

Designing Psychoeducation Groups

Although psychoeducation group designs vary in their overall purpose, all include common goals and objectives that govern the group. *Goals* are broad concepts that denote a desired outcome or result, whereas *objectives* are measurable functions to achieve smaller wins toward the completion of a larger goal. For example, a mental health goal could be to reduce stress and anxiety; an objective to meet this goal is to exercise daily for 30 minutes.

Several factors must be accounted for to create an effective psychoeducation program. First, a psychoeducation group design is structured and often time limited in its approach. Psychoeducation groups are typically designed as either open or closed groups, meaning the group either remains open to new members joining each session and does not routinely function with an end date, or the group does not accept new members during the course of the group and has a defined beginning and end date (AGPA, 2007). In addition, therapeutic interventions in a psychoeducation group can be thought of as dosages during a particular group session. Thinking of each group session as a dose enables group facilitators to structure each session with clearly defined short-term goals and objectives, group member activities or exercises, and the potential for a component regarding thoughts, feelings, and experiences associated with the interventions.

Group design also involves the construction of a group agenda that addresses specific goals and corresponding objectives through a diligent rationale and planning. In addition, attention must be applied to cultural privilege, not least in the case of groups that focus on LGBTQ sexual orientation and gender identity. Group facilitators will, ideally, be equipped to deconstruct potential oppression associated with LGBTQ sexual and gender identity within the group (Burnes & Ross, 2010). The planning process should also include an assessment of the facilitator's ability to be flexible, to monitor, and to modify groups as appropriate (Conyne, Crowell, & Newmeyer, 2008). Such a facilitation process ensures attention to the group objectives, with the setting and population, as well as multicultural considerations, as salient focus points (Conyne et al., 2008).

How Can Psychoeducation Groups Help LGBTQ Communities?

Psychoeducation groups are founded on teaching principles and offer the opportunity for group members to advance their knowledge in various domains of psychological well-being. A psychoeducation group's focus on education, awareness, and acquisition of skills can help clients to address psychological and psychosocial stressors that affect their lives. It is common for group members to identify domains in their cultural and developmental worldviews that they may wish to address via psychoeducational modalities during times of self-exploration. When identifying such domains, it is probable that group members will have access to various resources from facilitators as well as fellow group members during these sessions. Thus, learning about how one's specific cultural identities, such as sexual orientation and gender identity, affect psychological wellness can be a direct goal of a psychoeducation group.

Heck, Croot, and Robohm (2015) outlined how group work can help transgender participants learn information related to the transition process and challenge notions that transgender people experience the transition process in similar ways (e.g., concerns, needs for support). In a safe environment, psychoeducation groups can strive to provide connection and support against such stressors through universality, or one's sense of emotional connectedness and shared experience with fellow group members (Yalom & Leszcz, 2005), an increased sense of self (Brown, 2011), and knowledge of mental health issues that disproportionately affect LGBTQ communities (Mayer, Mimiaga, VanDerwarker, Goldhammer, & Bradford, 2007). For example, bisexual individuals who have experienced biphobia from gay and lesbian individuals can connect with each other in a psychoeducation group while learning about how internalized biphobia may increase symptoms of depression (e.g., isolation, depressed mood). McLean (2008) suggested that these connections to the LGBTQ community assist attendees in reducing "the stigma individuals attach to being homosexual or bisexual" (p. 64). Furthermore, LGBTQ people with minimal social support are afforded "a chance to meet others with similar experiences and who can help them come to see [their identities] as legitimate sexual identities" (McLean, 2008, p. 64). Therefore, psychoeducation groups function to increase feelings of acceptance, self-esteem, self-confidence, and pride in one's sexual identity and/or gender identities (Medeiros, Seehaus, Elliott, & Melaney, 2004).

In addition to connection and support, psychoeducation groups can combine teaching and education about how to cope with and advocate against societal oppressions that contribute to the negativity experienced by many who identify as LGBTQ. According to Russell and Bohan (2007), LGBTQ clients enter into therapy to address concerns "related to their status as members of a particular social group (and as individuals who claim an identity) that is widely regarded as" (p. 62) atypical or against societal norms. Kelleher (2009) noted that LGBTQ young people experience harassment and victimization in school, home, work, and community settings (p. 374), which increases the potential for mental illness symptoms.

Psychoeducation groups dedicated to competent and intentional service delivery for the LGBTQ population increase the ability to receive access to care while simultaneously decreasing stigma and judgment (Whitehead, Shaver, & Stephenson, 2016). Group members may begin to address their initial discomfort, challenge the societal misperception and lack of informed knowledge, and learn ways to assess their thoughts, feelings, and behaviors regarding oppression. For example, psychoeducation groups for individuals who are HIV-positive, a condition that disproportionately affects "gay, bisexual, and other men who have sex with men" (Centers for Disease Control and Prevention, 2014, p. 4) in the LGBTQ community (Burnes, 2014), have been shown to promote "positive parenting and lifestyle changes" (Mason et al., 2014, p. 80).

Specific Competency and Expertise Needed to Facilitate Psychoeducation Groups

Competency in a variety of domains is necessary when developing and facilitating a psychoeducation group (Conyne, 2010). Because of the adaptation of social, economic, and cultural diversity factors over time, mindfulness regarding requirements of the population serves as a focal point of ethical and professional psychological practice (Conyne, 2010; Conyne et al., 2008). Psychoeducation groups cannot be run like psychotherapy groups. Individuals who facilitate psychoeducation groups require competence in the practice of facilitating learning. It is critical for psychoeducation group facilitators to possess expertise in the process of learning, classroom management, and lesson plan design, implementation, and evaluation. The AGPA (2007) has been instrumental in devising a platform for service providers and treatment settings in which to design group work.

With such calls and mandates for competence and expertise from professional organizations, scholars (e.g., Conyne, 2010) have suggested that facilitators should be required to obtain specific training in the use of a variety of different psychoeducational approaches. There is increasing empirical research to support the idea that group workers (and in particular psychoeducation group facilitators) will benefit from engaging in rigorous training to competently lead such groups and learning the specific skills required to run psychoeducational groups in a variety of different contexts (Nimmanheminda, Unger, Lindemann, & Holloran, 2010). Although there is limited documentation of either the existence or the effectiveness of such training (Ward & Crosby, 2010), the focus for MHPs to learn psychoeducational group design continues to be an aspirational goal.

In addition, training psychoeducational group facilitators to work specifically with LGBTQ clients and communities is also of increased importance (Horne et al., 2014). How these facilitators create a learning environment in which LGBTQ people begin to examine their awareness and learn about issues that disproportionately affect their community is a topic that is absent from the psychological literature. Specifically, training facilitators to balance the teaching of mental well-being to clients while making sure to create a space that is safe for clients' multiple socio-cultural identities, learning styles, and knowledge bases is a pedagogical tension that is not well documented in the teaching of group psychology or the teaching of LGBTQ studies.

Current Literature on Psychoeducational Groups in LGBTQ Communities

Scholars (e.g., Fischer, Sherman, Han, & Owen, 2013) have suggested that psychoeducation is a proven and effective method for teaching about issues related to psychological well-being. Specifically, psychoeducation has been documented as an effective teaching tool in psychology to raise awareness about issues related to multicultural mental health at a broad level (Brown, 2011; Fann, Jarsky, & McDonough, 2009). However, it is still imperative for empirical studies to show how psychoeducation can be effective in increasing knowledge, attitudes, and skills related to sexual orientation and/or gender identity. It is also important to distinguish psychoeducation about LGBTQ communities from psycho-education programs attended by LGBTQ people that are about general healthy sexuality, stress, or a variety of other topics.

Although there is little information that documents the importance of psychoeducation in LGBTQ communities, some research does exist related to the use of group work with LGBTQ individuals and communities (Horne et al., 2014). There is evidence to support the use of specific teaching strategies in helping individuals to learn about LGB people, including using panels (Rogers, Rebbe, Gardella, Worlein, & Chamberlin, 2013) and writing assignments, both in class and outside of class (Burnes, 2007). Panels have been shown to be effective for teaching groups of health care professionals about transgender issues (Parkhill, Mathews, Fearing, & Gainsburg, 2014). In addition, the use of psychoeducation in group modalities has been a teaching strategy that has been proven to be effective in shaping knowledge, attitudes, and skills about MHPs (Goodrich & Luke, 2010). In addition, there is some information about the use of theoretical frameworks in psychoeducation groups: Many psychoeducation groups use a variety of different theoretical frameworks, including cognitive behavioral (Brouzos, Vassilopoulos, & Baourda, 2015) and family systems (Villalba, Gonzalez, Hines, & Borders, 2014) theories of psychology.

There is increasing evidence in the literature for specific group design strategies that may be effective in teaching specific issues in a psychoeducational format (Hackethal et al., 2013). Like all groups with the goal of increasing psychological wellness, psychoeducational groups hope to increase wellness through the acquisition of knowledge in a structured environment. Therefore, these groups (like other types of psychological services provided in a group modality) are designed to encourage learning from other members of the group, give members the opportunity to share knowledge with each other, and help them learn through a variety of structured activities and resources (Troutman & Evans, 2014).

POSITIVE PSYCHOLOGY CONTRIBUTIONS

There is some theory-driven evidence on psychoeducation group design that, although not specific to LGBTQ individuals, has strong implications for group design with these populations. Specifically, positive psychology research allows for a more optimistic and strength-based approach for individuals. According to Aspinwall and Tedeschi (2010), "events that are stressful or traumatic may appear to be chaotic, random, and inexplicable and thus pose a challenge" for people (p. 5). When experiencing a challenging life stressor, "if people perceive that they have the resources necessary to cope with or manage" the stressor, individuals will perceive these difficulties as less stressful (p. 5). When combined with optimism or "a generalized expectancy for positive outcomes that appears to be trait-like and predicts how people cope with stress" (p. 5), psychoeducational groups can use positive psychology as a theoretical framework to ensure constructive and demonstrable learning outcomes for attendees. Instructors may thus devise learning activities to help attendees increase their positive coping skills in dealing with challenges such as homophobia, transphobia, and intersecting oppressions.

In addition to positive psychology theory, the few studies on psychoeducational groups have often used specific theoretical formulas grounded in psychology as a way to provide structure and ensure accurate learning does occur. In designing psychoeducational groups, prevention and early intervention are two focal points that are frequently addressed. Groups are often effective in their approach to promoting community member cohesion, empathy, and trust while assisting in the development and practice of learned skills. In addition to such effectiveness, there are numerous economic advantages and the ability to impart information to many individuals simultaneously instead of in a single group session for a series of individual clients (Conyne, 2010).

INCIDENCE REDUCTION FORMULA

One effective group design strategy is the incidence reduction formula developed by Albee (1982), a hallmark addition to the psychoeducation group literature. Albee and Gullotta (1997) argued that individual treatment is not as efficacious as health-focused group education when attempting "to reduce the incidence (new cases) in the population . . . [where] efforts at individual treatment . . . [do] nothing to reduce the rate [and] the incidence (new cases) in the population" (p. 4). Conyne (2010) adapted and expanded Albee's model, creating the incidence reduction formula as a salient theoretical framework for the design and implementation of psychoeducational groups. In this mode, groups function with a specific direction and purpose, leading to a successful outcome for group members. The purpose is to identify target areas of problematic symptoms for a group of people while decreasing deficits (negative environmental factors) and increasing strengths (positive personal factors) to reduce the incidence of identified stressors (Conyne, 2010). For example, to reduce LGBTQ bullying in a school system, an MHP may design a psychoeducation group for psychologists working in school settings using Conyne's formula. In such a workshop, the facilitator would reduce oppressive language and powerlessness in the school (negative environmental factors) while strengthening community norms of safety, respect, and community cohesion (positive, personal factors). Although this example involves a psychoeducation group used to train school psychologists, the development of this group has a community focus at its core. Thus, if the school psychologists who attend this group are empowered to in turn create their own psychoeducation group interventions on these topics with teachers, other staff, students, and parents, the MHP's initial intervention is amplified to positively affect future groups that historically have had fewer opportunities because of negative environmental factors.

THE HEALTH BELIEF MODEL

Outside the discipline of health service psychology, the health belief model (HBM) is often used as a theoretical framework in psychoeducational groups in public health and social work that are geared toward the acquisition of health-related behaviors and/or assistance in decreasing negative health-related behaviors (Glanz & Bishop, 2010; Strecher & Rosenstock, 1997). There is documented evidence to suggest that minority stress may increase the likelihood of negative health behaviors for LGBTQ people, including substance use (Hughes & Eliason, 2002) and unprotected sex (Laing & Gaffney, 2014). Also, lack of connection or support related to one's sexual orientation or gender identity may also instigate an LGBTQ individual's decrease in health-related behaviors, including routine medical care (Riggle, Rostosky, McCants, & Pascale-Hague, 2011; Vaughan & Waehler, 2010). The HBM is a structural framework that is helpful in assisting psychoeducation group facilitators in their approach to designing groups that can ameliorate health issues in LGBTQ communities while addressing these types of behaviors using a psychoeducation modality.

The HBM asserts that several factors contribute to an individual's acceptance and commitment to health-related interventions: susceptibility, seriousness, benefits of and barriers to a behavior, cues to action, and self-efficacy (Champion & Skinner, 2008, p. 46). Therefore, if people believe they are susceptible to a mental health disorder, accept this information as pertinent and believe that the benefits of gaining knowledge about the disorder are greater than the hindrance or monetary cost, they are more inclined to act for betterment and are motivated to change their stressor (Champion & Skinner, 2008). Thus, the HBM allows psychoeducation group facilitators to design effective groups that affect attendees' perceived severity of a mental health problem, perceived susceptibility to the problem, perceived benefits and barriers (to mental wellness), cues to action, and self-efficacy (Carpenter, 2010).

Recognizing Intergroup Differences

These descriptions of theoretical models highlight distinct teaching strategies that can be used in psychoeducational group design in LGBTQ communities. Despite having these models, it is also necessary to address the unique teaching and learning differences in sexual orientation and gender diversity that often occur in psychoeducation. It is important to acknowledge that group differences exist within the LGBTQ community. Scholars have called on MHPs to create and deliver psychoeducational groups that can specifically address within-group differences in LGBTQ communities and promote members' empowerment and sense of self, which can remove barriers to other forms of treatment (Heck et al., 2015).

When structuring a psychoeducational group and its interventions, understanding intragroup or within-group differences is imperative to the success of the group (Burnes & Ross, 2010). AGPA (2007) noted, "seasoned group facilitators recognize that the success of individual group members is intimately linked to the overall health of the group-as-a-whole" (p. 12). Therefore, the multiple identities of a group's member–learners, including but not limited to race, class, gender, and sexual orientation, must be acknowledged by the group facilitator to understand how learning by the group will be affected by context (Burnes & Chen, 2012). Such acknowledgment has been documented to affect the learning of attendees—in particular, those with multiple marginalized identities. For example, Kelleher (2009) stated that the expectation of many was for LBQ women "to form a strong alliance because of their common marginalization in the heterosexist and sexist society" (p. 214). This is interesting to note because of the perception that members of the LGBTQ population would find commonality and strength from common experiences. Taking intragroup differences into consideration is essential and leads to more successful therapeutic outcomes for members.

As facilitators begin to design psychoeducation programs tailored to specific individuals or topics of sexual orientation and/or gender diversity, it is important to consider the multiple identities and contexts of subgroups in the LGBTQ communities. For example, although facilitators might be designing a psychoeducation group for bisexual women, the many races, ethnicities, and ages of potential women participants in this group may provide a wide range of experiences that may not match the perceived expectations or experiences of facilitators. In another example, facilitators may be asked to design a psychoeducation group for gay men and immediately plan activities for this group that center on safe sex; such a stereotype may appropriately anger some men who actually want to learn more about love and intimacy within a committed relationship. Many psychoeducation groups fail to address the unique psychosocial experiences of bisexual individuals, thereby increasing their isolation (Horne et al., 2014). For transgender individuals, psychoeducation groups are helpful in learning about various topics, including physical transition, changing identification documents, and sexual self-empowerment during the transition process. Therefore, it is imperative for the facilitators to consider the diverse and intersecting histories, experiences, needs, and desires of subgroups with the LGBTQ community when designing psychoeducation programs.

Case Examples

This review of the existing literature highlights the nascent research and scholarship related to using psychoeducational groups as a format for teaching LGBTQ psychology. For the authors of this chapter, the need to provide concrete examples of effective strategies can be challenging when such little documented teaching exists using this specific type of instruction format. Although a search of the Internet can provide teaching materials, it is difficult to ascertain whether the material is effective, for what age group the material is intended, and what specific competencies an instructor might require to engage successfully with that material. Therefore, the psychoeducation group program *Exploration of Gender: Creativity Versus Gender Identity*, designed by the first author for children, adolescents, and parents to learn about gender identity in a children's hospital setting, is used as an example (Burnes, 2016). The program has two goals and two corresponding objectives related to increasing awareness of one's gender. It is arranged in three modules (2 hours each), and facilitators can choose to spend from 1 week to 1 month per module depending on the age and cognitive capacity of group attendees (for learning and memory encoding purposes).

In the first module, the facilitators use a structured activity to help individuals learn the differences between sexual orientation, gender identity, gender expression, and biological sex. Attendees then work in small groups to complete a series of worksheets to understand the specifics of gender identity. In the second module, attendees review the concepts from the first module and begin to explore their sense of self with respect to gender. Attendees work in different small groups (groups with different members than in the first module) to share their internal sense of gender (e.g., "Who am I? What do I like? What gender makes me comfortable, or what genders make me comfortable? What are the community and societal gender roles I express without realizing it?"). The attendees then process this activity in a large group and understand that they can create and define their gender(s). In the third module, the facilitator begins to empower attendees to take action steps to be and love their gender(s). Then, a panel of two to four people addresses their respective processes of learning about their genders. The panelists are asked to share concrete action steps they each took to embody their respective gender identities. Attendees then break into a third set of small groups and create their own action steps for how they can begin to emulate the gender(s) to which they know they belong, either through continuing certain existing behaviors or creating new ones. Depending on the attendees' group, bibliotherapy resources (e.g., Brill & Pepper, 2008, for parents and providers of children) are provided. The outcomes of this group demonstrate increased learning about gender diversity by attendees. This is certainly feasible in a variety of settings, including elementary teacher training, hospital settings, and religious education classes for high school students. Summative evaluation feedback for this children's hospital group was collected and showed the program to be effective. Formative evaluation data collected noted that safety was one of the most frequently mentioned topics by attendees of this group (Burnes, 2016).

Teaching Tips and
Activity Ideas

In designing the group, facilitators should ensure that the group caters to member–learners of various levels of "intellectual, cognitive, and social functioning and to the cultural values of participants [which] helps to assure program acceptance if not success" (Conyne, 2010, p. 37). Many facilitators incorrectly design a group by first selecting activities in which the group attendees can engage. Instead, facilitators are encouraged to first construct goals and corresponding objectives to specify attendees' learning and how the facilitators will measure such learning. Next, facilitators can construct activities that aid in the attendees' learning and corresponding objectives. Activities must be derived from goals and objectives, be applicable to the skill level of the group members, be within the facilitator's competence, and increase participation for all group members (Trotzer, 2004). It is also important to take into consideration various other factors, such as the overall size of the group, the time allotment for each meeting, and the length and "structural" considerations in the group that may affect the activities a facilitator chooses when deciding which activities are appropriate for the group. When designing activities, facilitators are urged to consider learning activities that cater to diverse learning styles and identities. Facilitators may not know the learning styles of their attendees and, therefore, must use a range of activities that they can choose from and incorporate to meet the multiple learning styles of the group. Examples of such learning-style-focused activities include visual (PowerPoint slides, whiteboard, film clips), interpersonal (small group discussion, pair-and-share), kinesthetic (experiential, movement-based), and/or audio (panel discussions, music).

For groups specific to LGBTQ attendees, facilitators should ascertain within-group differences in the LGBTQ community. Prescreening group members before the group begins is essential to ensure that the members' needs and learning goals match those of the facilitators and the group. Prescreening questions for psychoeducation groups of exclusively LGBTQ members should consider an attendee's identity development, developmental age, and perceptions of psychoeducation group work to increase engagement and establish trust while simultaneously meeting the goals and objectives of the established program. Prescreens should be done individually and in-person so that the facilitators can collect baseline data about a potential member's interpersonal functioning. In addition, attending to issues of within-group social justice is paramount. LGBT affirmative facilitators should bring up and address these factors in a consistent way to mediate and abolish oppressive processes that take place in group settings on both microaggressive and macro-aggressive levels (e.g., comments, nonverbal behavior, harassment; Burnes & Ross, 2010).

Facilitators improve outcomes by ensuring that they create, clearly state, and enforce ground rules at the beginning and throughout the psychoeducational group process. Unlike a traditional classroom setting or an ongoing psychotherapy group, the facilitator may only be with psychoeducational group attendees for two sessions that are 4 hours each; nonetheless, it is important to establish and restate ground rules to promote safety in the group. These ground rules can be co-created with attendees and then written on a poster or a white-board for reference if facilitators and/or participants have to refer-ence them.

Activities for LGBTQ-focused psychoeducational groups are wide and diverse in regard to their purpose and other educational variables, such as level of knowledge of participants and time allotment. Activities and exercises may be used for several functions in a psychoeducational group, including to "initiate the focus and interaction of a group at the beginning of the overall group process, at the start of an individual ses-sion, or to interject a new or different direction in the group" (Trotzer, 2004, p. 80). Exercises used for attendees who are themselves LGBTQ are often different from those for allies (parents, friends, service provid-ers) who want to support LGBTQ people. Also, activities and exercises can reduce worry of group members if the group facilitator takes the lead regarding the activity because there is more direction, and a sense of trust and security can be established. Next, we discuss three examples of often-used activities.

The Gender Unicorn (see Activity 7.1 at the end of this chapter; Trans Student Educational Resources, 2016) assists participants to learn various terminologies related to sexual identity, gender identity, and gender expression. The activity can be introduced in a short lecture to explain different terms, with the facilitators providing the activity as a handout. The handout can also be an accompaniment to a panel discus-sion with panelists of various LGBTQ identities who share their identity development stories. Facilitators will improve the group outcome if the handout is explained in detail rather than only given to individuals as a post-workshop handout. For LGBTQ attendees, the Gender Versus Sexual Orientation Worksheet (see Activity 7.2) is a useful learning tool as well as a process-oriented activity. This worksheet can be used for a variety of purposes, such as meeting goals (and corresponding objectives) related to increasing self-awareness, differentiating between sexual orientation and gender identity, and learning concepts and lan-guage. Using the comfort level of the group as context, facilitators can ask, "What was it like to complete this worksheet? What did you learn by doing this activity?" (at a low-comfort level) or "Where did you place yourself on each of these lines? How did you make your decisions?" (at a high-comfort level). Large group process can follow as appropriate. The Internalized Oppression Outline (see Activity 7.3) is another activity that can be used in psychoeducation groups with LGBTQ attendees. This worksheet can be used for a variety of purposes to meet goals (and corresponding objectives) related to increasing self-awareness, differentiating between sexual orientation and gender identity, or learning related terminology and concepts.

Conclusion

The authors of this chapter highlighted the need for future research that empirically validates the effectiveness of psychoeducation groups in LGBTQ individuals' learning about their mental well-being. Specifically, using innovative program evaluation methods (Kettner, Moroney, & Martin, 2016) can provide documentation about the effectiveness of specific programs that teach LGBTQ individuals about psychological well-being and resilience specific to their communities. There is continual hope that scholars will feel supported in addressing this gap in the current research literature.

We addressed several factors, such as the utility of psychoeducational groups, the importance of conceptualizing group designs through frameworks, and the implementation of carefully selected interventions and activities. Ultimately, it is critical that psychoeducation groups with LGBTQ individuals be studied and that the number of psychoeducation groups specifically targeting LGBTQ communities be increased by designing groups that aim to increase the resilience of specific subgroups in the LGBTQ communities while also creating systemic change using empowerment and social justice. Further, the need for facilitators of psychoeducation groups to incorporate online and virtual learning as part of their groups' designs and agendas is paramount. Given the diversity of online learning that occurs within LGBTQ communities about identity and wellness (DeHaan, Kuper, Magee, Bigelow, & Mustanski, 2013; Magee, Bigelow, DeHaan, & Mustanski, 2012), it is critical to understand the many ways that online learning can expand psychoeducation groups for LGBTQ people. Such an increase in empirical knowledge will assist in promoting wellness and resiliency in a community in need of compassionate care and continued advancements within this domain of psychology.

ACTIVITY 7.1

The Gender Unicorn

Directions: Use this activity in psychoeducational groups or larger community settings. Give a copy of the figure of the Gender Unicorn (from http://www.transstudent.org/gender) to each learner and ask him or her to place him- or herself on each of the lines by placing an *X* on each line. Facilitators can then process questions about what different lines mean, how learners decided where to put themselves on each line, and so forth.

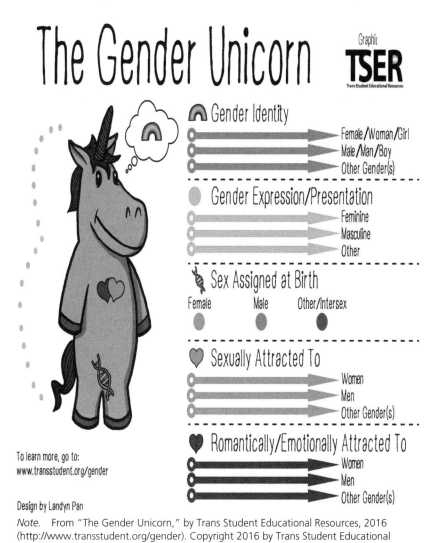

Note. From "The Gender Unicorn," by Trans Student Educational Resources, 2016 (http://www.transstudent.org/gender). Copyright 2016 by Trans Student Educational Resources. Reprinted with permission.

ACTIVITY 7.2

Gender Versus Sexual Orientation Worksheet

Directions: Each attendee engaging in the activity needs a printed worksheet and a writing instrument. Attendees are instructed to look at each of the five continua and to "place" themselves on the continua where they believe they are by marking themselves with an *X*. Instructors may wish to explain the worksheet by saying, "As you can see from this diagram, which represents only a few of the aspects of sex and gender, identity is composed of multiple, independent factors, and each factor has multiple places which individuals can inhabit." Attendees can then break into small groups and be given structured prompts to discuss what they feel comfortable sharing.

Biological sex (anatomy, chromosomes, hormones)

Male	Intersex	Female

Gender identity (psychological sense of self)

Man	Third sex, Trans, Bi-gendered, Genderqueer, Other	Woman

Gender expression (communication of gender)

Masculine	Androgynous	Feminine

Sexual orientation (identity of erotic response)

Attracted to women	Attracted to both, neither, trans, genderqueer, other	Attracted to men

Sexual behavior (sexual behavior)

Sex with women	Sex with both, trans, genderqueer, other	Sex with men

Note. From "Diagram of Sex and Gender," by Center for Gender Sanity, 2009. Retrieved from http://www.gendersanity.com/diagram.html. Copyright 2009 by Center for Gender Sanity. Adapted with permission.

ACTIVITY 7.3

Internalized Oppression Outline

Directions: Each attendee engaging in the activity needs a printed worksheet and a writing instrument. Participants are instructed to write different identities that they hold outside of the figure at the top of the page. Participants are then asked to write messages they have received from the outside world (family, friends, media, school, organizations) inside the figure. Attendees can then break into small groups and are given prompts to discuss what they feel comfortable sharing. Large group process can follow as appropriate.

References

Albee, G. W. (1982). Preventing psychopathology and promoting human potential. *American Psychologist, 37*, 1043–1050. http://dx.doi.org/10.1037/0003-066X.37.9.1043

Albee, G. W., & Gullotta, T. P. (1997). Primary prevention works. In G. W. Albee & T. P. Gullotta (Eds.), *Issues in children's and families' lives: Vol. 6. Primary prevention's evolution* (pp. 3–22). New York, NY: Sage.

American Group Psychotherapy Association. (2007). *Guidelines for ethics: Practice guidelines for group psychotherapy.* Retrieved from http://www.agpa.org/home/practice-resources/ethics-in-group-therapy

Aspinwall, L. G., & Tedeschi, R. G. (2010). The value of positive psychology for health psychology: Progress and pitfalls in examining the relation of positive phenomena to health. *Annals of Behavioral Medicine, 39*, 4–15. http://dx.doi.org/10.1007/s12160-009-9153-0

Brill, S., & Pepper, R. (2008). *The transgender child: A handbook for families and professionals.* San Francisco, CA: Cleis Press.

Brouzos, A., Vassilopoulos, S. P., & Baourda, V. C. (2015). Therapeutic factors and members' perceptions of co-leaders' attitudes in a psychoeducational group for Greek children with social anxiety. *The Journal for Specialists in Group Work, 40*, 204–224. http://dx.doi.org/10.1080/01933922.2015.1017065

Brown, N. W. (2011). *Psychoeducational groups: Process and practice* (3rd ed.). New York, NY: Taylor & Francis.

Burnes, T. R. (2007). Queering college writing: Writing students' learning of LGB issues using the Internet as an instructional tool. *Journal of Gay & Lesbian Issues in Education, 4*, 75–88. http://dx.doi.org/10.1300/J367v04n02_06

Burnes, T. R. (2014). Psychological services with consumers living with HIV: Changing contexts and intersecting, thematic understandings. *National Register of Psychologists Report, 40*, 34–38.

Burnes, T. R. (2016). *Exploration of gender: Design, implementation, and evaluation of a psychoeducation program for gender nonconforming children.* Manuscript submitted for publication.

Burnes, T. R., & Chen, M. (2012). Multiple identities of transgender individuals: Incorporating a framework of intersectionality to gender crossing. In R. Josselson & M. Harway (Eds.), *Navigating multiple identities: Race, gender, culture, nationality and roles* (pp. 113–128). http://dx.doi.org/10.1093/acprof:oso/9780199732074.003.0007

Burnes, T. R., & Ross, K. (2010). Applying social justice to oppression and marginalization in group process: Interventions and strategies for group counselors. *Journal for Specialists in Group Work, 35*, 169–176. http://dx.doi.org/10.1080/01933921003706014

Carpenter, C. J. (2010). A meta-analysis of the effectiveness of health belief model variables in predicting behavior. *Health Communication, 25,* 661–669. http://dx.doi.org/10.1080/10410236.2010.521906

Center for Gender Sanity. (2009). *Diagram of sex and gender.* Retrieved from http://www.gendersanity.com/diagram.html

Centers for Disease Control and Prevention. (2014). *HIV risk, prevention, and testing behaviors—National HIV Behavioral Surveillance System: Men who have sex with men, 20 U.S. Cities, 2011* (HIV Surveillance Special Report 8). Retrieved from http://www.cdc.gov/hiv/pdf/hssr_8_nhbs_msm_pdf-03.pdf

Champion, V. L., & Skinner, C. S. (2008). The health belief model. In K. Glanz, B. K. Rimer, & K. Viswanath (Eds.), *Health behavior and health education: Theory, research, and practice* (pp. 45–65). San Francisco, CA: Jossey-Bass.

Conyne, R. K. (2010). *Prevention program development and evaluation: An incidence reduction, culturally relevant approach.* http://dx.doi.org/10.4135/9781483349176

Conyne, R. K., Crowell, J. L., & Newmeyer, M. D. (2008). *Group techniques: How to use them more purposefully.* Upper Saddle River, NJ: Prentice Hall.

DeHaan, S., Kuper, L. E., Magee, J. C., Bigelow, L., & Mustanski, B. S. (2013). The interplay between online and offline explorations of identity, relationships, and sex: A mixed-methods study with LGBT youth. *Journal of Sex Research, 50,* 421–434. http://dx.doi.org/10.1080/00224499.2012.661489

Fann, A., Jarsky, K. M., & McDonough, P. M. (2009). Parent involvement in the college planning process: A case study of the P-20 collaboration. *Journal of Hispanic Higher Education, 8,* 374–393. http://dx.doi.org/10.1177/1538192709347847

Fischer, E. P., Sherman, M. D., Han, X., & Owen, R. P. (2013). Outcomes of participation in the REACH multifamily group program for veterans with PTSD and their families in the public domain. *Professional Psychology: Research and Practice, 44,* 127–134. http://dx.doi.org/10.1037/a0032024

Gladding, S. T. (2011). *Groups: A counseling specialty* (6th ed.). New York, NY: Merrill.

Glanz, K., & Bishop, D. B. (2010). The role of behavioral science theory in development and implementation of public health interventions. *Annual Review of Public Health, 31,* 399–418. http://dx.doi.org/10.1146/annurev.publhealth.012809.103604

Goodrich, K. M., & Luke, M. (2010). The experiences of school counselors-in-training in group work with LGBTQ adolescents. *Journal for Specialists in Group Work, 35,* 143–159. http://dx.doi.org/10.1080/01933921003705966

Hackethal, V., Spiegel, S., Lewis-Fernández, R., Kealey, E., Salerno, A., & Finnerty, M. (2013). Towards a cultural adaptation of family psychoeducation: Findings from three Latino focus groups. *Community Mental Health Journal, 49*, 587–598. http://dx.doi.org/10.1007/s10597-012-9559-1

Heck, N. C., Croot, L. C., & Robohm, J. S. (2015). Piloting a psychotherapy group for transgender clients: Description and clinical considerations for practitioners. *Professional Psychology: Research and Practice, 46*, 30–36. http://dx.doi.org/10.1037/a0033134

Horne, S., Levitt, H. M., & Wheeler, E. (2014). Group work with gay, lesbian, bisexual, and transgender clients: Discussing invisible differences. In J. L. DeLucia-Waack, D. A. Gerrity, C. R. Kalodner, & M. T. Riva (Eds.), *Handbook of group counseling and psychotherapy* (pp. 253–263). Thousand Oaks, CA: Sage.

Hughes, T. L., & Eliason, M. (2002). Substance use and abuse in lesbian, gay, bisexual, and transgender populations. *The Journal of Primary Prevention, 22*, 263–298. http://dx.doi.org/10.1023/A:1013669705086

Kelleher, C. (2009). Minority stress and health: Implications for lesbian, gay, bisexual, transgender, and questioning (LGBTQ) young people. *Counselling Psychology Quarterly, 22*, 373–379. http://dx.doi.org/10.1080/09515070903334995

Kettner, P. M., Moroney, R. M., & Martin, L. L. (2016). *Designing and managing programs: An effectiveness-based approach* (5th ed.). Thousand Oaks, CA: Sage.

Laing, M., & Gaffney, J. (2014). Health and wellness services for male sex workers. In V. Minichiello & J. Scott (Eds.), *Male sex work and society* (pp. 260–286). Binghamton, NY: Harrington Park Press.

Magee, J. C., Bigelow, L., DeHaan, S., & Mustanski, B. S. (2012). Sexual health information seeking online: A mixed-methods study among lesbian, gay, bisexual, and transgender young people. *Health Education & Behavior, 39*, 276–289. http://dx.doi.org/10.1177/1090198111401384

Mason, S., Vazquez, D., & Mason, R. (2014). Focused and motivated: A psychoeducational group for parents living with HIV. *Journal of HIV/AIDS & Social Services, 13*, 79–96. http://dx.doi.org/10.1080/15381501.2013.864176

Mayer, K. H., Mimiaga, M. J., VanDerwarker, R., Goldhammer, H., & Bradford, J. B. (2007). Fenway Community Health's model of integrated, community-based LGBT care, education, and research. In I. H. Meyer & M. E. Northridge (Eds.), *The health of sexual minorities* (pp. 693–715). New York, NY: Springer.

McLean, K. (2008). Inside, outside, nowhere: Bisexual men and women in the gay and lesbian community. *Journal of Bisexuality, 8*, 63–80. http://dx.doi.org/10.1080/15299710802143174

Medeiros, D. M., Seehaus, M., Elliott, J., & Melaney, A. (2004). Providing mental health services for LGBT teens in a community adolescent health clinic. *Journal of Gay & Lesbian Psychotherapy, 8*, 83–95.

Nimmanheminda, S. U., Unger, R., Lindemann, A. M., & Holloran, M. C. (2010). Group therapy training at Naropa University's contemplative counseling psychology program. *Group, 34*, 309–318.

Parkhill, A. L., Mathews, J. L., Fearing, S., & Gainsburg, J. (2014). A transgender health care panel discussion in a required diversity course. *American Journal of Pharmaceutical Education, 78*, 81. http://dx.doi.org/10.5688/ajpe78481

Rasmussen, H. N., & Lavish, L. (2014). Broad definitions of culture in the field of multicultural psychology. In J. T. Pedrotti & L. Edwards (Eds.), *Perspectives on the intersection of multiculturalism and positive psychology* (pp. 17–30). http://dx.doi.org/10.1007/978-94-017-8654-6_2

Riggle, E. D. B., Rostosky, S. S., McCants, L. E., & Pascale-Hague, D. (2011). The positive aspects of transgender self-identification. *Psychology and Sexuality, 2*, 147–158. http://dx.doi.org/10.1080/19419899.2010.534490

Rogers, A., Rebbe, R., Gardella, C., Worlein, M., & Chamberlin, M. (2013). Older LGBT adult training panels: An opportunity to educate about issues faced by the older LGBT community. *Journal of Gerontological Social Work, 56*, 580–595. http://dx.doi.org/10.1080/01634372.2013.811710

Russell, G. M., & Bohan, J. S. (2007). Liberating psychotherapy: Liberation psychology and psychotherapy with LGBT clients. *Journal of Gay & Lesbian Psychotherapy, 11*, 59–75.

Strecher, V. J., & Rosenstock, I. M. (1997). The health belief model. In A. Baum, S. Newman, J. Weinman, R. West, & C. McManus (Eds.), *Cambridge handbook of psychology, health, and medicine* (pp. 113–116). Cambridge, England: Cambridge University Press.

Trans Student Educational Resources. (2016). *The Gender Unicorn.* Retrieved from http://www.transstudent.org/gender

Trotzer, J. P. (2004). Conducting a group: Guidelines for choosing and using activities. In J. L. DeLucia-Waack, D. A. Gerrity, C. R. Kalodner, & M. T. Riva (Eds.), *Handbook of group counseling and psychotherapy* (pp. 76–90). http://dx.doi.org/10.4135/9781452229683.n6

Troutman, O. A., & Evans, K. M. (2014). A psychoeducational group for parents of lesbian, gay, and bisexual adolescents. *Journal of School Counseling, 12*, 1–25.

Vaughan, M. D., & Waehler, C. A. (2010). Coming out growth: Conceptualizing and measuring stress-related growth associated with coming out to others as a sexual minority. *Journal of Adult Development, 17*, 94–109. http://dx.doi.org/10.1007/s10804-009-9084-9

Villalba, J., Gonzalez, L. M., Hines, E. M., & Borders, L. D. (2014). The Latino Parents-Learning About College (LaP-LAC) program: Educational empowerment of Latino families throughout psychoeducational group work. *Journal for Specialists in Group Work, 39*, 47–70. http://dx.doi.org/10.1080/01933922.2013.859192

Ward, D., & Crosby, C. (2010). Using an observation model for training group therapists in a community mental health setting. *Group, 34*, 355–361.

Whitehead, J., Shaver, J., & Stephenson, R. (2016). Outness, stigma, and primary health care utilization among rural LGBT populations. *PLoS ONE, 11*(1), e0146139. http://dx.doi.org/10.1371/journal.pone.0146139

Yalom, I. D., & Leszcz, M. (2005). *The theory and practice of group psychotherapy* (5th ed.). New York, NY: Basic Books.

Cadyn Cathers, Caroline Carter, and Susan P. Landon

Teaching LGBTQ Psychology in Community Settings

8

G ender diverse and sexually diverse individuals have existed throughout history and are part of all cultures. These individuals deserve to be accepted and appreciated for being their authentic selves and deserve to experience a sense of freedom to live a life in which they are valued. When their unique lived experiences, identities, and needs are honored, gender diverse and sexually diverse individuals and their communities (and the community at large) are strengthened (Bockting, Miner, Swinburne Romine, Hamilton, & Coleman, 2013). In our work in community settings, we have often found that community members want to create places of safety and connection with gender and sexually diverse individuals but are unsure how to do this. As mental health professionals (MHPs) who focus on training others in the areas of gender and sexual diversity, we work within communities to help facilitate changes in their unique settings that will create the desired outcome of safety and connection. These settings

Special thanks to Katie Havener for graphic design of the activities and figures and to Tessa Babcock and Melissa Dellens for their additional support.

http://dx.doi.org/10.1037/0000015-008
Teaching LGBTQ Psychology: Queering Innovative Pedagogy and Practice, T. R. Burnes and J. L. Stanley (Editors)

include, but are not limited to, hospitals, community mental health clinics, public and private schools, higher education settings, workplace environments, religious settings, and government agencies.

To date, there is little research on teaching gender and sexual diversity within community settings; likewise, information that explores gender and sexuality within historical and ecological models is scarce. Resources that include tools for community training on gender and sexual diversity have predominantly been developed for use in K–12 school settings (Brill & Pepper, 2008; Bryan, 2012). Genderspectrum.org and GLSEN.org are examples of websites with resources for K–12 settings. Though many of these school-focused tools can be used outside of educational settings, there is not a more general training guide for teaching gender and sexual diversity in communities. This chapter provides useful teaching activities for those who desire to teach about gender and sexual diversity in community settings. The activities primarily serve to focus participants' awareness on the struggles and challenges many lesbian, gay, bisexual, and queer (LGBQ) and gender expansive and trans (GET) people experience. They lend themselves to the discussion of strengths sexually diverse and gender diverse people bring to communities while also placing a strong focus on building awareness of exclusion and privilege. Many of the activities in this chapter are taken from our personal teaching tool kits. When approaching the implementation of any particular training, it is important to consider the contextual factors of the setting, including the unique needs of the particular community. This chapter intends to provide some foundational tools that can be used with additional material to meet the specific needs of the various communities that educators are entering.

Most of the time when MHPs are asked to facilitate training, it is to raise basic awareness for a particular community (e.g., school, workplace setting, clinic) because a student, employee, client, or member has come out. However, there are some trainings that are designed and implemented to go beyond basic awareness. Sometimes, communities or agencies request more specialized training to cater to the specific needs of their population. For example, leaders in a workplace may want to brainstorm with an MHP regarding policy development for transgender employees at that specific organization and then also may want to train their staff. In another example, a mental health clinic may want training that is designed to understand the unique intersections of the population served at that clinic (e.g., residential, addiction, rape survivors) and LGBQ and GET populations.

There are many unique aspects to consider when teaching about LGBQ and GET populations in community settings compared with academic settings. In academic settings, there is often more time to focus on the intricacies of terminology and discussion of privilege over the course of a term, whereas in community settings, training sessions are often only 1 to 3 hours in length. Regardless of setting, most training should cover the basics of terminology and privilege, though the focus may shift according to the needs of a particular setting. For example, training at a church may have an additional focus on the intersection of religion and LGBQ and GET identities; training at a workplace may additionally address awareness of current state and federal laws relating to employment; training in a health care setting may focus on improving patient care.

One of the most important distinctions when providing training in community settings is that instructors have to consider the variety of knowledge bases of the participants. For example, some participants can have extensive knowledge about LGBTQ mental wellness, whereas others might be struggling with their own homophobia, biphobia, and transphobia. Assessing the knowledge of the participants prior to training can be helpful in developing the design. In addition, some participants may be mandated to attend (e.g., required training at a company), whereas some may be attending voluntarily. The design of a particular training should take all of these factors into consideration. We cannot stress advance preparation enough, especially when deciding how much self-disclosure to encourage among participants.

The amount of self-disclosure encouraged from participants depends on the type of setting and the time allotted for the training. Mandated training should encourage less self-disclosure than voluntary training. For example, the privilege walk (see Activities 8.7 and 8.8) could be done without participants having to self-disclose by simply reading the various heterosexual and monosexual privileges (Activity 8.7) and/or cisgender privileges (Activity 8.8) while people stay silent and just absorb the information rather than disclosing through taking steps. Adjusting the exercises in this chapter to meet the specific needs of the setting and participants will help make a better training session. Discussion around all the nuances of specific training is outside the scope of this chapter because of the varied aspects of training, including location, population, and/or audience.

Community organizations often approach us after learning about our training services through online searches and after visiting our website; thus, marketing often happens through informal networking or through a previous engagement in one of our community-focused learning environments. Also, we have found that as MHPs begin providing training in community settings, awareness of the training spreads via word of mouth. Using social media, such as Facebook, and contacting specific community and organizational listservs can help disperse information about the training. Because reviewing every possible type of community-based training is outside the scope of one chapter, we have chosen to focus this chapter on community-based training of basic awareness, terminology, and addressing privilege in LGBTQ psychology. Even when we do more advanced training, we often include these basic exercises as the foundation of our education sessions.

Sex, Gender, and Sexuality

In community presentations, it is important to differentiate early in the learning process the many terms that define (for attendees) sex, gender, and sexuality. *Sex* is understood as one's biology, which includes genitalia, hormones, chromosomes, and secondary sex characteristics. *Gender identity* is defined as one's internal sense of being a man, woman, both, neither, or something else entirely. *Gender expression* describes communication of gender through culturally defined mannerisms, clothing, hairstyle, and so forth. Part of gender expression is people's pronouns, which might be he/him/his, she/her/hers, ze/zir/zirs, and they/them/their/theirs or another pronoun combination. There are numerous pronouns that people might use, and conjugations can be different. Sexuality is a combination of a minimum of three factors: sexual orientation, sexual identity, and sexual behavior. *Sexual orientation* can be understood as who one is attracted to. *Sexual identity* is often conflated with sexual orientation, but they are different. Sexual identity is how one's sexuality is described on the basis of one's sexual orientation, race, age, culture, political affiliation, and internalized homophobia or biphobia. *Sexual behavior* simply describes a person's sexual activities with men, women, genderqueer folk, more than one gender, or no one.

When leading training sessions on sexuality or gender, instructors should allow time for questions so that participants can process their thoughts and feelings. It is important that facilitators use correct language (e.g., *woman* for gender, *female* for sex) to minimize confusion for participants. It is also important for facilitators to prepare for the variety of feelings that can come up for individuals during the training. Creating a space of safety for participants is essential. For many participants, this may be their first time thinking about gender and sexuality in a nuanced way. It may also be their first time examining the privileges of their identities. As such, guilt, shame, anger, and confusion are common feelings participants might experience. It is important to be prepared for these arising feelings and to allow time to process them.

Before facilitating learning about gender and sexual diversity with one's audience, it is important that MHPs review the traditional cultural understanding of gender and sexuality which is rooted in a binary model of sexuality and gender (Johnson & Repta, 2012). Within the binary model, only two options are available for each of the categories: sex (male or female), gender (man or woman), gender expression (masculine or feminine), and sexual identity (heterosexual or gay/lesbian, which is solely based on one's sexual attractions or orientation and behaviors). It is important to note that a binary approach views biological sex as predictive not only of gender identity and expression but also of one's sexual orientation, sexual identity, and sexual behavior. In other words, if someone is assigned as male at birth, the binary model imposes expectations that this person will identify as a man, be masculine, be attracted to women, have sexual relations with women, and identify as heterosexual. These expectations and norms are powerful and can greatly inhibit and negatively affect those who experience authenticity outside the traditional sexuality and gender binary.

The goal of instruction early on in the training is to begin to problematize culture's traditional understandings of gender and sexuality. Because the binary model limits a greater understanding of gender, it is important for instructors to only review this model briefly with their audience members (so as to not spend time reinforcing it). Instructors should spend more time explaining the spectrums model of sex, gender, and sexuality, which is discussed in the upcoming sections. As instructors are preparing their audience for a more inclusive understanding of gender and sexuality, it is important for attendees to see that the traditional model inevitably excludes the experience and identities of many, not simply individuals who may self-identify as LGBQ or GET. Activity 8.1 is a brief free-association writing exercise that is designed to accompany the explanation of the binary model. Instructors should openly ask learners to share as much as they feel comfortable sharing. Instructors might explain to learners that by openly considering their identities and experiences in relation to the binary model they can further strengthen their understanding of its limitations.

Contemporary discussions about gender have argued that sex cannot be seen as wholly predictive of one's gender (Dreger, 1998; Fausto-Sterling, 1993, 2000; Harris, 2005). Sex, gender identity, gender expression, sexual orientation, sexual identity, and sexual behavior must be seen as distinct from one another while also having the capacity to connect, group, and align in many unique ways. An expansive model, the spectrums model of sex, gender, and sexuality (Cathers, 2012), offers a more expansive representation and is visually represented in Figure 8.1. This model was developed from the Klein Sexual Orientation Grid (Klein, 1993) and Storms's (1980) bidimensional model of sexuality and the Gender Unicorn (Trans Student Educational Resources, 2016). In the spectrums model of sex, gender, and sexuality, sex, gender identity, gender expression, sexual orientation, sexual identity, and sexual behavior are divided into a three-axis system. The third axis is time, which allows attendees to learn how these attributes can change over time. Rather than having all aspects of gender and sexuality defined solely by biological sex, each graph represents a different aspect of a person.

Individuals can be located on any one graph with a small point or a large shape, depending on how static or fluid that particular attribute is for

FIGURE 8.1

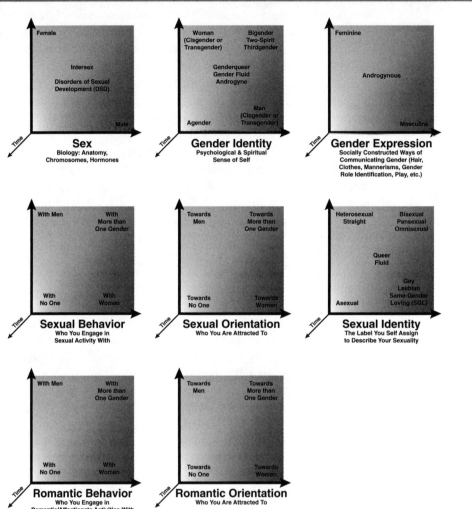

Spectrums model of sex, gender, and sexuality (see Cathers, 2012).

an individual. The graph has an axis for time to signify how individuals' identities can change over time. For example, someone may be attracted to and sexually active with women during his/her/zir/their adolescence and early adulthood but later come out as bisexual and have attractions and sexual behaviors with men and women in middle and late adulthood.

Activity 8.2 offers various options for using the spectrums model of sex, gender, and sexuality (Figure 8.1) as a teaching tool in community-based settings. Teaching this model can be done in a multitude of ways, but it is important to note that because of its complexity (compared with the binary model), people can struggle to follow and expand their thinking. For this reason, instructors should develop a strong understanding of this model before attempting to teach it. It is recommended that instructors take time to gain comprehension of this model by thoroughly applying it to themselves. In addition, they are encouraged to practice teaching this model to their colleagues and requesting feedback in areas in which they might have to offer more clarity. Adequate practice and preparation will ensure that instructors have the knowledge and skills to teach this model effectively and field their audience members' questions.

Depending on how much time is available and how large the audience is, the instructor can either present the model (as a handout or in a presentation) and lecture on the topic, or the instructor can draw empty three-axis grids with the labels at the bottom (sex, gender identity, gender expression, sexual orientation, sexual identity, and sexual behavior). The instructor can then work with the audience to fill in the graphs with the axes and also show where certain labels may fall on each graph. It is important that instructors explain each separate graph in detail to provide clarification to audience members. If comfortable, instructors may disclose where they fall on each of the graphs or invite people to do the same. Audience members can be asked to think about their location on the graphs. Alternatively, depending on their comfort level, audience members can be broken into small groups or dyads where they can share with one another as they feel comfortable where they fall on each of the graphs.

Usually, instructors need 45 minutes to over 2 hours to teach this model, depending on how interactive the audience is, how detailed the instructor is, how knowledgeable the audience is, and how much discussion the instructor and the attendees generate about other related concepts. The length of discussion may also depend on participants' comfort in disclosing personal information. Throughout this exercise, it is important to gauge the audience's level of comfort and always remind members that self-disclosure is optional.

When explaining the spectrums model of sex, gender, and sexuality, educators should be certain to highlight the following key elements. To describe sex, instructors should point out that the vertical axis represents biological characteristics that are typically seen with people assigned as female at birth (estrogen, vagina, breast development, etc.). The horizontal axis represents biological characteristics in individuals who are assigned as male at birth (testosterone, penis, testicles, facial hair, etc.). Clarifying these axes can lead the audience into a conversation about intersex people or people with differences of sexual development. These are called disorders of sexual development in some literature. Intersex people have chromosomal differences (e.g., XXY sex chromosomes), hormonal differences (e.g., androgen insensitivity syndrome), or anatomical differences (e.g., a child born with a scrotum divided into two, so it resembles a labia). For gender identity, the horizontal axis represents a psychological sense of oneself as a man, whereas the vertical axis represents a sense of oneself as a woman. Identification as a woman is separate from female sex. Both transgender and cisgender women fall within the gender identification of woman. Individuals may be represented on the graph as identifying strongly as both man and woman (and may identify as bigender, two-spirit, third gender, or other label), or individuals may not strongly identify as either a man or woman (and may self-label as agender, nongender, or other term). Individuals who identify with a combination of man and woman may identify as genderqueer, gender nonconforming, genderfluid, androgyne, genderfuck, or other label.

In addition to the axes on the figure, educators can begin to explore the similarities and differences between related concepts. For example, gender expression can be feminine, masculine, or androgynous, and many individuals may make the assumption that a man who presents with feminine gender expression is gay or that a woman who presents with masculine gender expression is a lesbian. Both of these assumptions reinforce the binary model and instructors can facilitate a discussion of how people have likely made these assumptions.

Facilitation of a discussion about how transphobia, homophobia, biphobia, and misogyny are intertwined in these assumptions can be helpful here as well. Misogyny plays into why feminine men and transgender women often face more discrimination than masculine women and transgender men. Another assumption that can be discussed is that an individual who is born female and who has sex with women must identify as a lesbian. This assumption might be challenged by reminding audience members that this individual might identify as bisexual. The instructor might further explain that such an assumption can result in *bisexual erasure*, when people who identify as bisexual are often made invisible in society. Opportunities to explore assumptions often arise when educating about these topics in community settings.

It is also important that audience members understand that language related to sexuality and gender can often intersect and be affected by individuals' multiple and intersecting identities, as well as additional contextual and personal factors (Cole, 2009). Race, ethnicity, age, religion, geographic location, internalized homophobia or biphobia, and other cultural factors influence the language that someone uses to self-identify their sexuality. As such, discussion about how these can influence individuals' identities can expand participants' learning even further. For example, *pansexual* and *omnisexual* both describe someone who is attracted to more than one gender. In addition, *same-gender-loving* is another label to describe men of color who are attracted to men. This specific identity emerged as a result of many men of color (who were attracted to men) feeling that the term *gay* was too commonly associated with White men who are attracted to men. *Queer* is a term that may still be considered offensive by older individuals but has been reclaimed by younger generations. All of these nuances can help to further expand your audience's understanding of the spectrum of gender and sexual identities, their intersection with cultural identities, and the corresponding terminology.

Sexual orientation, sexual identity, and sexual behavior are further separated to describe sexuality. Although *sexual orientation* refers to whom someone is attracted, and *sexual behavior* refers to whom someone is engaging in sexual activity with, these are often collapsed into *sexual identity*. It is important for instructors to highlight the complexity of sexual identity. For example, many individuals assume that as soon as a man has had any sexual activity with another man, he must be gay. Not only does this conflate behavior with identity and orientation, but it also reinforces a binary understanding of gender and sexuality, while also resulting in bisexual erasure. It is possible that this man may have had sexual activity with another man due to particular circumstances (e.g., prison culture, experimenting in college). As such, this man's behavior does not necessarily mean that he will or has adopted a gay or bisexual identity. It is possible that audience members struggle with ideas such as this. Depending on the community setting, we have found that it can be a novel concept for participants that someone might have sexual behavior that does not align with their sexual orientation. Again, it is important to take time and to promote a space of safety and curiosity to explore these assumptions.

Inclusive Language

When leading a training on gender and sexual diversity, it is important for instructors to use the most current terminology and inclusive language. The traditional use of language around gender and sexuality has been rooted in the language of the binary (Fausto-Sterling, 2000). This excludes the diversity of experiences and identities that do not fit within this language. For this reason, constructing new language has been and continues to be essential for the identity development of gender diverse and sexually diverse communities, as well as their inclusion in dominant culture.

When teaching your audience about language, it is important to convey that the use of appropriate and inclusive language for specific GET and LGBQ communities provides a container or accurate signification for individual community members' experience and/or self-concept (i.e., identity). Such language also conveys respect and, when used, often signals some level of relational safety for LGBQ and GET individuals. When used by others (e.g., friend, parent, doctor, teacher) or within the dominant culture (e.g., political or legal system), language has the power to recognize and validate or foreclose and invalidate the lived reality of another (Lev, 2004). For this reason, language is incredibly important in the GET and LGBQ communities. When running an event, training session, or community organizing session, we recommend your nametags include a location for both name and gender pronouns (e.g., he/him/his, she/her/hers, they/them/their/theirs, ze/zir/zirs). Activity 8.3 provides an example of nametags that can be used by participants.

It is also important to be aware of the many identities and corresponding words and definitions that have emerged from and have been created by GET and LGBQ communities. Research shows that an awareness of inclusive, respectful, and correct terminology not only respects the diversity of gender, sexual experiences, and identities but also reduces individual and communal microaggressions toward GET and LGBQ individuals (Nadal, Rivera, & Corpus, 2010). *Microaggressions* can be understood as subtle forms of discrimination that are often unconscious within the person speaking but can result in experiences of minority stress by GET and LGBQ individuals. A matching quiz can be used to educate about language used in GET and LGBQ communities. A sample quiz is included in Activity 8.4. This can be used to introduce and educate audience members about inclusive and appropriate language. Facilitators can make their own versions to update the quiz. Terms may be removed or added because language is always evolving and changing as society changes. Instructors can also adjust the quiz's length to fit within the amount of time they have available for their training.

Heteronormativity and Cissexism

Microaggressions can also result from the unquestioned assumptions that individuals have about others and what culture considers normative gender and sexuality. The cultural assumption that all individuals fall neatly into the gender binary is understood as *cissexism*, and the assumption that all individuals are heterosexual is *heteronormativity*. Combined with these types of oppression is the generalized assumption that an individual with "male" genitalia must hold a gender identity as a man, perform stereotypical "male" roles, be attracted to (its binary opposite) "females," identify as heterosexual, and engage in sexual expression solely with females. Activity 8.5 can help learners to identify these assumptions.

It is important for educators teaching about gender and sexual diversity to help community-based learners realize that heteronormativity and cissexism are often unconscious. The beliefs, attitudes, and assumptions within culture manage social behavior and enforce understandings of a "normative" sexuality and gender. Heteronormativity is consistently created and maintained by our cultural "institutions, structures of understanding, and practical orientations" making heterosexuality and binary genders "seem not only coherent . . . but also *privileged*" (Berlant & Warner, 1998, p. 548). They are privileged in that they have come to "possess implicit norm status in our society" (Prieto, 2009, pp. 30–31). Binary genders and heterosexuality serve as an "unquestioned bases for which other demographic traits are explicitly judged and compared against" (Prieto, 2009, pp. 30–31). This can be easily seen in the current binary cultural options such as men's or women's restrooms, which privilege cisgender bodies. Further, heteronormativity and cissexism can be seen in the assumption that only people with cis-female bodies need baby-changing tables in their restrooms. One might also argue that this is a reflection of cultural sexism.

When teaching gender and sexual diversity, it is important for MHPs to develop an awareness of the ways in which our culture, professional mental health field, and even our institutions promote heteronormativity. Activity 8.6, Heteronormativity and Cissexism Bingo, includes examples of heteronormativity and cissexism. After reviewing the activity, instructors may feel that alternate examples would be more fitting for specific community members. If this is the case, they are encouraged to revise the provided bingo game. In our work within community settings, we have found that this activity strengthens participants' understanding of these concepts while also being somewhat enjoyable.

Heterosexual and Monosexual Privileges

Heteronormativity is a cultural phenomenon that leads to heterosexual people having privileges that LGBQ people do not have, whereas cisgender privilege (discussed further later) gives privileges to cisgender people that GET people do not have. Individuals with monosexual identities (straight, gay, and lesbian) have privileges that individuals with non-monosexual identities (e.g., bisexual, pansexual, omnisexual) do not have, and in many cases, monosexual individuals do not realize they have these privileges (Case, Hensley, & Anderson, 2014).

When discussing heterosexual and monosexual privileges, some attendees of community-based workshops and learning environments can feel a great deal of guilt for having privileges they did not previously know they had. It is important to allow these feelings to enter the learning environment while still creating mutual space for the LGBQ and GET individuals (who have an intersecting LGBQ identity) to share their experiences. It is also essential that the LGBQ and GET people in the room do not become tokenized by being asked questions about being LGBQ and GET. To help prevent tokenization, instructors can share with audience members that "feeling tokenized" can often be the experience of LGBQ and GET individuals when they are called out in such situations. If instructors still find that participants tokenize LGBQ and/or GET individuals in the audience, it can be helpful for instructors to gently to point it out in a way that avoids shaming while protecting the tokenized audience member. For example, initiating responses such as, "Do you know that all individuals in that community feel as you state, or might there be another perspective?" Instructors must also aim to develop the ability to answer participants' questions while being attuned to the presence of possible homophobia, biphobia, and privilege that may be inherent in their inquiries. The instructor should aim to shed light on the possible bias while holding a position of non-judgment and curiosity. The exploration of bias in a non-shaming way is essential when exploring privilege and is key as instructors seek to expand participant worldviews.

Providing a list of different examples of privilege can be helpful in pointing out ways that society has offered privilege to some but not to others. Activity 8.7 is a list of heterosexual and monosexual privileges and can be used as a teaching tool. Additional lists for other identities that are outside the scope of this chapter (e.g., non-monogamy) can be found online, and these activities can be adapted to them.

Cisgender Privilege

In the dominant culture, those who are heterosexual do not often have to think about their sexual identity. Their identities are assumed to be normative and thus can fade into the background of their life. In other words, it is a privilege to be unaware. When it comes to gender, cisgender people have this privilege. They make choices throughout the day that assume safety, acceptance, and respect that GET people do not consistently receive. Gaining understanding of how GET people deal with lack of privilege can be a useful way for cisgender individuals to develop more empathy and compassion for the gender diverse experience.

Activity 8.8, Cisgender Privilege, can help facilitate a discussion about how easily a cisgender person can function in our world and maintain emotional wellness compared with a GET person who, throughout the day, has to maintain consistent vigilance to remain safe.

Assessing Participant Learning

To assess the acquired learning and/or satisfaction of audience members following training, instructors may choose to administer an evaluation, or posttest. Evaluations should include questions that include evaluation about both the training content and process. Specifically, assessment should reflect an audience member's perceptions of the instructor's teaching style, competence, and/or responsiveness to participant questions and comments. Additional evaluation questions could also assess how audience members will apply their new understanding of LGBQ and GET individuals within their communities. These questions may also assess whether the participants feel that their knowledge about these populations has increased and/or whether they would recommend the training to others. When evaluating an audience's experience of a facilitated training session, we often use questions with numbered Likert scales. This allows us to later perform statistics on data reflecting audience members' satisfaction and gain more quantifiable clarity on where we might strengthen our training for the future. Instructors may also choose to administer a posttest to assess acquired knowledge, skills, and changes to attitudes and/or beliefs following the training. Such posttest questions can be constructed from specific content used in the training and can include fill-in-the-blank or multiple-choice responses.

Conclusion

When children are born into a binary society, their sex, gender, and sexuality are conflated, and, as a result, they are subject to binary "rules": names; pronouns; clothing; what colors you like; what public spaces, including bathrooms and locker rooms, you should use; how your emotional life should be experienced and how you should express it; what courses in school should be interesting to you; what profession you should hope to embark on; and even who you should be attracted to and develop intimate romantic relationships with. The activities we have presented are meant to shift the view and experience we have of our society. They illustrate that sex and gender must be understood as distinct and that the traditional understanding we have been taught to assume is limited and limiting. These activities are meant for the audience to expand their awareness of the diversity of ways individuals in our society can express gender and sexuality and also understand that they may have a more diverse definition of self than they had previously realized. By recognizing and accepting these differences, it is our hope that communities will promote and applaud inclusion and not accept exclusion. It is also our hope that these tools might inspire and be tested in future research to shape further efficacy for educating about LGBTQ people and their experiences and culture within community settings.

ACTIVITY 8.1

Exploring the Limitations of the Binary Model

Directions: This activity can be done with small or large groups. Allow time for participants to process the information presented and ask questions.

Read the following statement aloud:

The binary model of gender and sexuality has been assumed because of the belief that gender and sexual identity are biologically based. For example, a baby is born, male genitalia are immediately identified, and the child is assigned a male gender and socialized to be masculine. Such work appears to be a "natural" conclusion. Biology is seen as determinative of one's gender, further resulting in gender and sex being seen as synonymous. Sex and gender are conflated in an attempt to bring order to a diverse world. As such, order is found when a body with a penis is labeled boy, and a body with a vagina is labeled girl.

Spend some time in your group discussing the following questions:

1. How does the gender binary view transgender, genderqueer, or gender nonconforming individuals? Or does it ignore them entirely?
2. In what ways do you fit into the binary?
3. In what ways do you not fit into the binary?
4. When you haven't fit into the binary, how have other people reacted?
5. How have you felt oppressed or restricted by the binary model?
6. In what ways have you enforced the binary in yourself? In others?

ACTIVITY 8.2

Spectrums Model of Sex, Gender, and Sexuality

Directions: The goal of this activity is to have participants gain an understanding of the spectrums model of sex, gender, and sexuality (Cathers, 2012; see Figure 8.1) through application and discussion. There are a few variations of this activity, depending on how many people you have in the group and time constraints:

1. Leaders can create a large poster of the graphs and vocabulary words provided in this chapter. Participants can then place the words onto the graphs (with tape or markers), and the facilitator can correct and discuss as words are placed on the graphs.
2. Leaders can print out blank copies of the graphs for each participant to fill out by themselves or fill out within a small group. Discussion can center on how people struggled with placing the words correctly on each graph.
3. Leaders can also draw or post the graph on the board and ask several participants to graph their identities and expressions in different colored markers.
4. Audience members can also be asked to graph themselves on a single sheet of paper while remaining seated and then decide if they want to share what they learned about themselves.

ACTIVITY 8.3

Sample Name Tag

NAME

PREFERRED PRONOUN

Preferred Pronoun Examples		
Subjective Case	Objective Case	Possessive Case
He	Him	His
She	Her	Her/Hers
Ze	Zir	Zir/Zirs
They	Them	Their/Theirs

ACTIVITY 8.4

LGBTQ Language Quiz

Match the following words with their corresponding definition.

Advocate	Affirm	Ally
Androgynous	Asexual	BDSM
Bear	Bisexual erasure	Binding
Biological sex	Biphobia	Bisexual
Bottom	Cisgender	Coming out
Cross dresser	Disorder of sexual development (DSD)	Drag king
Drag queen		Dyke
Gay	Gender binary system	Gender dysphoria
Gender expression	Gender identity	Genderqueer
Heteronormativity	HIV stigma	Homophobia
Intersex or differences of sexual development	Lesbian	Non-monogamy
Omnisexual	Open relationship	Packing
Pansexual	Polyamorous	Queer
Same gender loving	Social transition	Stud
Switch	Top	Transgender and gender expansive
Transgender	Transition	Transphobia

1. A person who actively works to end intolerance and educate others and who supports social equity for a group or groups.
2. Someone who confronts heterosexism, homophobia, biphobia, transphobia, heterosexual, and genderstraight privilege in themselves and others; a concern for the well-being of lesbian, gay, bisexual, transgender and gender expansive (GET), and intersex people; and a belief that heterosexism, homophobia, biphobia, and transphobia are social justice issues.
3. Refers to having honest, usually nonpossessive relationships with multiple partners; this can include open relationships, polyfidelity (which involves multiple romantic relationships with sexual contact restricted to those), and subrelationships (which denote distinguishing between a "primary" relationship or relationships and various "secondary" relationships; Green & Peterson, 2006).
4. Refers to people's understandings of themselves regarding gender categories such as man and woman, boy and girl, transgender, genderqueer, and many others.
5. The external presentation of gender, through clothing, idiosyncrasies, social behavior, and other factors, which may or may not conform to socially defined behaviors and characteristics typically associated with being either masculine or feminine (Human Rights Campaign, n.d.).
6. A persistent distress with one's physical sex characteristics or assigned birth sex role (TransYouth Family Allies, 2008).
7. Historically, this was a derogatory term used for LGBTQ individuals. This term has recently been reclaimed by many within the LGBTQ community and is used as an umbrella term to include anyone who feels that their identity or self-expression lands outside societal norms for gender or sexuality.

ACTIVITY 8.4 (*Continued*)

8. A gender expansive person whose gender identity is neither male nor female, is between or beyond genders, or is some combination of genders. Often includes a political agenda to challenge gender stereotypes and the gender-binary system (Green & Peterson, 2006).

9. A person presenting with a gender expression that is either mixed or neutral (Green & Peterson, 2006).

10. Someone who wears clothes of another gender/sex (Green & Peterson, 2006).

11. Anyone whose gender identity and/or gender expression differs significantly from what is expected of them in their culture based on their sex assigned at birth. This broad category includes transgender, transsexual and genderqueer people, cross-dressers, drag queens and kings, masculine women and feminine men, and more (Think Again Training and Consultation, 2014).

12. Describes people whose gender identity matches the biological sex they were assigned at birth (Think Again Training and Consultation, 2014).

13. A traditional dualistic view of gender that limits options to "man" and "woman."

14. The process by which one accepts someone else's sex, sexuality, or gender identity. This can be a continual, life-long process for gay, lesbian, bisexual, queer, GET, and intersex individuals (Green & Peterson, 2006).

15. Can refer to any of the medical, social, legal, spiritual, and personal processes a GET person may go through to live their life in a way that feels congruent with their internal sense of gender (Think Again Training and Consultation, 2014).

16. Changes in appearances, presentation, pronouns, name, and/or other arenas to express one's gender identity (TransYouth Family Allies, 2008).

17. A man who has facial/body hair and a cuddly body. However, this term means many things to different people, even within the movement. Many men who do not have one or all of these characteristics define themselves as such, making the term a loose one. This term is often defined as more of an attitude and a sense of comfort with natural masculinity and bodies (Green & Peterson, 2006).

18. A person who identifies as someone who is emotionally, romantically, and/or sexually attracted to more than one gender. This attraction does not have to be equally split between genders, and there may be a preference for one gender or gender expression (Green & Peterson, 2006).

19. A person who is said to take a more dominant role during sexual interactions (Green & Peterson, 2006).

20. The assumption, in individuals or institutions, that everyone is heterosexual, and that heterosexuality is superior to homosexuality and bisexuality (Green & Peterson, 2006).

21. A type of interpersonal relationship in which an individual forms multiple and simultaneous sexual or romantic bonds ("Non-Monogamy," 2015).

22. Sometimes referred to as *leather*, this includes deriving pleasure from inflicting or receiving pain, often in a sexual context, and playing with various power roles in both a sexual and social context. These practices are often misunderstood as abusive but when practiced in a safe, sane, and consensual manner can be a part of healthy sex life (Green & Peterson, 2006).

23. The medical terminology for the group of congenital conditions of intersex people. Many intersex people dislike this phrase ("Disorders of Sex Development," 2015).

24. This may refer to the process by which one accepts one's sex, gender identity, or sexuality, or it may also refer to the process by which one shares one's sex, sexuality, and/or gender identity with others. This can be a continual, life-long process for lesbian, gay, bisexual, transgender, queer, questioning, intersex, and asexual people (Green & Peterson, 2006).

25. The process of flattening one's breasts to have a more masculine or flat-appearing chest (Green & Peterson, 2006).

(*continued*)

26. A person who performs femininity theatrically (Green & Peterson, 2006).
27. Wearing a phallic device on the groin and under clothing for any purpose, including the validation or confirmation of one's masculine gender identity (for someone without a biological penis), seduction, and/or sexual readiness (for one who likes to penetrate another during sexual intercourse; Green & Peterson, 2006).
28. The fear of, discrimination against, or hatred of bisexuals, which is often related to the current binary standard. This can be seen within the gay and lesbian community, as well as in general society (Green & Peterson, 2006).
29. The irrational fear of those who are gender variant and/or the inability to deal with gender ambiguity (Green & Peterson, 2006).
30. A term sometimes used by members of the African American/Black community to express an alternative sexual orientation without relying on terms and symbols of European descent. The term emerged in the early 1990s with the intention of offering Black women who love women and Black men who love men a voice, a way of identifying and being that resonated with the uniqueness of Black culture (Green & Peterson, 2006).
31. A person who identifies as a member of a gender other than the one associated with the sex they were assigned at birth (Green & Peterson, 2006).
32. A person who is said to take a more submissive role during sexual interactions (Green & Peterson, 2006).
33. A person who is not sexually attracted to anyone or does not have a sexual orientation (Green & Peterson, 2006).
34. A masculine African American and/or Latina lesbian (Green & Peterson, 2006).
35. An interpersonal relationship in which the parties agree that a romantic or intimate relationship with another person is accepted, permitted, or tolerated. The parties involved have two or more romantic or sexual relationships occurring at the same time either as a short-term relationship such as dating or a long-term relationship such as marriage ("Open Relationship," 2015).
36. A variation in sex characteristics including chromosomes, gonads, or genitals that do not allow an individual to be distinctly identified as male or female. Such variation may involve genital ambiguity, and combinations of chromosomal genotype and sexual phenotype other than XY-male and XX-female (Intersex Society of North America, 2008).
37. A person who is sexually attracted to all or many gender expressions. This word is derived from an Ancient Greek term meaning "all" or "every" (Green & Peterson, 2006).
38. A person who is both a "top" and a "bottom"; there may or may not be a preference for one or the other (Green & Peterson, 2006).
39. A term used in some cultural settings to represent males who are attracted to males in a romantic, erotic, and/or emotional sense, though not all men who engage in "homosexual behavior" identify as this, and as such this label should be used with caution. It is also used to refer to the LGBTQI community as a whole or as an individual identity label for anyone who does not identify as heterosexual (Green & Peterson, 2006).
40. The tendency to ignore, remove, falsify, or reexplain evidence of bisexuality in history, academia, news media, and other primary sources. In its most extreme form, this can include denying that bisexuality exists. It is often a manifestation of biphobia, although it does not necessarily involve overt antagonism ("Bisexual Erasure," 2015).
41. A person who performs masculinity theatrically (Green & Peterson, 2006).

ACTIVITY 8.4 (*Continued*)

42. The irrational fear or hatred of homosexuals, homosexuality, or any behavior or belief that does not conform to rigid sex role stereotypes. It is this fear that enforces sexism as well as heterosexism (Green & Peterson, 2006).
43. The physical structure of one's reproductive organs that is used to assign sex at birth, additionally determined by chromosomes, hormones, and internal and external genitalia. Must be seen as a spectrum or range of possibilities rather than a binary set of two options (Gender Spectrum, 2015).
44. Used to refer to lesbians, most often those with masculine gender expression. Although often derogatory, it has been reclaimed by some who might use it to self-identify. Unless it is someone's identity, it is considered rude to use this word (Green & Peterson, 2006).
45. Another term to describe someone who is attracted to "all genders." The word is derived from the Latin meaning "all."
46. The experience of discrimination by those infected or affected by HIV or AIDS.
47. A term to describe a person who identifies as a woman (regardless of her biological sex) and is attracted to women.

Answers

1	Advocate	14	Affirm	2	Ally
9	Androgynous	33	Asexual	22	BDSM
17	Bear	40	Bisexual erasure	25	Binding
43	Biological sex	28	Biphobia	18	Bisexual
32	Bottom	12	Cisgender	24	Coming out
10	Cross dresser	23	Disorder of sexual development (DSD)	41	Drag king
26	Drag queen			44	Dyke
39	Gay	13	Gender binary system	6	Gender dysphoria
5	Gender expression	4	Gender identity	8	Genderqueer
20	Heteronormativity	46	HIV stigma	42	Homophobia
36	Intersex or differences of sexual development	47	Lesbian	21	Non-monogamy
45	Omnisexual	35	Open relationship	27	Packing
37	Pansexual	3	Polyamorous	7	Queer
30	Same gender loving	16	Social transition	34	Stud
38	Switch	19	Top	11	Transgender and gender expansive
31	Transgender	15	Transition	29	Transphobia

ACTIVITY 8.5

Ten Assumptions About Males and Females

Directions: Each column has 10 rows. Take 90 seconds to write down the first 10 things that come to mind that describe males and females in each column respectively. Do not spend too much time thinking about it or try to censor yourself. Just write down the first thing that comes to mind about the word *male* under the column labeled *Male* and the first thing that comes to mind about the word *female* under the column labeled *Female*. If you cannot come up with any more terms, leave the rest of the rows blank.

Female	Male
1	1
2	2
3	3
4	4
5	5
6	6
7	7
8	8
9	9
10	10

After 90 seconds, have the participants break into dyads or small groups to discuss their lists and ask them the following discussion questions.

1. *Sex* is a term describing the biology of a person. These characteristics include anatomy, hormones, and chromosomes, and the most common categories include male and female. People who do not neatly fit into the category of male or female are called intersex. How many characteristics were actually related to sex?
2. *Gender identity* refers to a person's psychology and spiritual sense of being a man, woman, both, neither, or something else entirely. How many characteristics were actually related to gender identity?
3. *Gender expression* refers to how people communicate gender. This is culturally defined. How masculinity is defined in the Unites States is different from how it is defined in Asia or Africa. Gender expression includes hairstyle, clothing, voice intonations, gait, interests, and hobbies. It is divided into masculine, feminine, and androgynous. How many characteristics were actually related to gender expression?
4. *Sexuality* refers to a variety of things, including sexual behavior, sexual orientation, and sexual identity. *Sexual behavior* describes who someone is having sex with (e.g., with men), *Sexual orientation* describes someone's attractions (e.g., toward men), and *sexual identity* is the term someone uses to describe his or her sexuality (e.g., lesbian, gay, bisexual, heterosexual). How many characteristics were actually related to sexuality?
5. How are these words limiting to people who don't fit the binary?
6. Any personal reactions to differentiating sex, gender, gender expression, and sexuality?

ACTIVITY 8.6

Heteronormativity and Cissexism Bingo

Directions: This activity works best in larger groups and can be a great icebreaker. Give each member of your audience a bingo card. They will have to mingle with other members of the group and find others who can answer the questions or affirm the statements in the boxes. When someone can affirm a statement, they write his/her/zir/their name in the box. A person can only provide one answer for the full board. First person to GET five in a row wins! After the game, discuss with the group what thoughts and feelings came up for them while playing the game. Can audience members identify other areas of their life (home, places of work, school, and religious spaces) where heteronormativity and cissexism is present?

Can you find someone who . . . ?				
B	I	N	G	O
Has a gender neutral bath-room at work or school	Can give an example of an LGBTQ couple in an advertisement	Learned about sexual diver-sity in high school health class	Was asked by someone "Are you married?" in the last month	Can name two lesbian TV characters
Can name a bisexual celebrity	Knows someone who was kicked out of the house for being LGBTQ	Has been part of a gendered baby shower	Can sing a song about a boy/man and girl/woman falling in love	Has been stared at when affectionate in public with a significant other
Grew up watch-ing Disney princess movies	Has been teased or gossiped about because of gender expression	FREE SPACE	Has been stopped and told by a stranger that he/she/ze/they were walking into the wrong bathroom	Had parents who assumed he/she/ze/they were heterosexual
Has some diverse gender expres-sion (e.g., man with long hair, woman who likes cars)	Has seen an elder LGBTQ couple holding hands in public	Has played with at least three gender neutral toys as a child	Doesn't want to have children	Has been misgendered
Knows at least two stay-at-home dads	Knows what the term *gender-queer* means	Knows a religious space that welcomes LGBTQ individuals	Has been made fun of because of his/her/zir/their gendered job (e.g., male teacher, female construction worker)	Knows someone who is HIV+

Heterosexual and Monosexual Privilege

Directions: This teaching tool works best in groups of 15 to 30, so if you have a larger group, you may choose to have some volunteers demonstrate in front of the group or have people just stand up rather than step forward. If you are using the stepping forward method, make sure that you have enough room for everyone to spread out. It may be important for you to alert participants that they might disclose information in this activity and that it is up to individual participants whether they want to disclose or not.

Read the following statement: "Privileges are unearned benefits someone gains on the basis of their perceived identity. Heterosexual and monosexual privilege include all the unearned privileges that are gained simply for being heterosexual or monosexual, respectively. The following activity helps people see the ways they might have privilege as a heterosexual that lesbian, gay, bisexual, and queer people might not have. Many people do not realize that they have privilege. Heterosexual, gay, and lesbian people have monosexual privileges that bisexual, pansexual, omnisexual, queer, fluid, or other identities don't have. I am going to read some statements and if the statement is true, please step forward (or for large groups, stand up and sit down when asked)."

After the activity, a pattern should develop in which some people (who identify more as straight) will have moved farther ahead than other participants. Gay and lesbian people have monosexual privilege, so they may have stepped forward in some places that bisexual people did not. Discuss with the group what their experiences were of learning about where they might have privilege that they did not know they had (or lack of it).

1. I can kiss, hug, or hold hands with my partner(s) in public without fear of being objectified or fetishized.
2. I don't fear hostile or potentially violent reactions from others when I am affectionate with my partner.
3. I can easily find role models that represent my sexuality.
4. I have been accepted by my family.
5. I have been accepted by my friends.
6. I have never been asked about how I have sex with my partner by strangers.
7. I have never been asked to join a threesome because of my sexual identity.
8. I have never been fired from my job because of my sexuality.
9. I have never been evicted from my housing because of my sexuality.
10. I have never had to be concerned that if my partner was in the hospital, I might not be able to be at his or her bedside.
11. I have never had to worry that if my spouse were to pass away, I wouldn't inherit our mutual assets.
12. I have never had my basic civil rights denied because of my sexuality.
13. I have never had anyone call me a "dyke," "faggot," or other slur based on sexuality.
14. I have never been called a "slut," "whore," or other slur based on the fact that I am attracted to more than one gender.
15. I have been able to find community resources for people who have the same sexual identity as me.
16. I have been able to move to another part of the country without worrying about my safety or that my legal rights have changed because of my sexuality.
17. I have never worried that my partner couldn't be the legal guardian of the child we are raising together.
18. No one has ever asked me when I knew what my sexual orientation or identity is.
19. I have never needed to defend my sexuality to anyone.
20. I have never thought that I will leave my partner for someone of another gender.
21. I have never worried about telling my doctor or therapist about my sexuality for fear of being shamed.
22. I have never felt tokenized because of my sexuality.

ACTIVITY 8.8

Cisgender Privilege

Directions: This teaching tool works best in groups of 15 to 30. There are two different ways instructors can implement this exercise. One way is by having audience members stand, line up, and take a step forward each time they identify with a statement read by the instructor. Another method is to have audience members stay at their seats and simply stand up when they identify with a statement read. Depending on the method chosen, it can be helpful for instructors to demonstrate briefly what is expected from the audience. If you are using the stepping forward method, make sure you have enough room for individuals to spread out. In addition, it is important to make sure that the activity is accessible for everyone; instructors might say something like, "If it is difficult or physically uncomfortable for you to walk (or stand up), we welcome you to find another way to participate that works for you." If you have a smaller group, you might choose to have the participants read the statements aloud and process each of them as you go along. Because some audience members may not feel safe or comfortable with the level of self-disclosure required for this exercise, instructors should always give participants the option of not participating.

Read the following statement: "Privileges are unearned benefits that someone gains on the basis of their perceived identity. Cisgender means that one has a gender identity which aligns with the sex they were assigned at birth. Cisgender privilege is, therefore, all the unearned privileges that are gained simply for having this alignment. The following activity aims to highlight the privileges that cisgender individuals have and that gender expansive and transgender (GET) individuals do not have."

The instructor should state, "By participating in this activity, you may disclose some personal information about yourself. We encourage you to take care of yourself and decide what you feel safe disclosing as you participate in this activity. It is OK if you choose not to participate and simply reflect on the exercise as others participate. Please pay attention to what you are feeling during the activity. I am going to read some statements. If the statement is true for you, then please step forward" (or, if using the other method, "please stand up." Participants should then sit down before the next statement).

After the activity is completed, a pattern should have developed in which most cisgender individuals will have moved farther ahead of GET participants (or if using the stand-up method, participants with more privileges will have stood more). Discuss with the group what their experiences were during the exercise. What did they learn? Are there privileges they did not know they possessed? Are there privileges they realized they lack compared with other participants? Instructors might also choose to have participants initially debrief in smaller groups before facilitating a larger group discussion.

Cisgender Privileges Activity

Below is a list of 25 cisgender privileges. We suggest reading 15 to 25 privileges for this activity.

1. Please step forward if you are able to use a public restroom without fear of violence or harassment because of your gender identity or perceived gender identity.
2. Please step forward if the gender and the name listed on your driver's license match your gender identity and your name.
3. Please step forward if you can tell others your name without being asked what your "real," "legal," or birth name is.

(continued)

4. Please step forward if you can expect that your health insurance will cover routine doctor's visits for all needed treatment.
5. Please step forward if you feel accepted by all your family members.
6. Please step forward if you are able to meet someone for the first time and do not have to worry that they will use incorrect gender pronouns when speaking to you.
7. Please step forward if people you have just met do not ask you personal questions about your body (including what surgeries you have had), personal history, and identity.
8. Please step forward if your gender identity has been respected your whole life by doctors, parents, teachers, professors, relatives, classmates, and employers.
9. Please step forward if you have never been fired from any job due to your gender identity and/or perceived gender identity.
10. Please step forward if you have never been evicted from housing because of your gender identity and/or perceived gender identity.
11. Please step forward if you are able to go through security at the airport calmly, without fear of being questioned about your gender identity and/or "patted down" by someone of the opposite gender.
12. Please step forward if you have never had a waiter or waitress or food server incorrectly gender you when you went out to eat.
13. Please step forward if you have never paid for cosmetic surgery to feel more congruent with your gender in your body.
14. Please step forward if you are able to walk into a department store and feel confident that you will not be harassed for shopping in the women's or men's section.
15. Please step forward if you have never had your basic civil rights denied because of your gender identity.
16. Please step forward if you have never been called a slur such as "trannie," "he–she," or "hermaphrodite."
17. Please step forward if you are able to use a gym locker room or store changing room without fears that you will be stared at or pointed at.
18. Please step forward if you are able to find mentors and role models who reflect your gender identity.
19. Please step forward if you are easily able to find community services for people with a similar gender identity as yourself.
20. Please step forward if you have been able to move to another part of the country without worrying about your safety or that your legal rights will change because of your gender identity.
21. Please step forward if you have your gender as an option on most forms.
22. Please step forward if no one has ever asked you when you "knew" that you were your gender.
23. Please step forward if you are able to find clothes (including shoes) that fit your gender expression and you do not have to place special orders to get items in your size.
24. Please step forward if you do not have to worry about old photographs not reflecting your true self.
25. Please step forward if others do not use you as a scapegoat for their unresolved gender issues.

References

Berlant, L., & Warner, M. (1998). Sex in public. *Critical Inquiry, 24,* 547–566. http://dx.doi.org/10.1086/448884

Bisexual erasure. (2015). In *Wikipedia.* Retrieved from http://en.wikipedia.org/w/index.php?title=Bisexual_erasure&oldid=687937125

Bockting, W. O., Miner, M. H., Swinburne Romine, R. E., Hamilton, A., & Coleman, E. (2013). Stigma, mental health, and resilience in an online sample of the U.S. transgender population. *American Journal of Public Health, 103,* 943–951. http://dx.doi.org/10.2105/AJPH.2013.301241

Brill, S. A., & Pepper, R. (2008). *The transgender child.* San Francisco, CA: Cleis Press.

Bryan, J. (2012). *From the dress-up corner to the senior prom: Navigating gender and sexuality diversity in pre-K–12 schools.* Lanham, MD: Rowman & Littlefield Education.

Case, K. A., Hensley, R., & Anderson, A. (2014). Reflecting on heterosexual and male privilege: Interventions to raise awareness. *Journal of Social Issues, 70,* 722–740. http://dx.doi.org/10.1111/josi.12088

Cathers, C. (2012, March). *Transference and countertransference with transgender, genderqueer, and gender non-conforming clients.* Paper presented at the PRIDE conference, Ontario, CA.

Cole, E. R. (2009). Intersectionality and research in psychology. *American Psychologist, 64,* 170–180. http://dx.doi.org/10.1037/a0014564

Disorders of sex development. (2015). In *Wikipedia.* Retrieved from http://en.wikipedia.org/w/index.php?title=Disorders_of_sex_development&oldid=672804958

Dreger, A. D. (1998). "Ambiguous sex"—or ambivalent medicine? *The Hastings Center Report, 28,* 24–35. Retrieved from Intersex Society of North America website: http://www.isna.org/articles/ambivalent_medicine

Fausto-Sterling, A. (1993). The five sexes: Why male and female are not enough. *The Sciences, 33,* 20–24. http://dx.doi.org/10.1002/j.2326-1951.1993.tb03081.x

Fausto-Sterling, A. (2000). *Sexing the body: Gender politics and the construction of sexuality.* New York, NY: Basic Books.

Green, E., & Peterson, E. N. (2006). *LGBTTSQI terminology.* Retrieved from http://www.trans-academics.org/lgbttsqiterminology.pdf

Harris, A. (2005). *Gender as soft assembly.* Hillsdale, NJ: Analytic Press.

Human Rights Campaign. (n.d.). *Sexual orientation and gender identity definitions.* Retrieved from Human Rights Campaign website: http://www.hrc.org/resources/entry/sexual-orientation-and-gender-identity-terminology-and-definitions

Intersex Society of North America. (2008). *What is intersex?* Retrieved from http://www.isna.org/faq/what_is_intersex

Johnson, J., & Repta, R. (2012). Sex and gender: Beyond the binaries. In J. Oliffe & L. Greaves (Eds.), *Designing and conducting gender, sex, and health research* (pp. 17–39). http://dx.doi.org/10.4135/9781452230610.n2

Klein, F. (1993). *The bisexual option*. New York, NY: Haworth Press.

Lev, A. I. (2004). *Transgender emergence: Therapeutic guidelines for working with gender-variant people and their families*. New York, NY: The Haworth Clinical Practice Press.

Nadal, K. L., Rivera, D. P., & Corpus, M. J. H. (2010). Sexual orientation and transgender microaggressions in everyday life: Experiences of lesbians, gays, bisexuals, and transgender individuals. In D. W. Sue (Ed.), *Microaggressions and marginality: Manifestation, dynamics, and impact* (pp. 217–240). New York, NY: Wiley.

Non-monogamy. (2015). In *Wikipedia*. Retrieved from http://en.wikipedia.org/w/index.php?title=Non-monogamy&oldid=673720185

Open relationship. (2015). In *Wikipedia*. Retrieved from http://en.wikipedia.org/w/index.php?title=Open_relationship&oldid=671776912

Prieto, L. R. (2009). Teaching about diversity: Reflections and future directions. In R. A. R. Gurung & L. R. Prieto (Eds.), *Getting culture: Incorporating diversity across the curriculum* (pp. 23–39). Sterling, VA: Stylus.

Storms, M. D. (1980). Theories of sexual orientation. *Journal of Personality and Social Psychology, 38*, 783–792. http://dx.doi.org/10.1037/0022-3514.38.5.783

Think Again Training and Consultation. (2014). *Gender and sexual orientation terminology*. Retrieved from http://thinkagaintraining.com/wp-content/uploads/2014/10/TermsDefinitions2014.pdf

Trans Student Educational Resources. (2016). *The Gender Unicorn*. Retrieved from http://www.transstudent.org/gender

TransYouth Family Allies. (2008). *Terminology and glossary*. Retrieved from TransYouth Family Allies website: http://www.imatyfa.org/resources/youth-resources/terms/

Tiffany O'Shaughnessy and Nicholas Ladany

LGBTQ-Affirmative Training in Clinical Settings

9

Effective lesbian, gay, bisexual, transgender, and queer (LGBTQ)–affirmative supervision practice helps mental health providers (MHPs) consolidate the knowledge and awareness gained through more didactic forms of teaching and allows for the deep development of clinical skills to support the growth and development of LBGTQ clients (Halpert, Reinhardt, & Toohey, 2007). Although there have been promising findings in the literature about an increase in MHPs' enhanced knowledge and awareness about LGBTQ issues (Graham, Carney, & Kluck, 2012), there have also been concerns that this has not produced an equivalent increase in improved counseling skills with LGBTQ clients (O'Shaughnessy & Spokane, 2013). Given the continued experiences of microaggressions by LGBTQ clients in psychotherapy (Shelton & Delgado-Romero, 2013), it is clear that MHPs still have much progress to make in creating therapeutic spaces that are not recreating harmful and oppressive structures seen in the larger environment.

http://dx.doi.org/10.1037/0000015-009
Teaching LGBTQ Psychology: Queering Innovative Pedagogy and Practice, T. R. Burnes and J. L. Stanley (Editors)

A widely agreed on definition of *clinical supervision* was outlined by Bernard and Goodyear (2014):

> An intervention provided by a more senior member of a profession to a more junior colleague or colleagues who typically (but not always) are members of the same profession. This relationship is evaluative and hierarchical, extends over time, and has the simultaneous purpose of enhancing the professional functioning of the more junior person(s); monitoring the quality of professional services offered to the clients . . . and serving as a gatekeeper for the particular profession the supervisee seeks to enter. (p. 9)

Bernard and Goodyear (2014) further noted that, although clinical supervision is a distinct intervention, a good supervisor may draw from the similar roles of teacher, counselor, and consultant as appropriate to meet the developmental needs of a supervisee. The teacher role may be particularly salient in LGBTQ-affirmative supervision given the documented, continued relegation of training in competency with LGBTQ clients to a single multicultural course (Graham et al., 2012) that frequently excludes information about the specific needs of gender expansive and transgender (GET) communities (O'Hara, Dispenza, Brack, & Blood, 2013).

Fewer than 10% of students have access to a course on LGBTQ-affirmative therapy during their training programs (Sherry, Whilde, & Patton, 2005). It is likely that MHPs in training will reach practicum, internship, or various other training experiences in the field, depending on the discipline, without adequate exposure to the literature on effective work with LGBTQ clients and little direct experience providing services to the LGBTQ community. By engaging in the teaching role, clinical supervisors can address this educational gap and help deepen trainee knowledge and skills for working with the LGBTQ community (Halpert et al., 2007).

Although the intention of supervision is both to assist the trainee in developing competence and to protect mental health consumers, supervision has all too often gone poorly. A complete review of the literature on harmful and inadequate supervision is beyond the scope of this chapter; however, it is important to note that an LGBTQ-affirmative approach to supervision must start with what Ellis and colleagues (2014) described as "minimally adequate clinical supervision" (p. 437). This type of supervision includes maintaining ethical boundaries, serving as a gatekeeper, providing appropriate evaluation, being consistent and on time, maintaining supervisee confidentiality when appropriate, being attentive to cultural issues, and having proper credentials. Unfortunately, supervision can go beyond simple inadequacy and move into harmful supervision (i.e., "supervisory practices that result in psychological, emotional, and/or physical harm or trauma to the supervisee"; Ellis et al., 2014, p. 440).

Burkard, Knox, Hess, and Schultz (2009) examined LGB supervisees' experiences of LGB affirmative and nonaffirmative supervision. Participants who experienced affirming supervision described feeling supported in their work with clients and noted that the affirming events positively affected the supervisory relationship and client outcomes. In an affirming supervisory environment, supervisees were able to process their feelings toward clients and develop new insights and clinical knowledge. Alternately, in the nonaffirming supervision, supervisees felt that supervisors were biased or oppressive toward the supervisee or client based on LGB concerns or identity. The supervisees experienced these nonaffirming events, many of which fit the definition of harmful supervision, as negatively affecting the supervisees, the supervisory relationship, and the clinical outcome. This study speaks to the importance of developing a supervisory relationship that is affirming of supervisees' identities in order to foster receptiveness to the knowledge the supervisor can share.

Another important precursor for being able to provide effective LGBTQ-affirmative supervision is for the supervisor to hold a balanced and nuanced view of the needs, strengths, and resources of the LGBTQ community. A qualified supervisor should be familiar with Meyer's (2003) minority stress model and how this model has been expanded to reflect the needs of the GET communities (e.g., Testa, Habarth, Peta, Balsam, & Bockting, 2015). Specifically, supervisors should be aware of the ways that violence, rejection, and discrimination (Velez, Moradi, & DeBlaere, 2015) directed toward the LGBTQ community affect mental health and be comfortable examining how this may be recreated in both the therapy and supervision contexts (Blumer & Barbachano, 2008). By helping supervisees see these concepts playing out in clients' lives, you will help to bring these concepts to life and model how to integrate this knowledge into appropriate clinical intervention. In addition, Vaughan and Rodriguez (2014) noted that although awareness of the negative impact of minority stress is essential, it has often come at the expense of recognizing the strengths, resilience, and resources of the LGBTQ community. Thus, a skilled supervisor should be able to utilize a "both/and" perspective and embrace the resilience and growth within the community.

A final preliminary consideration before examining models of supervision is the importance of attending to power dynamics in LGBTQ-affirmative supervision (Green & Dekkers, 2010). The intersections between the cultural identities of the supervisee, supervisor, and client may increase the potential for microaggressions or harmful supervision, particularly when the supervisor and/or client come from more socially privileged identities. Singh and Chun (2010) provided examples of the complex interplay of identities for queer people of color supervisees and supervisors. They emphasized that a focus on resilience, as well as the development of both the supervisor and supervisees' multicultural competence, is essential in helping to reduce the likelihood of re-creating oppressive supervisory environments.

Models of Supervision

A number of models of supervision have been proposed over the past 3 decades, most of which have attended to an aspect of the supervisory work (e.g., Bordin, 1983; Overholser, 2004). A handful of models offer a comprehensive scope of supervision, and of these, three were developed or revised over the past decade. These models include the integrative developmental model (IDM; Stoltenberg & McNeill, 2010), the competency-based approach to clinical supervision (CBACS; Falender & Shafranske, 2004), and the critical events in supervision model (CES; Ladany, Friedlander, & Nelson, 2016). In this section, we briefly review each model and indicate the manner in which LGBTQ issues are addressed. We also provide a case that illustrates the application of the critical events in supervision model to a supervision context involving LGBTQ issues.

INTEGRATIVE DEVELOPMENT MODEL

The IDM has been a long-standing and evolving model of supervision (e.g., Stoltenberg, 1981). The authors proposed that supervisors are able to assess trainee developmental level by examining three overarching structures across eight domains of professional practice. The three structures are (a) self- and other-awareness: cognitive and affective (e.g., cognitive complexity and emotional attunement), (b) motivation (e.g., interest and investment), and (c) autonomy (e.g., trainee independence). Domains consist of (a) intervention skills competence (e.g., therapeutic confidence and competence), (b) assessment techniques (e.g., assessment confidence and competence), (c) interpersonal assessment (i.e., therapist uses self to assess client), (d) client conceptualization (e.g., diagnosis), (e) individual differences (e.g., demographic differences such as ethnicity), (f) theoretical orientation, (g) treatment plans and goals, and (h) professional ethics (including personal ethics). Structures and domains vary across levels of trainee development, which run across four levels from Level 1 (e.g., limited experience in a particular domain) to Level 3i (e.g., integration across domains).

A primary domain in the IDM is individual differences, which includes traditional diversity variables such as gender, race, and sexual orientation. The authors point to changes in understanding of demographic variables over time that seem similar to multicultural identity models; however, details about how a supervisor would approach moving a trainee along this domain are limited, particularly in relation to LGBTQ issues. Bruss, Brack, Brack, Glickhauf-Hughes, and O'Leary (1997) adapted this model into an LGB-affirmative supervision model; however, Halpert et al. (2007) noted that even with this adaptation, it lacked an emphasis on how to address homophobia and transphobia. Halpert and colleagues proposed the integrative affirmative supervision (IAS) model, which takes the strengths of the IDM and supports this with additional theoretical approaches that emphasize supervisee empowerment, affirmation of sexual orientation, and the importance of addressing transference, countertransference, and coming out. The IAS model is a promising and well-articulated model that has yet to be subjected to empirical scrutiny.

COMPETENCY-BASED APPROACH TO CLINICAL SUPERVISION

The CBACS sets as a foundation that the primary goal of supervision is to develop competencies in the trainee that consist of knowledge, skills, and values. The trainee and supervisor work together to decide which competencies they will address in supervision, and formative and summative evaluations are used to assess the trainee's progress toward competence. Four subordinate values are considered critical to the work: (a) integrity-in-relationship, (b) ethical values–based practice, (c) appreciation of diversity, and (d) science-informed practice. The authors note the importance of addressing LGBTQ issues in supervision; however, the manner in which the supervisor operates within their model is unclear. Bieschke, Blasko, and Woodhouse (2014) attempted to extend the CBACS by adding Halpert and colleagues' (2007) IAS model; however, a fully developed approach to LGBTQ issues within CBACS is warranted.

CRITICAL EVENTS IN SUPERVISION MODEL

According to the CES model, supervision can be observed as a series of critical events, each of which contains a chain of tasks in which the supervisor and trainee engage that results in successful to unsuccessful outcomes. The model is intended to be pantheoretical, cross-disciplinary, and interpersonal (i.e., beyond case management) and assumes that events have an identifiable beginning, middle, and end. There are four primary components of a critical event: (a) the supervisory working alliance, (b) the marker, (c) the task environment, and (d) the resolution. The supervisory alliance (based on Bordin's, 1983, model) consists of three factors: (a) agreement between the supervisor and trainee about the goals of supervision, (b) agreement between the supervisor and trainee about the tasks of supervision, and (c) an emotional bond between the supervisor and trainee. The supervisory working alliance serves as a figure–ground in relation to a critical event, such that it becomes more prominent when the relationship is challenged or new and falls into the background once it is stable. Importantly, addressing the intersections of relatively privileged and oppressed aspects of the supervisor and supervisee identities is essential in establishing a quality emotional bond.

The marker is a trigger that the supervisor notices that points to the beginning of a critical event. For example, the trainee may ask for guidance with a client who is questioning her own sexual identity. A different kind of marker may be the supervisor noticing that a trainee becomes uncharacteristically nervous when discussing a client who is bisexual. In each case, the marker serves as the entry point for the task environment, which includes a set of possible interactional sequences in which the supervisor may choose to engage. These interactional sequences include focus on the supervisory alliance, focus on the therapeutic process, exploration of feelings, focus on countertransference, attend to parallel processes, focus on self-efficacy, normalize experience, focus on skill, assess knowledge, focus on multicultural awareness, and focus on evaluation. Finally, the task environment results in a resolution or outcome that falls on a continuum of successful to unsuccessful in relation to self-awareness, knowledge, skills, or the supervisory alliance.

A salient critical event that has been identified is heightening multicultural awareness, and sexual orientation and gender identity are considered important multicultural variables that have been illustrated in the model (Ladany et al., 2016). A process model was created for a multicultural event such that, following the marker, the typical interactional sequences that make up the task environment include focus on the supervisory alliance, exploration of feelings, focus on multicultural awareness, focus on skill, and normalize the experience.

Case Example

Using the CES model, the following case illustrates heightening multicultural awareness in relation to LGBTQ issues in supervision when working with supervisees and their clients. Interspersed among the dialogue are comments that address the process taking place. The supervisor is Ben, a 42-year old White, queer, transgender man who has 15 years of therapy experience and 5 years of supervision experience. He works as a staff therapist and supervisor at a community mental health center. His trainee is Diana, a 24-year-old Latina, cisgender woman who is in her second year of practica. Diana carries a caseload of 10 clients, and she presents one in particular for discussion in supervision. The client, Linda, is a 40-year-old Latina questioning/bisexual woman who is considering leaving her husband and is significantly distressed over the decision.

> Ben: So, what would you like to learn today? [*This initial question sets the stage for empowering the trainee to discuss what her concerns are for supervision and thus*

> *take responsibility for the direction. In addition, it rein-*
> *forces the task component of the supervisory alliance.*]

Diana: Well, I have this one client, who I'm having trouble sorting out. I'm really stuck with her. [*In this case, the marker is pretty clear: Diana is feeling "stuck." However, it is less clear what type of event they are moving into.*]

Ben: Tell me more about this client and the place you are feeling stuck.

Diana: My client, Linda, is thinking of leaving her husband. She's really upset when considering this decision. Recently, she said that she realizes that she's bisexual, although she's not 100% sure. It sounds like she can't make up her mind about a number of things. [*Laughs.*] I mean, how can she not know? She's been married for almost 20 years, and now she realizes it.

At this point Ben hypothesizes that the event is a heightening multicultural awareness event because of the judgmental statements Diana made. Ben makes a mental note of his emotional reaction to Diana's words "how can she not know," which connect to his experiences of microaggressions from others while coming out around his GET and queer identities.

FOCUS ON THE SUPERVISORY WORKING ALLIANCE

Ben: It sounds like maybe her confusion is leading you to feel a bit confused as well.

Diana: Sure. I think she should figure out her sexual orientation first, and then decide if she wants to leave her husband. He sounds like a good guy.

Ben: It sounds like you wonder if leaving him would be a premature mistake.

Diana: Yes. What if she decides tomorrow she's really heterosexual? Then what will she do?

Ben: I wonder if it would be OK with you if we delve into this a bit deeper?

Diana: Sure.

Ben has attempted to use empathy and reflections of feelings and thoughts to strengthen the bond component of the alliance. From there, he seeks to strengthen the task component by seeing whether Diana is willing to explore things further. Her acquiescence indicates that the alliance is strong enough to proceed.

EXPLORATION OF FEELINGS

Ben: You mentioned feeling confused. Talk about what's happening when that comes up for you.

Diana: I don't know. It's like I feel like she should first decide what her sexual orientation is and then decide to make a life-altering decision so it doesn't mess everyone else in her life up. She has two kids also. I know that sounds harsh.

Ben: That's OK, your honesty is important here. When you mention that she should make a decision before messing everyone else up, what are you feeling?

Diana: You mean right now? I don't tell her that, of course.

Ben: Of course, but yes, right now what do you feel?

Diana: Frustrated. I also feel bad for her kids and her husband.

Ben: Keep going.

Diana: Well, her poor kids don't deserve that. I don't like the idea of a family getting broken up.

Ben: It sounds like family is really important to you.

Diana: You know I'm Latina, and it's all about the family; something feels wrong to me that this Latina woman is considering walking away from her family—and for what?

We begin to see the intersectionality of two multicultural variables that Diana is managing: race (i.e., the trainee's racial identity; Ancis & Ladany, 2010) and sexual orientation (i.e., the client's sexual identity and orientation). This leads Ben to begin determining how much of the multicultural challenges are knowledge and how much has to do with awareness, with the goal of enhancing Diana's multicultural awareness.

ASSESS MULTICULTURAL AWARENESS

Ben: I know we've talked before, and you certainly have a great understanding of your Latina culture and how this culture plays a role in the counseling work you do. At the same time, there's a sexual orientation piece where there seem to be some struggles.

Diana: Yeah, I think so.

Ben: You mentioned frustration about her breaking up the family but didn't speak about her bisexuality. How do you feel about sexual orientation as a counseling topic?

Diana: I thought I was fine with it. I like to think of myself as gay affirmative, and I've had gay clients and lesbian clients. But honestly, I've never worked with a bisexual client. Can people really change midlife, or could that just be an excuse?

Ben: I would say that people's sexual orientation can be fluid; Lisa Diamond's work on the fluidity of women's sexuality supports that this can change over time [*see Diamond, 2009*]. Or, in the case of this client, may have always been there for her but she is just now discovering herself. We just don't know. At the same time, why does knowing why make a difference in how you'll work with her?

Diana: I suppose it shouldn't; I know that intellectually and I want to support her where she's at.

Ben: That's good. Then perhaps it's the family issue that is causing most of the angst.

Diana: I think you are right.

Although more work is to be done, particularly on the racial issues (Ancis & Ladany, 2010), the supervisor can use his teaching role and dispel a potential myth about sexual orientation and provide an external resource for further exploration while also not solving the puzzle completely. The supervisor can then move on to attending to how Diana may be able to change how she works with the client next session.

FOCUS ON SKILL AND NORMALIZE THE EXPERIENCE

Ben: So, with this knowledge, how might you approach Linda differently in the next session?

Diana: Well, for one, I think I'll be less distracted with my own reactions. But also, I feel like I'll be in a better place with just accepting her where she's at.

Ben: How might you do that?

Diana: I think sometimes I encouraged her to focus on her family, and she wanted to talk more about her sexual orientation. I suppose I could start there. I just wish I hadn't missed this.

Ben: Yes, that would be a fine change to make. I also want you to know that it's always tough to realize things we haven't in the past. And that's common, particularly with multicultural issues. I commend you on your work and disclosures in this area. Also, in the future, there may be other aspects of sexual orientation, gender identity, and racial identity that we can discuss.

Diana: I would appreciate that.

The supervisor helps set the stage for the work in the next counseling session as well as future discussions about sexual orientation and identity. The event is partially resolved because, clearly, more work needs to be done. At the same time, it is fortunate that Diana is a relatively compliant trainee whose openness should continue to serve her well in her professional development. Ben may consider asking Diana to complete the process note at the end of the chapter (see Activity 9.1) to help deepen the discussion about these issues in future sessions.

Practical Teaching Strategies, Interventions, and Activities

These supervision models are useful maps for the overall process of clinical supervision; in this section, we provide specific strategies and interventions that a supervisor may use when facilitating LGBTQ therapy competence via clinical supervision.

ASSESSMENT MEASURES

A useful strategy for developing a clear understanding of supervisees' knowledge, awareness, skills, and self-efficacy for engaging in LGBTQ-affirmative therapy is to have them complete a formal assessment at the start of supervision. Ascertaining this information at the outset can help strengthen the working alliance by supporting the development of collaborative goals based on the supervisee's areas of lower confidence or efficacy revealed in the assessment. It also helps the supervisor determine how much the teacher versus consultant role is needed. Supervisees with low self-reported knowledge and efficacy will likely benefit from more direct instruction whereas those with higher levels of knowledge are likely more able to spend time examining deeper process issues related to working with LGBTQ clients. Giving the same assessment at the end of the supervision relationship is a useful strategy to examine areas of growth. Examining pre and post measures focusing on changes in knowledge, awareness, skills, and self-efficacy and outlining remaining growth edges can be a powerful way to terminate a supervisory relationship. Unfortunately, there are no published validated measures for assessing self-efficacy for working with GET clients at this time (O'Hara et al., 2013); however, we describe next two recently developed assessment measures that can be used for these purposes in working with LGB clients.

The Lesbian, Gay, Bisexual Working Alliance Self-Efficacy Scales (Burkard, Pruitt, Medler, & Stark-Booth, 2009) is a 32-item measure that assesses supervisees' sense of self-efficacy in forming an emotional bond, engaging in appropriate tasks, and setting appropriate goals for working affirmatively with LGB clients.

The Lesbian, Gay, and Bisexual Affirmative Counseling Self-Efficacy Inventory—Short Form (LBG–CSI–SF; Dillon et al., 2015) is a 15-item measure that assesses the supervisee's self-efficacy for engaging in LGB affirmative therapy across the domains of (a) application of knowledge, (b) advocacy skills, (c) self-awareness, (d) relationship, and (e) assessment.

PROVIDING TRAINING FOR ALL STAFF

The literature on effective LGBTQ-affirmative therapy practices is still relatively new and is constantly changing. It is likely that staff members, even those who are recent graduates, may not have seen the most current information on affirmative approaches to working with LGBTQ clients. Establishing article reading groups or providing clinical training updates that allow all current staff and trainees to examine the current literature can be a useful strategy to help create a climate more conducive to LGBTQ-affirmative supervisory practices.

LGBTQ-AFFIRMATIVE THERAPY PROCESS NOTES

When a supervisor wants a supervisee to take a deeper look at the interactional process occurring between client and therapist, particularly to uncover areas of bias or countertransference, assigning process notes can be a useful teaching strategy (Bernard & Goodyear, 2014). Included in Activity 9.1 is a process note template adapted for examining deeper issues that may arise while working with LGBTQ clients. The intention of the template is to provide ideas for key areas of focus to help open the supervisory dialogue, including cultural beliefs and conflicts, countertransference, quality and strength of the working alliance, and opportunities for social justice advocacy at the individual, community, and public levels outlined by Lewis, Arnold, House, and Toporek (2003).

AWARENESS OF RESOURCES AND CRITICAL KNOWLEDGE

As noted earlier, awareness of community resources and immersion in the LGBTQ-affirmative therapy literature is essential for competent practice across disciplines. Included in Activity 9.2 is a handout that the supervisor can tailor to share essential readings in LGBTQ-affirmative therapy and to encourage the supervisee to become familiar with local community resources for the LGBTQ community.

Conclusion

The clinical supervision relationship is an ideal place to help MHPs deepen their understanding of how their own identity statuses influence their work with their diverse clients. It is one of the few places where clinical education is tailored specifically to the needs of the supervisee and the clinical population being served; thus, a well-prepared, self-reflective, and ethical supervisor can help trainees (a) understand their own experiences of oppression and privilege, (b) see how this is interacting with their clients and in the supervision relationship, and (c) move toward an ability to provide adequate, effective, and positive clinical experiences for the LGBTQ community. As illustrated with Ben and Diana in the case example, the supervisor cocreates a learning environment that allows the supervisee to develop their knowledge, awareness, and skills in working with the LGBTQ community. To do this, supervisors from all disciplines must be dedicated to examining their own biases, be willing to address power dynamics regularly within the supervisory session, and be continuously engaged with the LGBTQ-affirmative therapy literature to model and support effective practices. At its best, LGBTQ-affirming supervisory practices foster professional growth and promote safety and support for the LGBTQ community.

ACTIVITY 9.1

Process Note Template for LGBTQ Affirmative Supervision

Client: Session #:
Therapist: Date:

1. Issues presented in session:
2. Themes emerging across multiple sessions:
3. Cultural beliefs and conflicts
   (a) Client's identity statuses (e.g., race, ethnicity, sexual orientation, gender identity, sex, ability status, social class, subculture identification)
   (b) Therapist's identity statuses (e.g., race, ethnicity, sexual orientation, gender identity, sex, ability status, social class, subculture identification)
   (c) How are the similarities and differences influencing the work in the therapy room? What knowledge, awareness, and/or skills do you need to enhance this work? How are you broaching these issues in session?
   (d) Transference, countertransference, and biases: How is the client reacting to you? How are you reacting to the client that seems uncharacteristic or distorted, or atypical?
   (e) Strength and quality of working alliance (e.g., mutual agreement on goals and tasks, client's perception of empathic bond, ruptures, or repairs in session?)
   (f) Client's sources of resilience and strength
   (g) Advocacy: Considering the client's presenting concerns in an ecological context, what potential areas for advocacy (e.g., acting with or on behalf of your client at individual, community, and public levels for empowerment and change; Lewis, Arnold, House, & Toporek, 2003).

ACTIVITY 9.2

Key Resources for LGBTQ-Affirmative Therapy

List local LGBTQ community centers, support groups, gathering places, and health providers for easy access

Useful national resources	Lambda Legal: http://www.lambdalegal.org Human Rights Campaign: http://www.hrc.org National Center for Transgender Equality: http://www.transequality.org Affirming religious organizations and congregations: http://geneq.berkeley.edu/lgbt_resources_religion_and_spirituality POZ (resource for HIV+ folks): http://www.poz.com Mautner Project (lesbian health project): http://www.mautnerproject.org
Key affirmative therapy readings	American Psychological Association. (2012). Guidelines for psychological practice with lesbian, gay, and bisexual clients. *American Psychologist, 67*, 10–42. Bieschke, K. J., Perez, R. M., & DeBord, K. A. (Eds.). (2007). *Handbook of counseling and psychotherapy with lesbian, gay, bisexual, and transgender clients* (2nd ed.). Washington, DC: American Psychological Association. Meyer, I. H. (2003). Prejudice, social stress, and mental health in lesbian, gay, and bisexual populations: Conceptual issues and research evidence. *Psychological Bulletin, 129*, 674–697. Moradi, B., DeBlaere, C., & Huang, Y. (2010). Centralizing the experiences of LGB people of color in counseling psychology [Special issue]. *The Counseling Psychologist, 38*(3). Szymanski, D. M., Kashubeck-West, S., & Meyer, J. (2008). Internalized heterosexism [Special issue]. *The Counseling Psychologist, 36*(4).
Transgender and gender-expansive specific readings	Association for Lesbian, Gay, Bisexual, and Transgender Issues in Counseling. (2009). *ALGBTIC Competencies for counseling transgender clients.* Available from http://www.counseling.org/docs/competencies/algbtic_competencies.pdf?sfvrsn=3 Nadal, K., Skolnik, A., & Wong, Y. (2012). Interpersonal and systemic microaggressions toward transgender people: Implications for counseling. *Journal of LGBT Issues in Counseling, 6*, 55–82. Vanderburgh, R. (2009). Appropriate therapeutic care for families with pre-pubescent transgender/gender-dissonant children. *Child and Adolescent Social Work Journal, 26*, 135–154. World Professional Association for Transgender Health (WPATH) Standards of Care: http://www.wpath.org/
Couples and family therapy	Ariel, J., & McPherson, D. W. (2000). Therapy with lesbian and gay parents and their children. *Journal of Marital and Family Therapy, 26*, 421–432.

(continued)

ACTIVITY 9.2 (Continued)

Religion and spirituality	Green, R. J., & Mitchell, V. (2008). Gay and lesbian couples in therapy: Minority stress, relational ambiguity, and families of choice. In. A. S. Gurman (Ed.), *Clinical handbook of couple therapy* (4th ed., pp. 662–680). New York, NY: Guilford Press. Sanders, G. L., & Kroll, I. T. (2000). Generating stories of resilience: Helping gay and lesbian youth and their families. *Journal of Marital and Family Therapy, 26,* 433–442. Bartoli, E., & Gillem, A. (2008). Continuing to depolarize the debate on sexual orientation and religion: Identity and the therapeutic process. *Professional Psychology: Research and Practice, 39,* 202–209. Bozard, R. L., Jr., & Sanders, C. J. (2011). Helping Christian lesbian, gay, and bisexual clients recover religion as a source of strength: Developing a model for assessment and integration of religious identity in counseling. *Journal of LGBT Issues in Counseling, 5,* 47–74.

References

Ancis, J., & Ladany, N. (2010). A multicultural framework for counselor supervision: Knowledge and skills. In N. Ladany & L. Bradley (Eds.), *Counselor supervision* (4th ed., pp. 53–95). New York, NY: Routledge.

Bernard, J. M., & Goodyear, R. K. (2014). *Fundamentals of clinical supervision* (5th ed.). Boston, MA: Allyn & Bacon.

Bieschke, K. J., Blasko, K. A., & Woodhouse, S. S. (2014). A comprehensive approach to competently addressing sexual minority issues in clinical supervision. In C. A. Falender, E. P. Shafranske, & C. J. Falicov (Eds.), *Multiculturalism and diversity in clinical supervision: A competency-based approach* (pp. 209–230). http://dx.doi.org/10.1037/14370-009

Blumer, M. L. C., & Barbachano, J. M. (2008). Valuing the gender-variant therapist: Therapeutic experiences, tools, and implications of a female-to-male trans-variant clinician. *Journal of Feminist Family Therapy, 20,* 46–65. http://dx.doi.org/10.1080/0895280801907135

Bordin, E. S. (1983). A working alliance based model of supervision. *The Counseling Psychologist, 11*(1), 35–42. http://dx.doi.org/10.1177/0011000083111007

Bruss, K. V., Brack, C. J., Brack, G., Glickhauf-Hughes, C., & O'Leary, M. (1997). A developmental model for supervising therapists treating gay, lesbian, and bisexual clients. *The Clinical Supervisor, 15,* 61–73. http://dx.doi.org/10.1300/J001v15n01_05

Burkard, A. W., Knox, S., Hess, S. A., & Schultz, J. (2009). Lesbian, gay, and bisexual supervisees' experiences of LGB-affirmative and nonaffirmative supervision. *Journal of Counseling Psychology, 56*, 176–188. http://dx.doi.org/10.1037/0022-0167.56.1.176

Burkard, A. W., Pruitt, N. T., Medler, B. R., & Stark-Booth, A. M. (2009). Validity and reliability of the Lesbian, Gay, Bisexual Working Alliance Self-Efficacy Scales. *Training and Education in Professional Psychology, 3*, 37–46. http://dx.doi.org/10.1037/1931-3918.3.1.37

Diamond, L. (2009). *Sexual fluidity: Understanding women's love and desire.* Cambridge, MA: Harvard University Press.

Dillon, F. R., Alessi, E. J., Craig, S., Eber-Sole, R. C., Kumar, S. M., & Spadola, C. (2015). Development of the Lesbian, Gay, and Bisexual Affirmative Counseling Self-Efficacy Inventory—Short Form (LGB–CSI–SF). *Psychology of Sexual Orientation and Gender Diversity, 2*, 86–95. http://dx.doi.org/10.1037/sgd0000087

Ellis, M. V., Berger, L., Hanus, A. E., Ayala, E. E., Swords, B. A., & Siembor, M. (2014). Inadequate and harmful clinical supervision: Testing a revised framework and assessing occurrence. *The Counseling Psychologist, 42*, 434–472. http://dx.doi.org/10.1177/0011000013508656

Falender, C. A., & Shafranske, E. P. (2004). *Clinical supervision: A competency-based approach.* http://dx.doi.org/10.1037/10806-000

Graham, S. R., Carney, J. S., & Kluck, A. S. (2012). Perceived competency in working with LGB clients: Where are we now? *Counselor Education and Supervision, 51*, 2–16. http://dx.doi.org/10.1002/j.1556-6978.2012.00001.x

Green, M. S., & Dekkers, T. D. (2010). Attending to power and diversity in supervision: An exploration of supervisee learning outcomes and satisfaction with supervision. *Journal of Feminist Family Therapy, 22*, 293–312. http://dx.doi.org/10.1080/08952833.2010.528703

Halpert, S. C., Reinhardt, B., & Toohey, M. J. (2007). Affirmative clinical supervision. In K. J. Bieschke, R. M. Perez, & K. A. DeBord (Eds.), *Handbook of counseling and psychotherapy with lesbian, gay, bisexual, and transgender clients* (2nd ed., pp. 341–358). http://dx.doi.org/10.1037/11482-014

Ladany, N., Friedlander, M. L., & Nelson, M. L. (2016). *Essentials for the critical events in psychotherapy supervision model.* Washington, DC: American Psychological Association.

Lewis, J. A., Arnold, M. S., House, R., & Toporek, R. L. (2003). *ACA advocacy competencies.* Retrieved from http://www.counseling.org/Resources/Competencies/Advocacy_Competencies.pdf

Meyer, I. H. (2003). Prejudice, social stress, and mental health in lesbian, gay, and bisexual populations: Conceptual issues and research evidence. *Psychological Bulletin, 129*, 674–697.

O'Hara, C., Dispenza, F., Brack, G., & Blood, R. A. C. (2013). The preparedness of counselors in training to work with transgender clients: A mixed methods investigation. *Journal of LGBT Issues in Counseling, 7*, 236–256. http://dx.doi.org/10.1080/15538605.2013.812929

O'Shaughnessy, T., & Spokane, A. (2013). Lesbian and gay affirmative therapy competency, self-efficacy, and personality in psychology trainees. *The Counseling Psychologist, 41,* 825–856. http://dx.doi.org/10.1177/0011000012459364

Overholser, J. C. (2004). The four pillars of psychotherapy supervision. *The Clinical Supervisor, 23,* 1–13. http://dx.doi.org/10.1300/J001v23n01_01

Shelton, K., & Delgado-Romero, E. A. (2013). Sexual orientation microaggressions: The experience of lesbian, gay, bisexual, and queer clients in psychotherapy. *Psychology of Sexual Orientation and Gender Diversity, 1,* 59–70. http://dx.doi.org/10.1037/2329-0382.1.S.59

Sherry, A., Whilde, M. R., & Patton, J. (2005). Gay, lesbian, and bisexual training competencies in American Psychological Association accredited graduate programs. *Psychotherapy: Theory, Research, Practice, Training, 42,* 116–120.

Singh, A., & Chun, K. Y. S. (2010). "From the margins to the center": Moving towards a resilience-based model of supervision for queer people of color supervisors. *Training and Education in Professional Psychology, 4,* 36–46. http://dx.doi.org/10.1037/a0017373

Stoltenberg, C. D. (1981). Approaching supervision from a developmental perspective: The counselor complexity model. *Journal of Counseling Psychology, 28,* 59–65. http://dx.doi.org/10.1037/0022-0167.28.1.59

Stoltenberg, C. D., & McNeill, B. W. (2010). *IDM supervision: An integrative developmental model for supervising counselors and therapists* (3rd ed.). New York, NY: Routledge.

Testa, R. J., Habarth, J., Peta, J., Balsam, K., & Bockting, W. (2015). Development of the gender minority stress and resilience measure. *Psychology of Sexual Orientation and Gender Diversity, 2,* 65–77. http://dx.doi.org/10.1037/sgd0000081

Vaughan, M. D., & Rodriguez, E. M. (2014). LGBT strengths: Incorporating positive psychology into theory, research, training, and practice. *Psychology of Sexual Orientation and Gender Diversity, 1,* 325–334. http://dx.doi.org/10.1037/sgd0000053

Velez, B. L., Moradi, B., & DeBlaere, C. (2015). Multiple oppressions and the mental health of sexual minority Latina/o individuals. *The Counseling Psychologist, 43,* 7–38. http://dx.doi.org/10.1177/0011000014542836

Tania Israel and Jay N. Bettergarcia

Evidence-Based Teaching of LGBTQ Issues in Psychology

10

Evidence-based psychological practice integrates the "best available research with clinical expertise in the context of patient characteristics, culture, and preferences" (American Psychological Association, 2006, p. 273). Evidence helps mental health providers (MHPs) make decisions regarding treatment and provide effective services. Can an evidence-based approach offer guidance regarding teaching about lesbian, gay, bisexual, transgender, queer, and/or questioning (LGBTQ) issues in psychology? What are the benefits of drawing on research to inform teaching? What research has been conducted on this topic, and what can we learn from it?

One benefit of evidence-based teaching is that the more educators can demonstrate the importance and impact of such education, the more effective they are likely to be in gaining approval to develop LGBTQ-specific courses, soliciting support for others to integrate LGBTQ issues into non-LGBTQ-specific courses, and assuring that such courses and

http://dx.doi.org/10.1037/0000015-010
Teaching LGBTQ Psychology: Queering Innovative Pedagogy and Practice, T. R. Burnes and J. L. Stanley (Editors)

content are offered on a regular basis. Evidence may also be useful when advocating for, designing, and promoting community-based training (e.g., Israel, Willging, & Ley, 2016).

In addition to evidence regarding the importance and outcomes of teaching LGBTQ issues in general, it is helpful to have evidence to guide the content and pedagogical approaches to teaching LGBTQ issues in psychology. For example, as discussed in Chapter 4 ("Teaching Ethics in Relation to LGBTQ Issues in Psychology"), there have been several cases in which MHP trainees have refused to work with LGBTQ clients as part of a supervised field placement experience (Whitman & Bidell, 2014). It is crucial that MHPs understand the impact of training on LGBTQ issues and supervised experience with LGBTQ clients on trainees, especially those who have religious conflicts or are participating in training because of mandatory training requirements.

What kind of evidence can we draw on to guide the teaching of LGBTQ issues in psychology? In this chapter, we review studies of MHPs' training needs and experiences regarding LGBTQ issues, studies that investigate a single aspect of teaching on LGBTQ issues, and studies of multimodal training or courses on LGBTQ issues. We also draw on educators' descriptions of practice and expert recommendations for training to illustrate aspects of evidence-based teaching of LGBTQ issues in psychology.

Review of Empirical Literature on Teaching LGBTQ Issues in Psychology

The evidence for teaching and training MHPs regarding LGBTQ issues is limited, and much of the research focuses on an exploration of what is lacking, what is needed, and descriptions of what learners are or are not receiving from their training programs. Only a limited number of studies have investigated multimodal approaches to teaching about LGBTQ issues in psychology, and even fewer have examined the utility of specific activities or teaching methods. In the research that does exist, the emphasis is on lesbian and gay populations with less literature inclusive of or specific to bisexual and transgender people. These studies include participants who are MHPs, MHP trainees, peer helpers, and undergraduate students. The following sections provide a review of the empirical literature on teaching LGBTQ issues in psychology.

STUDIES OF MENTAL HEALTH PROVIDERS' NEEDS AND EXPERIENCES

Historically, graduate students in clinical and counseling psychology programs have received inadequate training regarding working with LGBTQ clients (Anhalt, Morris, Scotti, & Cohen, 2003; Phillips & Fisher, 1998), although more recent studies have suggested that such opportunities are increasingly available (Asta & Vacha-Haase, 2013). Many trainees have reported that they do not feel well-prepared to counsel lesbian and gay clients and even less prepared to work with bisexual clients (Phillips & Fisher, 1998) and transgender or gender questioning clients (Benson, 2013; Sennott & Smith, 2011). One study found that 90% of MHP trainees believed they would benefit from training in sexual orientation and gender identity concerns, with many noting that they would be more likely to feel comfortable with LGBTQ clients if they received additional training (Anhalt et al., 2003). In particular, trainees tend to self-report lower skills competencies and higher awareness and knowledge competencies with regard to working with LGB clients (Graham, Carney, & Kluck, 2012).

Receiving training improves trainees' assessments of their competencies, and specific types of training may be helpful for enhancing particular competencies. For example, those who work with LGB clients during practicum experiences tend to report higher skills competencies (Graham et al., 2012). In one study, counselors identified "experiential activities to facilitate growth and discussion concerning LGBT issues" and specific LGBT classes as components of effective training (Asta & Vacha-Haase, 2013).

The responsibility for training future professionals to work with LGBTQ clients may be spread across various training components, including coursework, practicum, internship, and supervision. Although many educators value the inclusion of LGBTQ issues in their curricula and describe their programs as integrating this material, it is likely that LGBTQ issues, if addressed, are covered in a single class period (Luke, Goodrich, & Scarborough, 2011). Such brief training is inconsistent with best practices in multicultural training (Luke et al., 2011) and is likely inadequate to cover the breadth and depth of knowledge, attitudes, and skills necessary to work effectively with LGB clients (Israel, Ketz, Detrie, Burke, & Shulman, 2003). The power of attending to LGBTQ issues during graduate education is highlighted by the lifelong impact such training can have on later career work (Johnson & Federman, 2014).

STUDIES OF MULTIMODAL TEACHING APPROACHES

Among the evidence-based teaching and training models for MHPs or MHPs-in-training on LGBTQ issues, many are multimodal, including some combination of didactic and experiential modalities. The goals of this training often include increasing knowledge, awareness, and skills (Bidell, 2013; Byrd & Hays, 2013; Rutter, Estrada, Ferguson, & Diggs, 2008) or decreasing homonegativity (Rye & Meaney, 2009). Of these, the most common goals for in-service and preservice training tend to include an explicit goal to increase knowledge, awareness, and skills related to providing mental health services for LGB, and sometimes transgender, individuals. The studies described next investigated a combination of training modalities and techniques, such as didactic presentations (e.g., PowerPoint lecture), group discussions about clinical case examples and an exploration of bias and beliefs, and skill-building experiential role-play activities. Many assessed outcomes using a pretest–posttest design, some of which also included a control condition, although few used random assignment or matched samples for the control.

One study tested a 3-hour manualized safe space training session offered to school counselor trainees (Byrd & Hays, 2013). The training included role-play exercises, case studies, and skill-building activities aimed at intervening in cases of anti-LGBTQ sentiments. Participants were randomly assigned to complete the posttest either before or following the training. The findings indicated a statistically significant increase in knowledge, awareness, and skills from pretest to posttest following the training.

Similarly, an LGB competency training program for advanced counseling students used didactic PowerPoint presentations, skill-building experiential role-plays, and clinical vignettes (Rutter et al., 2008). The researchers measured self-assessed knowledge, awareness, and skill competencies before and after training for students who received the training and for students in an introductory counseling class that did not receive the training. The study found that there was a significant increase in knowledge and skills, though not a significant increase in awareness scores from pretest to posttest and as compared with the control group. The comparison with the control condition should be considered with caution because the control was a nonequivalent class.

Another multimodal study focused on teaching graduate students in an LGBTQ counseling class that consisted of presentations about LGBTQ issues, LGBTQ community speakers sharing knowledge and experience, films, and time to discuss and reflect on reactions to the course materials (Bidell, 2013). This study evaluated self-assessed counselor competency before and after the course and compared the course participants with a matched sample of counselor trainees. The study found that self-reported counselor competency (including knowledge, awareness, and skills) and self-efficacy increased significantly from pretest to posttest compared with a control group.

A mixed-method, community-based training study of 37 paraprofessional peer advocates sought to improve knowledge and skills in supporting LGBTQ people (Israel et al., 2016). Participants took part in either an initial or a revised training program over 2 weekends that consisted of LGBTQ topics, including mental health, substance use, minority stress, protective factors, suicide prevention, cultural competence, LGBTQ subpopulations, and experiences of LGBTQ people living in rural communities. The training also included role-plays and interactive activities. The revised training integrated helping skills throughout the training modules and reduced didactic material, overly conceptual topics, and redundancies. Comparison of pretest and posttest scores showed an increase in self-efficacy for participants in both training sessions and an increase in knowledge for participants in the revised training session. The study also found that participants appreciated the opportunity to increase their knowledge and skills, especially concerning bisexual and transgender persons, and the opportunity to connect with others in the community who wanted to support LGBTQ people.

A multimodal two-part safe-zone training session was provided for graduate students in a professional psychology program across two semesters (Finkel, Storaasli, Bandele, & Schaefer, 2003). The first session included introductions, setting ground rules, icebreaker activities, a guided imagery experiential activity, and information about coming out and being an LGBTQ ally. The participants were also asked to take part in an intention activity in which they decided on three LGBTQ-affirming actions and committed to doing them before the second session. In the second training session, participants processed the intention activity and participated in role-play activities. Two thirds of the participants reported positive feedback about the training and approximately 40% reported positive attitudinal change from the first training session to the second, though the ratings for the first session were retrospective rather than a pretest–posttest design (Finkel et al., 2003).

In a descriptive pretest–posttest study, Pearson (2003) provided a 3-hour counselor training class seminar to teach about three main topics related to LGB issues: (a) sexuality and sexual identity development; (b) sexual minority oppression, discrimination, and marginalization; and (c) the role of counselors' attitudes, beliefs, and background on sexual minority clients (Pearson, 2003). Using class discussion, assigned readings, analysis of popular music lyrics, and information about counseling interventions with LGB people, the descriptive statistics indicated an overall increase in knowledge, interest in LGB topics, and more favorable attitudes about sexual orientation issues (Pearson, 2003).

An ethnographic study investigated the impact of cofacilitating gay–straight alliance (GSA) groups on 11 heterosexual, female, school counseling students (Goodrich & Luke, 2010). The GSA group facilitation was part of an effort to integrate training in social justice group work into an existent school counseling course. The training included information about research on LGBTQ issues, video clips of personal stories, and journaling. The findings indicated that the trainees expanded their knowledge, awareness (of biases, LGBTQ student needs, and necessity of advocacy), and skills related to LGBTQ adolescents.

Though many of these studies focused on training MHPs, others focused on teaching undergraduate students. One such study used a multimodal training approach to teach about LGB issues in a homonegativity awareness workshop with college students (Rye & Meaney, 2009). Using a quasi-experimental design with nonequivalent groups of college students, participants were less homonegative and erotophobic after attending the training session. Training consisted of the establishment of group rules, participant introductions, an imagery exercise to reflect on and explore attitudes, facilitator coming out stories, a question and answer discussion, myths about LGB people, and how to create nurturing environments for LGB people (Rye & Meaney, 2009).

In another study of undergraduates, 33 college students in a psychology of prejudice class completed attitude measures at the beginning and end of the course. There was a significant reduction in negative attitudes toward homosexuality, especially for students who were more engaged in the course (Pettijohn & Walzer, 2008).

One study investigated the impact of teaching about lesbian and gay issues on high school students (Van de Ven, 1995). In the study, 130 Australian ninth graders participated in six lessons, totaling 305 minutes and consisting of information, a gay and lesbian speaker panel, scenarios, and reflection. Lessons were administered once per week, and attitudes were assessed before, immediately following, and 6 weeks after the lessons. Posttest cognitive, affective, and behavioral attitudes were significantly more positive than pretest attitudes for all participants. Some of these changes were retained at follow-up, although less so for boys than for girls (Van de Ven, 1995).

In a meta-analytic study of training interventions aimed at reducing sexual prejudice, many studies used both education and contact with LGB people in the training design (Bartoş, Berger, & Hegarty, 2014). Of these studies, 27 explored a contact and education style intervention on sexually prejudiced attitudes, and they had a medium effect size. Three studies displayed positive effects on knowledge using a contact and education intervention; however, there were too few studies to provide a conclusion about their effects. Five contact and education studies that focused on the impact of the training on sexually prejudiced emotions were found to be effective. Finally, five studies examined contact and education interventions on intended behaviors and found a small to medium effect size, whereas two more focused on actual behavior and found more moderate results. Thus, the combination of education about LGB topics and contact with LGB people was moderately effective in improving attitudes, emotions, and behaviors toward LGB people.

STUDIES OF SPECIFIC TEACHING INTERVENTIONS

Research on specific teaching interventions is scarce, and most studies have focused on individual LGBTQ speakers or panels. Aside from investigations of speakers, only five studies of specific approaches to teaching were found, including investigations of participation in a research team, comparison of information delivery and attitude exploration, comparison of a logical and structured format with an action-oriented and affective format, comparison of a humanizing versus diagnosis-focused approach to learning about transgender people, and goal setting as part of training. The methods used to study specific teaching interventions included qualitative content analysis and randomized experimental design.

Speaker panels and individual speakers are commonly used approaches. Seven studies of LGBTQ speakers were found, some of which were reviewed by Croteau and Kusek (1992). Rather than describe each study individually, a summary follows. One study engaged social work students (Black, Oles, Cramer, & Bennett, 1999); the rest focused on undergraduates. Individual speakers or panelists typically spoke about their experiences and answered questions, and sessions lasted between 50 minutes and 3 hours. One study included these elements in a virtual, interactive lesbian and gay speaker panel intervention in which participants selected prerecorded videos of lesbian and gay speakers sharing their experiences and answering questions (Beasley, Torres-Harding, & Pedersen, 2012). Most studies investigated gay male and lesbian speakers, although one studied speakers who identified as cross-dressers (Penor Ceglian & Lyons, 2004) and another included speakers who were transgender (Walch et al., 2012). Attitudes were measured at various points in time, including before the speaker, immediately following the speaker, and several weeks after the hearing the speaker. Participants typically reported more positive cognitive and/or affective attitudes in comparison with pretest data or a control condition (Geasler, Croteau, Heineman, & Edlund, 1995; Grutzeck & Gidycz, 1997; Lance, 1987; Nelson & Krieger, 1997; Walch et al., 2012), although some reported no significant change (Black et al., 1999; Cotten-Huston & Waite, 1999; Grutzeck & Gidycz, 1997). Some attitude change differed by gender role (e.g., Grutzeck & Gidycz, 1997; Penor Ceglian & Lyons, 2004) or by what types of attitudes were measured (e.g., Beasley et al., 2012; Grutzeck & Gidycz, 1997). Taken together, these studies suggest that LGBTQ speakers are typically effective in changing participants' attitudes.

A meta-analytic study investigated teaching and training interventions aimed at reducing sexual prejudice (Bartoş et al., 2014). Across 32 studies, education was highly effective for increasing knowledge, moderately effective in reducing sexually prejudiced attitudes, and effective in reducing sexually prejudiced emotions. Contact with LGB people was also moderately effective in reducing prejudiced attitudes about them. Media and entertainment were used in 11 studies, and the results indicated a tendency for media to have a positive effect in reducing sexual prejudice.

In contrast to the multiple studies on LGBTQ speakers and on reducing sexual prejudice, most specific teaching interventions or approaches to teaching about LGBTQ issues have been investigated through a single study. One study used experimental design to compare the outcomes of providing information with exploring attitudes regarding LGB individuals (Israel & Hackett, 2004). In this study, 161 MHP trainees took part in a 2.5-hour training session. Participants were randomly assigned to one of four conditions: (a) information, (b) attitude exploration, (c) both information and attitude exploration, or (d) neither information nor attitude exploration (training on a different population). Posttest comparisons indicated that participants who received information had higher levels of knowledge regarding LGB issues, yet participants who explored attitudes reported less positive attitudes than those who did not.

Taking a slightly different angle on training approaches, another study randomly assigned 50 undergraduate students to one of three 2-hour sessions: two experimental conditions based on cognitive–experiential self-theory (experiential or rational) and a control condition (Guth, Lopez, Rojas, Clements, & Tyler, 2005). Similar material about LGB populations was delivered by either focusing on a logical and structured format or an action-oriented and affective format. Cognitive and affective attitudes were assessed 1 month before, immediately following, and 3 weeks after the session. Participants in the experiential workshop reported more positive cognitive and affective attitudes and increases in both positive and negative affect, compared with those in the rational and control conditions. The results suggest that experiential training may be more effective in reducing anti-LGB prejudice than training that uses a more rational focus.

A randomized experimental study of 100 undergraduates compared the impact of a humanizing condition (watching a video of a child with gender identity disorder[1] [GID] and writing a coming out letter as if

---

[1]The diagnosis of GID has since been replaced with gender dysphoria in the fifth edition of the *Diagnostic and Statistical Manual of Mental Disorders* (American Psychiatric Association, 2013) to emphasize the stress and anxiety associated with wanting to be another gender rather than wanting to be another gender as a disorder itself.

they were transgender) with a diagnosis-centered condition (reviewing GID criteria, watching an expert video, and writing down factual information about being transgender). Whereas participants in the humanizing condition reported reduced transprejudice and increased desire for social contact following the intervention, participants in the diagnosis-centered condition reported increased transprejudice following the intervention (Tompkins, Shields, Hillman, & White, 2015).

Madera, King, and Hebl (2013) evaluated the effectiveness of goal setting by 500 incoming college students and their mentors on diversity-training outcomes. Before the training, half the students were randomly assigned to set their own goals about appreciating diversity with regard to sexual orientation. Half the mentors were randomly assigned to set goals related to reinforcing students' diversity training. Trainers shared personal experiences in which they faced some challenge related to their identity (including sexual orientation identity). Attitudes and behaviors that support sexual orientation diversity (e.g., intervening when someone makes derogatory comments) were assessed 3 and 8 months posttraining. Researchers found that student goal setting, mentor goal setting, and participating in supportive behaviors were associated with more positive attitudes 8 months posttraining. Notably, behaviors changed more quickly than attitudes, providing evidence that behaviors can influence attitudes.

Finally, one study investigated motivations, experiences, and impact regarding participation on a research team about attitudes toward LGB people (Dillon et al., 2004). This qualitative analysis of reflections written by 10 graduate student research team members revealed aspects of participation in the research team that had a positive impact on the learning and growth of the members. Discussion of complexities of sexual orientation in a supportive environment, as well as opportunities to reflect on their own sexual orientation identity development and attitudes toward LGB people, played an important role in their growth over the course of the research project (Dillon et al., 2004).

Evidence-Based Strategies for Teaching LGBTQ Issues in Psychology

Taken as a whole, the results of the studies reviewed in this chapter offer guidance regarding content, format, context, and characteristics of instructors for teaching about LGBTQ issues. Recommendations for and descriptions of teaching methods can help to illustrate how these evidence-based approaches may be implemented. Additional guidance may be gleaned from other sources of information regarding teaching about diversity and teaching, more generally.

TRAINING CONTENT AND FORMAT

Overall, the evidence reviewed in this chapter includes a number of different teaching and training approaches, though the overlap among these teaching strategies is worth noting. The nature of the multimodal training research makes it difficult to ascertain the direct impact of a specific intervention on a specific outcome; however, as indicated by the specific intervention studies, insight can be garnered regarding what works when teaching about LGBTQ issues from the evidence. Taken together, the specific intervention studies and multimodal training studies provide the foundational stages of an evidence-based roadmap that supports the teaching and training methods an educator may choose to use.

The studies investigated training formats that ranged from short-term 3-hour training sessions as part of larger a course to entire LGBTQ courses delivered over a series of weeks. All these formats seemed to have some utility, and unfortunately, there are no studies that compare impact of length of training on outcomes. Therefore, length of training will likely be determined by the context of the training and the resources available.

Not surprisingly, providing information about LGBTQ issues seemed to increase knowledge as a single intervention (Israel & Hackett, 2004) and as part of multimodal training (Bidell, 2013; Pearson, 2003; Rutter et al., 2008). Types of information that may be particularly valuable are those identified in studies of counselor competencies and in professional guidelines (e.g., American Psychological Association, 2012; Association for Lesbian, Gay, Bisexual & Transgender Issues in Counseling, 2013; Coleman et al., 2012; Israel et al., 2003).

Exploration of attitudes is a common component of teaching about LGBTQ issues. Interestingly, the exploration of attitudes and awareness showed varied results. One study found that exploration of attitudes resulted in less positive attitudes (Israel & Hackett, 2004), another study found no change in attitude scores (Rutter et al., 2008), and three found an increase in awareness (Bidell, 2013; Byrd & Hays, 2013; Pearson, 2003). Some of these differences may be due to the types of activities used to explore attitudes and increase awareness during training and the research methods and outcome measures used to measure the results. However, Madera et al. (2013) found that engaging in supportive behaviors helped change attitudes, and behavioral change occurred more rapidly than attitudinal change.

Research has suggested that the content of cultural diversity training and the messages being delivered has some influence on increasing awareness; however, the differences are more substantial depending on the method of delivery (Brown, 2004). Brown (2004) wrote, "When students are passive participants or observers, they may understand the message but fail to connect it in meaningful ways" (p. 336). Perhaps an active behavioral component during teaching and training can be helpful in supporting attitude exploration and increasing awareness. Increasing awareness of privilege may also be a way of personalizing diversity material in a way that graduate students value (Cannon, Wiggins, Poulsen, & Estrada, 2012).

An increase in skill competencies has been demonstrated when using teaching interventions that include an active and experiential component. Role-plays (Byrd & Hays, 2013; Rutter et al., 2008), experiences working directly with LGBTQ individuals (Goodrich & Luke; 2010; Graham et al., 2012), and other experiential activities (Bidell, 2013) may be particularly helpful in increasing skill competencies. Kocarek and Pelling (2003) offered suggestions for skill-building role-play exercises that may increase empathy, help to explore attitudes, practice tangible skills, increase involvement and motivation for learning, and provide opportunities for immediate and direct feedback.

Training on LGBTQ issues may include some sharing of personal experiences by guest speakers or panelists. Panels may decrease discomfort and negative stereotypes about lesbians and gay men (Nelson & Krieger, 1997). To enhance the effectiveness of panels, it is better to have the panel consist of people who are peers of the students and involve interaction rather than didactic presentation of material (Nelson & Krieger, 1997). Presenters should be prepared for nuanced and personal questions that may differ from the examples included in teaching manuals (Peel, 2009). Chapter 6 of this volume offers suggestions for preparing students and invited speakers to maintain focus and appropriateness of student questions.

It is important to include content about each LGBTQ subpopulation because some knowledge, attitudes, and skills are population specific. Education can combat invisibility of bisexuality within LGBTQ communities, elicit attitudes and explore monosexist biases, and develop skills to address the unique needs of bisexual clients (Israel, 2007). Bi-affirming approaches to instruction include using inclusive language (e.g., "same-sex relationships" rather than "lesbian or gay relationships"), using examples that include bisexuals and that highlight their unique experiences and needs, providing accurate information about bisexuality, and modeling affirming attitudes toward bisexuals.

Approaches that have been described for teaching about transgender populations include accessing personal narratives through speakers (Rye,

Elmslie, & Chalmers, 2007), the Internet, conferences, films, and books (Chavez-Korell & Johnson, 2010), as well as through using film clips to illustrate various aspects of transgender experiences (Kalra, 2013). It can also be helpful to consider the training required to provide various levels of care for transgender clients; promoting accepting attitudes toward transgender people may not be adequate to prepare MHPs to help a client transition (Goldberg, 2008).

CONTEXT OF TRAINING

The results of a study of MHP trainees' experiences in graduate school suggested that the context of the training matters (Carlson, McGeorge, & Toomey, 2013). This retrospective study showed that classroom-based teaching and training were significantly associated with greater levels of knowledge and skills but not awareness. However, affirming LGB practices at the programmatic level were associated with greater levels of knowledge, awareness, and skills. The authors' recommendations for creating a more affirming training setting at the programmatic level included required ally training, a no-tolerance policy for homophobic language, opportunities for students to work directly with LGB clients, support for student research on LGB topics, and remediation procedures for those whose beliefs affected their ability to provide affirming counseling. They also suggested that curriculum include specific content about heterosexism, heterosexual privilege, heterosexual bias, and critical self-reflections on beliefs and privilege.

There may be ways to incorporate LGBTQ training into other types of training in meaningful ways. For example, one study described cofacilitation of GSA groups as a requirement for training on group process in an introductory school counseling course (Goodrich & Luke, 2010). Educators can look for opportunities to include knowledge, awareness, and skills training related to LGBTQ issues in a wide range of courses and venues for learning. Infusion of diversity material into general content courses has been recommended for multicultural and LGBTQ issues, although it is unclear whether inclusion of LGBTQ in multicultural courses is an effective means of assuring this material is included in training or whether it dilutes attention to racial and ethnic diversity (Israel & Selvidge, 2003).

Beyond content of courses, training environment may have an impact on students. Presence of LGBTQ faculty, research on LGBTQ issues, and LGBTQ-affirming university policies (e.g., benefits for same-sex partners), practices (e.g., use of preferred names and pronouns), and facilities (e.g., all gender restrooms) may also contribute to a context for effective education about LGBTQ issues (Israel & Selvidge, 2003).

It is also important to keep in mind the composition of the student population, which may be associated with the context for the training as being either required or an elective. Elective training is more likely to include only students who have already thought about LGBTQ issues and have generally positive attitudes (e.g., Dillon et al., 2004). Some students who choose to participate in training on LGBTQ issues are part of this population themselves. LGBTQ people can benefit from training on LGBTQ issues, especially when it attends to more marginalized aspects of these communities, such as bisexual and transgender people (Israel et al., 2016). When training is mandatory, some students may hold negative attitudes and resist participation in such training. Informing students during the admissions process about a program's LGBTQ-affirming stance and infusion of LGBTQ material is in line with ethical codes and may prevent later conflicts (Whitman & Bidell, 2014).

The sexual orientation and/or gender identity of instructors or presenters may have particular implications for training about LGBTQ issues. Students who are LGBTQ or allies may feel greater trust in and rapport with trainers who identify as LGBTQ themselves (Israel et al., 2016), and LGBTQ trainers sharing their own personal experiences has been shown to be effective in specific training environments (Madera et al., 2013). However, there are no studies that indicate how instructors in an academic course disclosing LGBTQ status may affect the teacher and students. The extent to which students perceive instructors to be credible can have an impact on whether students are likely to be persuaded by their messages (Pornpitakpan, 2004), but it is not clear how instructor LGBTQ identity affects credibility or what factors enhance credibility of non-LGBTQ instructors. Furthermore, LGBTQ instructors may have to make sure they have the support of their department or program before disclosing personal experiences in the context of an academic course.

Contributing to the Evidence Base for Teaching LGBTQ Issues in Psychology

An evidence base for teaching about LGBTQ issues in psychology is sorely lacking, but there are abundant opportunities to contribute to this body of knowledge. Developing an evidence base for teaching about LGBTQ issues in psychology should be easier than developing an evidence base for psychological practice with LGBTQ clients for several reasons: (a) participants are readily available in diversity and psychology courses, (b) gaining institutional review board approval will likely be relatively easy, and (c) gathering outcome data can be integrated into other means of evaluating student performance and course evaluation.

Some published work offers recommendations or describes approaches for teaching about LGBTQ issues, and these can be tested empirically. For example, assessing the effectiveness of recommended interventions for each stage of readiness for change (Tyler, Jackman-Wheitner, Strader, & Lenox, 1997) would contribute to theoretically driven, evidence-based teaching about LGBTQ issues in psychology. Consider evaluating teaching interventions on the basis of the recommendations, approaches, and activities described in this book. Activity 10.1 describes an assignment that can help students develop the skills to contribute to the evidence base in this way.

There are various research designs that may be particularly useful in developing this evidence base. Most of the studies we reviewed used either a pre–post within-subjects design (Israel et al., 2016; Pearson, 2003) or quasi-experimental design with a control (Bidell, 2013; Byrd & Hays, 2013; Rutter et al., 2008; Rye & Meaney, 2009). A few were experimental studies with random assignment to conditions (Israel & Hackett, 2004; Madera et al., 2013). One study used an ethnographic approach to investigate the impact of specific training activities (Graham et al., 2012). Given the prominence of LGBTQ issues in society and policy, it is important to keep in mind the potential impact of events external to the training if the training takes place over multiple sessions or if the impact is evaluated some time after the training ends.

In addition to the research approaches reflected in the extant literature, it may be particularly expedient to collect data using sources that are built into the course. If students are providing written responses to assignments, classroom activities, or readings, the instructor could conduct a content analysis of the written responses to identify types of reactions and learning that the students experienced. Instructors can assess the effectiveness of knowledge acquisition methods by varying the means of acquiring knowledge across sections, students, or courses taught in different academic terms. Information on knowledge acquired by students could be gathered via in-class student response systems, quizzes, tests, or anonymous online surveys. If items are included for the purpose of investigating various teaching approaches, it may be appropriate to exclude these items from the student's grade. It is notable that these means of data collection that do not involve additional measures or extensive manipulation of the learner's experience are entirely absent from the literature.

It is also important to consider what outcomes to assess. Research has indicated that behaviors may influence attitudes, that changes in both variables may take considerable time (3–8 months posttraining) to detect, and that it can be useful to measure both (Madera et al., 2013). Thus, immediate posttest training may not detect these changes. As it is sometimes not feasible to gather data several months after training takes place, it may be useful to assess immediately after the training a more proximal variable, such as self-efficacy, which contributes to future behavior (Israel et al., 2016).

As an educator, you may be in a good position to contribute to this knowledge base. If you teach a course on LGBTQ issues or diversity, if you do diversity training in the workplace, if you help train student leaders (e.g., resident advisors) on LGBTQ issues, you have an available source of participants. If you are reading this book, you likely have opportunities to gather data. We encourage you to do this research and to publish your work. By disseminating your results, you can help increase the effectiveness of teaching about LGBTQ issues in psychology, which will benefit teachers, trainers, students, and ultimately, LGBTQ people in our society.

ACTIVITY 10.1

Design a Study About Teaching LGBTQ Psychology

Directions: This activity would be appropriate for students in a research methods, evaluation, or graduate pedagogy course. It could be included in the course as an in-class group activity or as an individual or group assignment.

Review the teaching activities described in Burnes and Stanley, *Teaching LGBTQ Psychology: Queering Innovative Pedagogy and Practice* (2017). Choose one activity described in one of the chapters of the book and design a study evaluating the outcomes of the activity on student learning or learners' acquisition of knowledge, attitudes, or skills. You will have to determine or decide the following:

1. The goal(s) of the activity (identify one or more constructs related to learning about LGBTQ psychology and broadly describe the audience).
2. The learning objectives (what will the learners gain, in observable and specific terms).
3. The characteristics and recruitment of participants for the study, as well as where the participants are learning (traditional classroom setting, community-based workshop, etc.).
4. The research design.
5. Types of measures you will use to assess the learning outcomes and data collection procedure.
6. Approach to data analysis.

You may want to read Israel and Bettergarcia's chapter, "Evidence-Based Teaching of LGBTQ Issues in Psychology" (Chapter 10, this volume), in preparation for this assignment. The completed assignment should be between three and five pages (double-spaced) and should address the points above.

References

American Psychiatric Association. (2013). *Diagnostic and statistical manual of mental disorders* (5th ed.). Washington, DC: Author.

American Psychological Association. (2012). Guidelines for psychological practice with lesbian, gay, and bisexual clients. *American Psychologist, 67,* 10–42. http://dx.doi.org/10.1037/a0024659

Anhalt, K., Morris, T. L., Scotti, J. R., & Cohen, S. H. (2003). Student perspectives on training in gay, lesbian, and bisexual issues: A survey of behavioral clinical psychology programs. *Cognitive and Behavioral Practice, 10,* 255–263. http://dx.doi.org/10.1016/S1077-7229(03)80038-X

Association for Lesbian, Gay, Bisexual & Transgender Issues in Counseling. (2013). *Competencies for counseling with lesbian, gay, bisexual, queer, questioning, intersex, and ally individuals.* Retrieved from http://www.algbtic.org/competencies.html

Asta, E. L., & Vacha-Haase, T. (2013). Heterosexual ally development in counseling psychologists: Experiences, training, and advocacy. *The Counseling Psychologist, 41,* 493–529. http://dx.doi.org/10.1177/0011000012453174

Bartoş, S. E., Berger, I., & Hegarty, P. (2014). Interventions to reduce sexual prejudice: A study-space analysis and meta-analytic review. *Journal of Sex Research, 51,* 363–382. http://dx.doi.org/10.1080/00224499.2013.871625

Beasley, C., Torres-Harding, S., & Pedersen, P. J. (2012). The "virtual" panel: A computerized model for LGBT speaker panels. *American Journal of Sexuality Education, 7,* 355–377. http://dx.doi.org/10.1080/15546128.2012.740948

Benson, K. E. (2013). Seeking support: Transgender client experiences with mental health services. *Journal of Feminist Family Therapy: An International Forum, 25,* 17–40. http://dx.doi.org.proxy.library.ucsb.edu: 2048/10.1080/08952833.2013.755081

Bidell, M. P. (2013). Addressing disparities: The impact of a lesbian, gay, bisexual, and transgender graduate counselling course. *Counselling & Psychotherapy Research, 13,* 300–307. http://dx.doi.org/10.1080/14733145.2012.741139

Black, B., Oles, T. P., Cramer, E. P., & Bennett, C. K. (1999). Attitudes and behaviors of social work students toward lesbian and gay male clients: Can panel presentations make a difference? *Journal of Gay & Lesbian Social Services, 9,* 47–68. http://dx.doi.org/10.1300/J041v09n04_03

Brown, E. L. (2004). What precipitates change in cultural diversity awareness during a multicultural course: The message or the method? *Journal of Teacher Education, 55,* 325–340. http://dx.doi.org/10.1177/0022487104266746

Byrd, R., & Hays, D. G. (2013). Evaluating a safe space training for school counselors and trainees using a randomized control group design. *Professional School Counseling, 17,* 20–31. http://dx.doi.org/10.5330/PSC.n.2013-17.20

Cannon, E., Wiggins, M., Poulsen, S., & Estrada, D. (2012). Addressing heterosexist privilege during orientation: One program's experience. *Journal of LGBT Issues in Counseling, 6,* 3–17. http://dx.doi.org/10.1080/15538605.2011.598225

Carlson, T. S., McGeorge, C. R., & Toomey, R. B. (2013). Establishing the validity of the affirmative training inventory: Assessing the relationship between lesbian, gay, and bisexual affirmative training and students' clinical competence. *Journal of Marital and Family Therapy, 39,* 209–222. http://dx.doi.org/10.1111/j.1752-0606.2012.00286.x

Chavez-Korell, S., & Johnson, L. T. (2010). Informing counselor training and competent counseling services through transgender narratives and the transgender community. *Journal of LGBT Issues in Counseling, 4,* 202–213. http://dx.doi.org/10.1080/15538605.2010.524845

Coleman, E., Bockting, W., Botzer, M., Cohen-Kettenis, P., DeCuypere, G., Feldman, J., . . . Zucker, K. (2012). Standards of care for the health of transsexual, transgender, and gender-nonconforming people, version 7. *International Journal of Transgenderism, 13,* 165–232. http://dx.doi.org/10.1080/15532739.2011.700873

Cotten-Huston, A. L., & Waite, B. M. (1999). Anti-homosexual attitudes in college students: Predictors and classroom interventions. *Journal of Homosexuality, 38,* 117–133. http://dx.doi.org/10.1300/J082v38n03_07

Croteau, J. M., & Kusek, M. T. (1992). Gay and lesbian speaker panels: Implementation and research. *Journal of Counseling & Development, 70,* 396–401. http://dx.doi.org/10.1002/j.1556-6676.1992.tb01623.x

Dillon, F. R., Worthington, R. L., Savoy, H. B., Rooney, S. B., Becker-Schutte, A., & Guerra, R. M. (2004). On becoming allies: A qualitative study of lesbian-, gay-, and bisexual-affirmative counselor training. *Counselor Education and Supervision, 43,* 162–178. http://dx.doi.org/10.1002/j.1556-6978.2004.tb01840.x

Finkel, M. J., Storaasli, R. D., Bandele, A., & Schaefer, V. (2003). Diversity training in graduate school: An exploratory evaluation of the safe zone project. *Professional Psychology, Research and Practice, 34,* 555–561. http://dx.doi.org/10.1037/0735-7028.34.5.555

Geasler, M. J., Croteau, J. M., Heineman, C. J., & Edlund, C. J. (1995). A qualitative study of students' expression of change after attending panel presentations by lesbian, gay, and bisexual speakers. *Journal of College Student Development, 36,* 483–492.

Goldberg, J. M. (2008). Training community-based clinicians in transgender care. *International Journal of Transgenderism, 9,* 219–231. http://dx.doi.org.proxy.library.ucsb.edu:2048/10.1300/J485v09n03_10

Goodrich, K. M., & Luke, M. (2010). The experiences of school counselors-in-training in group work with LGBTQ adolescents. *Journal for Specialists in Group Work, 35*, 143–159. http://dx.doi.org/10.1080/01933921003705966

Graham, S. R., Carney, J. S., & Kluck, A. S. (2012). Perceived competency in working with LGB clients: Where are we now? *Counselor Education and Supervision, 51*, 2–16. http://dx.doi.org/10.1002/j.1556-6978.2012.00001.x

Grutzeck, S., & Gidycz, C. A. (1997). The effects of a gay and lesbian speaker panel of college students' attitudes and behaviors: The importance of context effects. *Imagination, Cognition and Personality, 17*, 65–81. http://dx.doi.org/10.2190/P8TW-KF4N-6U7W-7G8J

Guth, L. J., Lopez, D. F., Rojas, J., Clements, K. D., & Tyler, J. M. (2005). Experiential versus rational training: A comparison of student attitudes toward homosexuality. *Journal of Homosexuality, 48*, 83–102. http://dx.doi.org/10.1300/J082v48n02_05

Israel, T. (2007). Training counselors to work ethically and effectively with bisexual clients. In B. A. Firestein (Ed.), *Becoming visible: Counseling bisexuals across the lifespan* (pp. 381–394). New York, NY: Columbia University Press.

Israel, T., & Hackett, G. (2004). Counselor education on lesbian, gay, and bisexual issues: Comparing information and attitude exploration. *Counselor Education and Supervision, 43*, 179–191. http://dx.doi.org/10.1002/j.1556-6978.2004.tb01841.x

Israel, T., Ketz, K., Detrie, P. M., Burke, M. C., & Shulman, J. L. (2003). Identifying counselor competencies for working with lesbian, gay, and bisexual clients. *Journal of Gay & Lesbian Psychotherapy, 7*, 3–21. http://dx.doi.org/10.1300/J236v07n04_02

Israel, T., & Selvidge, M. M. D. (2003). Contributions of multicultural counseling to counselor competence with lesbian, gay, and bisexual clients. *Journal of Multicultural Counseling and Development, 31*, 84–98. http://dx.doi.org/10.1002/j.2161-1912.2003.tb00535.x

Israel, T., Willging, C. E., & Ley, D. (2016). Development and evaluation of training for rural LGBTQ mental health peer advocates. *Journal of Rural Mental Health, 40*, 40–62. http://dx.doi.org/10.1037/rmh0000046

Johnson, L., & Federman, E. J. (2014). Training, experience, and attitudes of VA psychologists regarding LGBT issues: Relation to practice and competence. *Psychology of Sexual Orientation and Gender Diversity, 1*, 10–18. http://dx.doi.org/10.1037/sgd0000019

Kalra, G. (2013). Using cinema to train mental health care trainees in transgender issues. *International Journal of Transgenderism, 14*, 39–48. http://dx.doi.org/10.1080/15532739.2013.791652

Kocarek, C. E., & Pelling, N. J. (2003). Beyond knowledge and awareness: Enhancing counselor skills for work with gay, lesbian, and bisexual clients. *Journal of Multicultural Counseling and Development, 31,* 99–112. http://dx.doi.org/10.1002/j.2161-1912.2003.tb00536.x

Lance, L. M. (1987). The effects of interaction with gay persons on attitudes toward homosexuality. *Human Relations, 40,* 329–336. http://dx.doi.org/10.1177/001872678704000601

Luke, M., Goodrich, K. M., & Scarborough, J. L. (2011). Integration of the K–12 LGBTQI student population in school counselor education curricula: The current state of affairs. *Journal of LGBT Issues in Counseling, 5,* 80–101. http://dx.doi.org/10.1080/15538605.2011.574530

Madera, J. M., King, E. B., & Hebl, M. R. (2013). Enhancing the effects of sexual orientation diversity training: The effects of setting goals and training mentors on attitudes and behaviors. *Journal of Business and Psychology, 28,* 79–91. http://dx.doi.org/10.1007/s10869-012-9264-7

Nelson, E. S., & Krieger, S. L. (1997). Changes in attitudes toward homosexuality in college students: Implementation of a gay men and lesbian peer panel. *Journal of Homosexuality, 33,* 63–81. http://dx.doi.org/10.1300/J082v33n02_04

Pearson, Q. M. (2003). Breaking the silence in the counselor education classroom: A training seminar on counseling sexual minority clients. *Journal of Counseling & Development, 81,* 292–300. http://dx.doi.org/10.1002/j.1556-6678.2003.tb00256.x

Peel, E. (2009). Intergroup relations in action: Questions asked about lesbian, gay, and bisexual issues in diversity training. *Journal of Community & Applied Social Psychology, 19,* 271–285. http://dx.doi.org/10.1002/casp.997

Penor Ceglian, C. M., & Lyons, N. N. (2004). Gender type and comfort with cross-dressers. *Sex Roles, 50,* 539–546. http://dx.doi.org/10.1023/B:SERS.0000023073.99146.2d

Pettijohn, T. F., II, & Walzer, A. S. (2008). Reducing racism, sexism, and homophobia in college students by completing a psychology of prejudice course. *College Student Journal, 42,* 459–468.

Phillips, J. C., & Fischer, A. R. (1998). Graduate students' training experiences with lesbian, gay, and bisexual issues. *The Counseling Psychologist, 26,* 712–734. http://dx.doi.org/10.1177/0011000098265002

Pornpitakpan, C. (2004). The persuasiveness of source credibility: A critical review of five decades' evidence. *Journal of Applied Social Psychology, 34,* 243–281. http://dx.doi.org/10.1111/j.1559-1816.2004.tb02547.x

Rutter, P. A., Estrada, D., Ferguson, L. K., & Diggs, G. A. (2008). Sexual orientation and counselor competency: The impact of training on enhancing awareness, knowledge and skills. *Journal of LGBT Issues in Counseling, 2,* 109–125. http://dx.doi.org/10.1080/15538600802125472

Rye, B. J., Elmslie, P., & Chalmers, A. (2007). Meeting a transsexual person: Experience within a classroom setting. *Canadian Online Journal of Queer Studies in Education, 3,* 1–10.

Rye, B. J., & Meaney, G. J. (2009). Impact of a homonegativity awareness workshop on attitudes toward homosexuality. *Journal of Homosexuality*, *56*, 31–55. http://dx.doi.org/10.1080/00918360802551480

Sennott, S., & Smith, S. (2011). Translating the sex and gender continuums
in mental health: A transfeminist approach to client and clinician fears.
Journal of Gay & Lesbian Mental Health, *15*, 218–234. http://dx.doi.org/
10.1080/19359705.2011.553779

Tompkins, T. L., Shields, C. N., Hillman, K. M., & White, K. (2015).
Reducing stigma toward the transgender community: An evaluation of
a humanizing and perspective-taking intervention. *Psychology of Sexual
Orientation and Gender Diversity*, *2*, 34–42. http://dx.doi.org/10.1037/
sgd0000088

Tyler, J. M., Jackman-Wheitner, L., Strader, S., & Lenox, R. (1997).
A change-model approach to raising awareness of gay, lesbian, and
bisexual issues among graduate students in counseling. *Journal of Sex
Education & Therapy*, *22*, 37–43.

Van de Ven, P. (1995). Effects on high school students of a teaching
module for reducing homophobia. *Basic and Applied Social Psychology*,
17, 153–172. http://dx.doi.org/10.1080/01973533.1995.9646137

Walch, S. E., Sinkkanen, K. A., Swain, E. M., Francisco, J., Breaux, C. A.,
& Sjoberg, M. D. (2012). Using intergroup contact theory to reduce
stigma against transgender individuals: Impact of a transgender speaker
panel presentation. *Journal of Applied Social Psychology*, *42*, 2583–2605.
http://dx.doi.org/10.1111/j.1559-1816.2012.00955.x

Whitman, J. S., & Bidell, M. P. (2014). Affirmative lesbian, gay, and bisexual counselor education and religious beliefs: How do we bridge the
gap? *Journal of Counseling & Development*, *92*, 162–169. http://dx.doi.org/
10.1002/j.1556-6676.2014.00144.x

Index

About the Editors

Theodore R. Burnes, PhD, MSEd, is an associate professor and the director of the LGBT specialization of Antioch University's clinical psychology master's program. He has constructed, facilitated, and evaluated undergraduate and graduate coursework in psychology, Black studies, writing, LGBT studies, poetry, women's studies, teacher education, and counseling in university settings for 15 years. He has been in directorial positions in both master's and doctoral programs in applied psychology for over 6 years. He is also a staff psychologist and the coordinator of continuing education for the Los Angeles Gender Center, a nonprofit organization that provides training around the country on best practices for supporting and affirming transgender and gender nonconforming individuals in clinical practice and other mental health work in mental health agencies, hospitals, schools, and university counseling centers. Dr. Burnes is a licensed psychologist and a licensed professional clinical counselor in private practice in Los Angeles. His professional expertise focuses on teaching pedagogy, LGBTQI individuals' mental health and wellness, accreditation and licensure in professional counseling and applied psychology, sexuality and sex-positivity, and clinical supervision. He provides consultation and training for educational institutions. Dr. Burnes's teaching evaluations consistently document his energy; high expectations of students;

creativity in designing learning assignments; and skill in navigating difficult dialogues about race, sexuality, and gender.

Jeanne L. Stanley, PhD, MSEd, is the executive director of Watershed Counseling and Consultation Services, LLC. She conducts training around the country on best practices for supporting and affirming LGBTQ individuals. She is also a licensed psychologist in private practice in the Chestnut Hill area of Philadelphia and has been on the faculty at the University of Pennsylvania for over 20 years. There, she was the director of the master's program in psychological services at the Graduate School of Education, founded and directed the Penn Center for Continuing Education for Counseling and Psychology, and taught over 50 graduate courses in counseling psychology. Dr. Stanley currently holds the position of adjunct professor at the University of Pennsylvania and was awarded the Outstanding Educator Award from the University of Pennsylvania's Graduate School of Education. She was also the director of the Bryson Institute of the Attic Youth Center, where she provided hundreds of trainings on the best practices for supporting LGBTQI youth in schools, universities, and religious communities. Her clinical, training, and research specialties focus on the intersection of individuals' sociocultural identities (including gender, race, ethnicity, sexual identity, religion, and disability), supporting and affirming LGBTQI individuals, expanding individuals' talents and strengths in work teams, procuring accreditation and licensure in counseling, and group dynamics in academic and business systems. She also provides consultation and training for companies and educational institutions as well as jury consulting for law firms. Dr. Stanley is also the founder and executive director of Grad School Coaching, LLC, where she assists students in applying and gaining admittance to, as well as completing, graduate programs.